GAEILGE

A Radical Revolution

First published in 2019 by
Currach Books
Unit 3B, Block 3, Bracken Business Park,
Sandyford, Dublin 18, Ireland
www.currachbooks.com

ISBN: 978-1-78218-907-7

Fourth Printing, 2022

Set in Freight Text Pro 10.5/14
Cover and book design by Alba Esteban | Currach Books
Printed by L&C Printing Group, Poland

GAEILGE

A Radical Revolution

CAOIMHÍN DE BARRA

CURRACH
BOOKS

Do Kathy, Aisling Searc agus Saoirse Samhain,
mo mhná maoiní.

CONTENTS

INTRODUCTION

<u>ÉIRE OR IRELANDSHIRE</u>

When it comes to the Irish language, there are two questions. Could it be revived? Should it be revived?

The language is a source of ongoing, heated debate in Ireland. But almost all discussion revolves around the second question. Should Irish be revived?

Champions of Irish argue that more needs to be done for the language because it is an essential part of Irish identity. They point out that the language has been spoken on our island for centuries, if not millennia, meaning it was spoken by our ancestors, both distant and more recent. They insist that the language is beautiful, romantic and unique, and that it is the birthright of all Irish people to have the opportunity to speak it.

Opponents of Irish contend that far too many resources are wasted on Irish. They acknowledge that the language was once widely used in Ireland, but that language shift is a natural part of evolution and it is pointless to try and reverse it. They note that despite extensive schooling in Irish, most of the Irish population simply does not speak it. While they are happy for those who speak Irish to continue doing so, they argue that it is simply not practical for the Irish state to spend time and money on a lost cause.

I could write a book on why Irish should be revived. Initially, that was what I thought this book was going to be about. But I realised that would be pointless. When it comes to the Irish language, indeed when it comes to most things in life, people already have their minds made up. I could write the most incredible piece of prose ever composed in the English language, but it wouldn't change anyone's mind about whether Irish is worth reviving. Those who support Irish would probably enjoy it, while those who take issue with the language would dismiss it as waffle. So, to save everyone time and effort, I will simply say that I believe Irish should be revived.

But could Irish be revived? That to me seems a more interesting question. Indeed, it should take precedence over the other one. After all, if Irish cannot be revived, then there is no point debating whether it should be.

This book, then, is going to explore whether Irish can be revived. Of course, this raises the question of what "reviving Irish" actually means. I will address that in more detail in the last chapter, but for now it will suffice to say that by "reviving Irish", I simply mean having it more widely spoken in Ireland than it currently is.

In order to evaluate whether Irish can be revived, some other questions also need to be answered. Why did Irish decline in the first place? Why isn't the language more widely spoken given that it is a compulsory subject in both primary and secondary school? Have other languages ever been revived? How many people actually speak Irish? And why is there such a hatred toward the language among some people?

I also want to discuss how these questions about Irish and attitudes towards it are shaped by ideology. What is ideology? It is defined as "a system of ideas and ideals". Each one of us has an individual view of the world we live in, but it is shaped and molded by the various ideologies we encounter. This is something we often lose sight of. When we use the word ideology, we tend to use it in a negative sense, and as such, we believe ideology is a word that doesn't apply to us. People who disagree with us – they are the people who can't think for themselves because they are blinded by ideology – unlike ourselves of course. And yet, whether we like it or not, our opinions and positions are just as ideologically motivated as the people we argue with.

In other words, there is no such thing as an absence of ideology. An important figure in understanding this concept is Karl Mannheim, a Hungarian sociologist. Mannheim pointed out that in any public debate, what is actually taking place is a contest between two ideologies. Generally speaking, these ideologies can be labeled as the legitimate or dominant ideology on the one hand, that is to say, the ideology that supports the powers that be and the way things are, and on the other, the challenging or utopian ideology, which seeks to alter the status quo.

Some examples are in order to make this clearer. Everyone can agree that socialism is an ideology – and it is usually a utopian ideology, seeking to bring about social and economic change. It is opposed by the dominant ideology, which is free market capitalism. This is a classic example of the dominant versus utopian ideologies that Mannheim was talking about.

Another example – feminism is clearly an ideology. It seeks to change the position of women in society relative to men. As such, it is challenging the status quo, and is opposed in these efforts by the dominant ideology – which we will label patriarchy.

So far, this is relatively straightforward. But Mannheim went a step further, and noted that the reason that dominant ideologies are successful is precisely because of their ability to deny that they are ideologies at all. Instead, the supporters of the dominant ideology maintain that their position is based on the plainest common sense, on the use of reason, logic and rationality. They deny that there are any ideological influences on their world view, while insisting that their opponents have been brainwashed by their ideology and can't think for themselves.

We can see this in the two examples mentioned above. Everyone accepts that socialism is an ideology, but in the western world we are a bit slower to see capitalism as one as well. Instead we depict capitalism as "just how the world works" or as the social model that "just is economic common sense". Similarly, no-one has any problem labeling feminism an ideology, but many people would deny that there is any such thing as an ideology that opposes feminism.

Our neighbours to the east in Britain have given us a wonderful example of how dominant ideologies mask their presence in two monumental referendums they held, on the question of Scottish independence in 2014, and the infamous Brexit vote in 2016. Using Mannheim's model, we can see the Scottish referendum was a contest between two ideologies, in this case, two nationalisms. The dominant ideology, British nationalism, was challenged by the utopian ideology, Scottish nationalism. But of course, this is not how the debate was depicted in the British media, or indeed the media of the English speaking world generally. Instead the referendum was framed as a battle between xenophobic, parochial, economically hair-brained nationalist zealots on the one hand, and inclusive, enlightened, fiscally responsible, outward looking and tolerant people on the other. As far as the general public was concerned, the Scottish referendum was a contest between ideologically-driven Scottish nationalism and basic common sense.

But when it came to the Brexit debate, we saw many of those who opposed Scottish independence make an about-face upon the principles that they supposedly based this opposition on. Millions of people across Britain who rejected the arguments in favour of Scottish independence, namely greater local political control and the potential of increased economic prosperity, now made the exact same arguments in favour of Britain leaving the European Union. Broadly speaking, the principles upon which one would argue against Scottish independence and against a British withdrawal from the European Union are very similar. The fact that so many people supported those principles in 2014 but argued against them in 2016 demonstrates that it is not logic or rationality that is forming these views, but rather ideology.

This is exactly what Mannheim was talking about. In the Scottish referendum debate, the dominant ideology was British nationalism and as such, it was able to mask its influence under the cover of "common sense" and "reason". But in the Brexit campaign, British nationalism was the utopian ideology, challenging the status quo, and as such, its existence, its presence was much more obvious than it had been in 2014.

Very well you might say, but what has all of this to do with the Irish language? The point is that we see the exact same patterns when it comes to the debate about the place of Irish in our society. Just as Scottish nationalists were derided as brain-washed cranks, associated with the worst excesses of human behavior, those who seek to promote the Irish language are subjected to similar, hyperbolic attacks. Frequently, people involved with the Irish language in some capacity are labelled Nazis. In *The Sunday Times* Kevin Myers called those who challenge his criticism of the state's policy toward the Irish language "brainless Gaeilgeoir skinheads", while in the *Sunday Independent* journalist Eilis O'Hanlon described Irish language summer camps in the Gaeltacht as a "vast network of concentration camps". In recent years, it has become fashionable to draw parallels between support for the Irish language and Islamic fundamentalism. Victoria White, in the *Irish Examiner*, has claimed that those who seek to promote Irish language rights "have gone at the language like the Taliban went at Islam", while in *The Irish Times*, Anne-Marie Hourihane claimed that the language was Ireland's "equivalent of the hijab". In 2007, the *Irish Examiner*, in response to making Irish the sole medium of instruction, described one new public school as "Finsbury Park Mosque by the sea". In this case, a few schools in Dingle had been amalgamated into one new institution called Pobalscoil Chorca Dhuibhne. It seems that, despite government legislation insisting that all schools in the Gaeltacht teach through Irish, the old schools had used English extensively. Certainly, there was merit in the concern some parents had about children who had largely been educated through English (in attending the old schools) suddenly being educated through Irish. But to compare the decision to comply with the law and teach solely through Irish to the ideology of a well-known radical London mosque that had produced several terrorists was embarrassingly over the top.

Yet such language is common in the discourse about Irish. In a televised debate in 2018 about the role of Irish in the education system, Ivan Yates referred to Bláthnaid Ní Chofaigh and Pearse Doherty, who were defending the inclusion of Irish in the national curriculum, as "cultural terrorists". In the *Sunday Independent* another journalist, Declan Lynch, has described the trend of people sending their children to Gaelscoileanna as "sinister", while claiming that "the vast majority of us cannot hear that language being spoken, in any context, without also hearing some distant echo of physical and sexual and psychological abuse". Even when the language used is less inflammatory, the message behind it is identical. In 2018, Pat Kenny claimed that those who support Irish-language signage in the Gaeltacht are "quite militant...activists". Kenny's choice of the word "militant" was telling. This automatically labels those who might disagree with him as aggressive, hardline zealots, lacking the cool, detached logical worldview of people like himself. This is a well-worn path used to discredit supporters of the Irish language. People depict them as frothing at the mouth in their eagerness to impose their wicked totalitarian nightmare upon us all. Those who oppose them, of course, are imagined as entirely sensible and rational, completely free of anything so sordid as an "ideology".

But this isn't true. Put simply, the debate on the Irish language is shaped by two competing ideologies. Of course, we immediately recognise that the argument to preserve and promote the Irish language is influenced by Irish nationalism. Speaking personally as someone who spent long hours learning the Irish language and who is raising my children through Irish, I am well aware that it is ideology driving me to do this.

It should be remembered, however, that those who oppose the state's Irish language policy are just as ideologically driven. This is often forgotten, or ignored. Those who identify as being in the anti-Irish camp argue that their position comes from reason-based analysis, logic and common sense. Undoubtedly, most of these people believe this to be the case, but many of the arguments they put forward don't always stand up as logical or consistent. This of course fits exactly with Mannheim's model that those who support the status quo (in this case, the dominant position of English in Ireland) deny an ideological influence in shaping their views. But one doesn't have to look too far to find it.

If you closely examine those who have claimed the enlightened high ground for themselves, their level-headedness can be something of a mirage as well. In 2017, I engaged in an online debate with a journalist who claimed he wanted a rational discussion on the state's Irish language policy. By the end, he was publicly proclaiming that he wanted to fight a pistol duel at dawn so he could put me six feet under, while simultaneously sending me abusive messages in private. So much for detached, emotionless logic.

When it comes to the Irish language and questions of Irish identity generally, what we are dealing with is not nationalism against common sense, but in fact two competing Irish nationalisms. What is nationalism? Nationalism is the idea that the people living in a state are a single entity, not just now, but in the past and the future as well. Nationalism is the story of a single people moving together through time. It uses the past to legitimise its current position, but it gets its energy from the promise that a brilliant future is just around the corner. Of course, that perfect future is never reached, as there is always something that needs to be corrected or amended. But the paradox of nationalism is that it looks backwards and forwards at the same time. We saw a magnificent example of this mindset perfectly encapsulated in 2016 in the form of the slogan of the Trump presidential campaign: "Make America Great Again".

Nationalism, like ideology, is a word with negative connotations. As with ideology, we recognise it in other people, but we often don't see it in ourselves. In his book entitled *Banal Nationalism*, psychologist Michael Billig points out that nationalism is the most successful ideology of all time.[1] This seems like an incredible claim at first, but Billig notes that the entire world is divided into states organised along nationalist lines. No political system or religion has ever spread to every corner of the globe in the way that nationalism has. Indeed, Billig notes that nationalism is so central to our existence that we are often oblivious to it. For example, Americans don't notice the fact that their national flag is absolutely everywhere in the United States, although visitors spot this immediately. Or supporters of international sport never give a second thought to why they become deeply emotionally invested in a group of well-paid professional athletes they have never met engaging in recreational activity, simply owing to the colour of the jersey they wear.

Nationalism is fueled by two things; a desire to establish a state that represents the nation or, once this state exists, to perfect the state according to nationalist principles. This is simple to grasp, but what is often not appreciated is that alternative visions for what the nation-state should be are in fact different nationalisms in competition. In other words, in any country, it is not just the flag-waving people who talk about limiting immigration who are nationalist, but also those who are repelled by excessive flag-waving and want to encourage multi-ethnic immigration to their homeland. Both groups have idealised versions of what their nation should be in the future, but the principles and ideals that underpin it are different.

....

1   Michael Billig, *Banal Nationalism (Theory, Culture and Society)*, New York: SAGE Publications, 1995.

Thus, the debate about the Irish language is not a clash between romantic sentimentality and logical pragmatism, as opponents of Irish like to frame it, but rather two competing ideas about what Ireland should be in the future. These forces can be called Éire nationalism and Irelandshire nationalism, respectively. Éire nationalism is what most people mean when they refer to Irish nationalism in the traditional sense. It emerged as a coherent ideology in the 19th Century and its main feature is the promotion of the idea that Ireland is culturally unique and distinctive, especially from Britain. Its version of Irish history stresses the struggle of Irish resistance to British rule, and geographically speaking it sees Ireland as completely separate from Britain, denying that there is any such thing as the "British Isles". Politically, it promotes the concept of a single, united Ireland. It celebrates Gaelic games as a marker of Irish identity, often accompanied with a suspicion of games like soccer or rugby that are seen as overtly English. It cherishes the Irish language and wishes to see its position within Irish society improve.

Irelandshire nationalism, on the other hand, owes its origins to the development of Irish unionism in the 19th Century. In many ways, it is a moderated form of unionism that accepts the reality of an independent Irish state. It celebrates the social and cultural connections between Ireland and Britain and sees itself as more inclusive in that regard. Its version of Irish history stresses the links and connections between Ireland and Britain, and downplays differences between the two. It promotes the concept of a 26 county Irish state, and is suspicious of efforts to bring about a political union between Ireland and Northern Ireland. It celebrates the international and cosmopolitan nature of sports like soccer and rugby, often accompanied with a sense that Gaelic games are inferior or parochial. It views the Irish language as a barrier in the relationship between Ireland and Britain, and as such it wishes to see its presence removed from Irish society.

These then are the two ideologies that shape the debate about what the Irish nation is, or what it should be. Just to be clear, I am not saying one should think of these in "either-or" terms, that everyone either falls into one camp or the other. Instead it would be better to think of these as being two ends of a spectrum. Certainly, you can find people who would tick all of the boxes on one side or the other, but the world view of most Irish people is formed by some combination of the two. So, it is possible to be a fan of Gaelic games but hostile toward the Irish language, or to support a 32 county Irish state and celebrate historic ties with Britain. Indeed, even within each of these categories, the extent to which someone cares for one of these things varies greatly from person to person. For example, for some people, an interest in Gaelic games means checking the scores of big games every now and again, while for others it might mean daily involvement in their local club. In the same vein, for some people, a disdain for the Irish language amounts to no more than an eye-roll whenever they hear a politician attempting the cúpla focal, whereas for others it involves regularly writing letters to newspapers protesting the state's Irish language policy.

It should also be noted that I am not saying that one of these nationalisms is better, more authentic or more Irish than the other. As a historian of nationalism, I am well aware of the fact that all national identities and nationalist visions are constructed, indeed, invented, to a large extent. Nor am I claiming that having competing forms of nationalism is unique to Ireland. Similar divisions can be found in every country, albeit with different points of focus to those in Ireland. Living in the United States for over a decade, I have observed how the political divide in that country is based on drastically different interpretations of America's past and contrasting hopes for its future. What is important to understand, however, is that there is more than one nationalist ideology at work in Ireland.

Finally, in reading this book, one may be struck by the relatively few references to both the Gaeltacht and Northern Ireland. This is very much by design. Firstly, there is a tendency among some elements of the Irish public to assume that Gaeltacht affairs and questions about the Irish language in the Gaeltacht are the same thing. Thus, when Joe McHugh, who didn't speak Irish, was appointed minister of state with responsibility for Gaeltacht in 2014, many people commenting online stated this was a good thing, because McHugh might have a new insight into why Irish was taught so badly in schools. This was the equivalent of saying that accelerating coastal erosion might help improve the quality of drinking water in Athlone. It might appear superficially that one is talking about the same thing (in this case, water), but in reality, they are not related at all. As such, this book will focus mostly on the Irish language as it exists outside the Gaeltacht. As someone who is not from the Gaeltacht and has not spent much time in the Gaeltacht, I do not feel qualified to address the complex issues involved in preserving Irish as a community language there. My hope is that if I can offer some ideas for how to improve the status of Irish generally, this would naturally help improve its position within the Gaeltacht as well. Regarding Northern Ireland, there has been an impressive movement working towards improving the position of Irish there since the late 1960s. But the issues addressed in this book will mostly be geared towards what happens in the 26 county state, where, in theory at least, all major political parties are committed to reviving Irish.

CHAPTER 1:

MISE AGUS AN GAEILGE

I thought the best place to start this book would be with an explanation of my own relationship with the Irish language. I have a few reasons for this.

Firstly, as someone who learned Irish in school, but really didn't become fluent in it until I was an adult, I hope to offer some encouragement, as well as practical tips, to those who wish to learn Irish. There are thousands of people who would love to be fluent in Irish but, for one reason or another, are not. I know the feeling, because I was one of those people, so hopefully my experience can offer a guiding light to others.

Secondly, I want fluent Irish speakers to understand just how difficult it is for people who didn't learn Irish well in school to pick it up. I have found that some people who speak Irish well don't always have much sympathy for those who want to speak Irish but feel they have missed their chance to learn it. "Just go ahead and learn it so", can often be the attitude of those who have been fluent for most of their lives. But many of those people fail to appreciate that, either by learning it at home or through immersion schooling, they had an opportunity to learn Irish naturally that most Irish people never get. So hopefully this can create a greater awareness amongst fluent Irish speakers for the struggle faced by learners.

Finally, as this book is about reviving Irish, I felt my own story was pertinent. To the extent that there has been an effort to revive Irish, I represent the success story. I grew up in an entirely English-speaking environment, learned Irish at school, became fluent and now speak Irish at home with my family. Apparently, that is what was supposed to happen with everyone who went through the Irish education system. Understanding what went right for me might help us figure out what goes wrong for everyone else.

As a young lad in Cloghroe National School in Cork, I hated Irish. Hated it. HATED IT! When I think back to my time in primary school, I still vividly remember the absolute frustration whenever I had to do any school work or homework in Irish. There were nights when I was literally crying with anger trying to tackle my Irish homework. My problem was that I was so weak at Irish, I couldn't do anything through the language, so any school work in Irish was always a nightmare.

I honestly have no recollection of beginning to learn Irish in school, so I don't know when exactly I started to fall behind my classmates in the subject, or fall short of my teachers' expectations. From the very beginning, I suspect. I only had the ability to use the barest fragments of Irish. If someone had asked me to write or speak just one correct sentence of Irish, I would have been unable to do that. I remember knowing that "Rith mé" meant "I ran", although I had no idea how to use this verb in other tenses. So I used "rith mé" for "I will run", "I would run", or anything else I was trying to say in Irish that involved running.

I liked going to the shop for sweets, so I knew what "siopa" was. I also knew what "urlár" meant. I spent a lot of time looking at the floor, especially during Irish, so perhaps that was why that one stuck. I knew of the word "tá" and knew that it was important and had to be used regularly, but I did not really know how it translated into English. So whenever I was trying to say something in Irish, it had to be built around "rith mé", "urlár", "siopa", "tá", and whatever other couple of words I was in the process of learning and forgetting at the time. Sentences like "Tá rith mé ag siopa" were fairly commonplace in my Irish writing, and an awful mess for any teacher to untangle.

Oddly, one Irish expression that stuck with me was "sméara dubha", or blackberries. I remember it sticking in my head immediately the day we learned it, and it never left. I was very fond of eating blackberries, so maybe that was why it made an impression with me. I never forgot it, even if I didn't get to use it very much. It was hard enough trying to make some sense in Irish while referring to the shop, I ran, and the floor, all the while trying to negotiate the ambiguous "tá", without random blackberries further confusing the situation. "Sméara dubha" then was the smallest of successes in years of toil with primary school Irish.

Even the most basic Irish expressions escaped my comprehension. One of the books we used for Irish was *Suas Liom*. It seemed so simple a title to translate, just two little words, but it was an odious expression to me, something I could not wrap my head around. Someone told me it meant "Up With Me". I was skeptical. Right enough, I knew that "suas" was up; I had been told enough times to stand up ("seas suas") to understand that word. But I also knew that me was translated as "mé", and since there wasn't a "mé" to be found in "suas liom", that didn't add up. Then again, the English word "me" seemed to have an awful habit of shape-shifting into many different forms in Irish. Sometimes it seemed to be "orm", then "agam", and at other times it was "dom". With the most basic of all concepts in any language, the expression "I/me", seemingly in a constant state of change without any rhyme or reason, what hope had I of making any kind of progression with Irish? It was only years later that I understood what a prepositional pronoun was and how "orm", "liom", "agam" and "dom" all did indeed refer to "me".

It should be noted that I was actually quite good at most other subjects, notably English and history. While I was probably the worst in my class at Irish for primary school, I was one of the strongest students, when it came to English. And I was very confident that I was the best history student in class. Three times in third class,

Mrs. Mannix held a history quiz, having the entire class stand up and asking us history questions one by one. If you got a question wrong, you had to sit down and you were out. Two out of the three times I was the last person left standing, my supremacy in history unquestionable! So, the question we might ask is, how can a student be so strong at some subjects, yet so, so weak at another? Especially at primary school, when you have the same teacher for all subjects?

Any examination of academic literature will tell you that the one clear factor that helps explain a student's success in school, more important than anything to do with the quality of teacher or access to facilities, is parental involvement. This certainly explains why I was so good at English and history, as my father fueled a passion for those two subjects at an early age. He always encouraged both my brother and myself to read, and every week without fail we were taken into the Mayfield library to pick up new books. I devoured books, reading at every opportunity I had. My father also always had us watching history programs, and was forever talking about history, Irish history especially, and how family members had been present for momentous historical occasions like the Battle of the Somme and Béal na mBláth. With this support at home, it is no wonder that I thrived at English and history in school.

But what of Irish? I later realised that my father actually had a reasonable amount of Irish, but I never had that sense as a child. I am sure he helped me with some of my homework, but certainly I never got the sense from him that Irish was important, apart from the time he told me that if I wanted to become a teacher or a Garda, I would need to learn it. Having spoken to him since about the language, I think it would be fair to describe his attitude toward Irish as "indifferent". Like a lot of Irish people, I am sure I picked up (in all kinds of subconscious ways) this indifference from my father, and obviously this did nothing to help my ability to learn Irish.

My mother, to my knowledge at the time at least, had no Irish at all, although I was later to realise that many of the words she used regularly in English (her Clare dialect of English had some different vocabulary compared to what I would regularly hear around Cork) were lifted directly from Irish. I was astonished to later learn that my mother's mother, my grandmother (who passed away when I was very young) was actually a fluent Irish speaker. Anyway, I never had the impression that my mother cared much for Irish either. She did, however, realise I was struggling badly in the subject, and some-time when I was in fifth or sixth class, she arranged for a nun she was friendly with from the convent in Blarney to come and give me some tutorials in Irish. The poor woman tried her best. From what I remember, she seemed to understand that I had no grasp at all of Irish, and tried to begin with the very basics. But for some reason, it would not sink in. I was willing to sit there and try and learn, but whether it was some kind of mental block, or I had just accepted subconsciously that I was thick stupid and would never learn the language, the tutorials did not improve my Irish at all.

So, in recap, I was miserable at Irish, and I hated it. Or perhaps it would be more accurate to say that I hated being miserable at Irish. For all my struggles with Irish, I don't think I ever hated the language itself. I never saw the language as useless or pointless, but rather a skill that I could not seem to acquire (usually I just assumed that I was too stupid to pick it up). Indeed, in attending Cloghroe school, the existence of Irish as a living language was always reinforced, in particular by the school headmaster, Pádraig Ó Conaill. In interact-ing with students on a daily basis, he was always throwing in Irish phrases here and there. I vividly remember travelling with him by car one day to a hurling match against Watergrasshill. The entire journey, there and back, Mr. Ó Conaill had Raidió na Gaeltachta on, and not only did us passengers have to sit silently and listen to the stream of Irish, but Paddy (as we called him behind his back), was taking a full part in the conversation, chattering away in Irish in response to whatever was being said on the radio. I understood nothing, but I was jealous for not understanding it, wishing (not for the first or last time) that I could speak Irish.

But it was not just Pádraig Ó Conaill who reminded me that Irish was a living language. At the time, Cloghroe N.S. had a two-way intercom system, meaning that, whenever Mr. Ó Conaill made an announcement from the office, the teacher in the classroom could press a button on the side of the intercom, and talk back to him, without the rest of the school hearing. These conversations between individual teachers and the headmaster took place regularly, several times a week at least, in front of students. And they were always in Irish, because, of course, they didn't want the pupils to know what was being said. Now, on the one hand, this best encapsulates the problems of Irish language instruction in primary schools, as the teachers who were responsible for teaching the language could carry on their secret conversations in Irish before the students, safe in the knowledge that the majority of them had no idea at all of what was being said. Yet, for me at least, the impact of watching these conversations take place regularly was profound. It reinforced the idea that Irish was a living language, and that possessing it was valuable.

Nevertheless, I ended up leaving Cloghroe with very little Irish. For secondary school, I headed into Christian Brothers College in Cork City. My Irish language ability certainly did not improve in my early years in the school, but it finally began to turn a corner as I entered third year. After struggling badly with Irish in second year, I had been placed in the ordinary level Irish class. This was taught by Mr. David Nolan, and he really helped me, and some of my other classmates, get to grips with Irish. I think his biggest strength as a teacher was acknowledging that we had almost no understanding of Irish, and he began teaching us from the ground up.

For me, this was a revelation. It was the first time in my life that Irish made any kind of sense at all to me. Not that I was becoming proficient at it – far from it, but compared to the impenetrable black fog that had been my understanding of Irish, now a kind of dim light could be seen in the distance. David Nolan also demonstrated a real passion in wanting us to succeed in the language, and it rubbed off on me. Slowly, Irish moved away from being my least favourite school subject. I actually began to enjoy going to class, and I certainly liked the sense of achievement I had in making some headway in the subject.

So, I did the ordinary level Irish paper for the Junior Certificate. What did I get? A D! A D in pass Irish, in the Junior Cert! Clearly, I wasn't the second coming of Peig Sayers just yet! I honestly don't remember what my expectation was for that exam, but I do remember being dissatisfied with a D. I actually met with David Nolan not long after that, and he also seemed a bit disappointed with my results. But I shudder to think that, if I barely passed the ordinary level paper after one year of reasonable grounding in Irish, how horribly would I have done if not for ending up in David Nolan's class?

My next stroke of luck (although I did not realise it at the time!) was ending up in Anne Barry Murphy's ordinary level Irish class in transition year. For anyone who attended CBC around the turn of the millennium, the formidable reputation of Ms. Barry Murphy needs no embellishing. Suffice to say, she was a demanding teacher with high expectations for her students. Plenty of stick without even the faintest hint of carrot. As a teacher, she was incredibly effective for some, but not for all. Indeed, she had been my maths teacher for my first two years of secondary school, and I don't think it was a pleasant experience for either of us. So, I was somewhat crestfallen when I heard she would be my Irish teacher. The teacher who frightened the life out of me teaching the subject I had struggled badly with all my life? It didn't seem like it was going to end well.

In hindsight, the three years I spent in her class was the makings of me as an Irish speaker. I had become more interested in Irish after

David Nolan's class, but I was still a very weak student. I remember that, even in fourth year, I had almost no understanding of what the relationship was between "tá" and "bhí" (the present tense and past tense form of the verb "to be"), and I used them interchangeably in writing and speaking Irish, not grasping the distinction between the two. That was all to change very quickly in Ms. Barry Murphy's class. Her teaching methodology was definitely old school. Basically, we had to learn off chunks of prose or poetry for homework, and then recite them in class. Ms. Barry Murphy would pick one student to begin reciting, and then ask the student next to him to take over. She would have each one of us reel off what we had learned for homework every day, so you could never take the risk not to learn it, because you would be on the receiving end of either a torrent of shouting or a withering, ice-cold, comment.

Of course, to a lot of people, rote-learning Irish prose out of fear of a teacher's wrath sounds like everything that is wrong with how Irish has been taught over the years. But memorisation was something I had always been good at (it was undoubtedly the reason I was so good at Mrs. Mannix's history quizzes), so from the beginning, it meant at least that I was doing well in my Irish homework. But Ms. Barry Murphy always went through the text we had to learn off for homework before the end of class, and she translated what it meant, so I wasn't learning text that I didn't understand. As time went on, my understanding of Irish improved immensely, because if I was trying to say something in Irish, I could often draw upon something I had rote learned and repurpose it. Indeed, even today, if I am looking for a certain way to phrase something in Irish, I often think of an Irish song I have learned to remember the wording I am looking for. Anyway, my growing confidence in my Irish ability only furthered my interest to learn more of it and to do well in the class. Some of the lads made fun of me for being a teacher's pet, but I made no apologies for that. I had been on the end of enough tongue-lashings in first and second year mathematics class to know that I was much happier as the teacher's pet. It was a weird feeling for me to see that Irish was becoming one of my strongest subjects, and after years of misery, I felt proud that I had a grasp on the language.

When it came to sitting the Leaving Cert, I got an A2 in ordinary-level Irish. Truth be told, I was a bit disappointed with that at the time, as I had hoped for an A1. Looking back today, I actually think getting the A2 was a big achievement. I had clearly travelled a considerable distance from being a very weak student of Irish when I sat the Junior Cert three years earlier. But with hindsight, I see there were big gaps in my Irish-language ability, gaps I didn't appreciate at the time because I was getting good scores on Irish exams. My ability to read and write Irish was reasonably good, although I didn't understand then that my vocabulary was fairly basic, and more suited for discussing literature than day to day life in Irish. For example, I didn't know how to say "I want" in Irish. I could say "I would like", but not "I want", and I think many people finish school with similar holes in their vocabulary.

I also understand now that while I could understand much of what I read in Irish, I hadn't properly learned how to phonetically pronounce written Irish, meaning that when I tried to say words that I read, I regularly mispronounced them. Given that, my spoken ability in Irish wasn't very strong, and I knew that my ability to understand other people speaking Irish was quite weak. I had always been at a loss for why I could read Irish relatively well, but struggled when people spoke Irish. I now know that because I had not fully learned the phonetic system of Irish, people were saying words that I would have known if they were written down, but did not recognise at all when they were spoken.

So, I had finished school with a greater appreciation and ability in Irish than I ever had in my life. But where would the journey go from here? I had wanted to study either Law or Arts at university, and I was offered a place in Arts in UCC after the Leaving Cert. In studying Arts, I had decided to be a secondary school teacher, with English and history as my subjects. In all honesty, by this time I was also interested in teaching Irish, but since I had only studied the subject at ordinary level for the Leaving Cert, I wasn't eligible to study it at UCC.

But I didn't want to abandon Irish either. The Ionad na Gaeilge Labhartha at UCC offered a voluntary course in Irish. The deal was you had to pay a deposit, but as long as you attended 80% of the classes, you got the money back, so I signed up for that. The course met once a week, and I never missed a class, but my Irish language journey stalled here. The issue was that the class mostly focused on spoken Irish, and to my disappointment, I found that I was one of the weaker students in the class. Some of my old concerns about whether I was too stupid to speak Irish came back, and having thought I had gotten the hang of Irish in doing the Leaving Cert, it was a bit demoralising to see how weak my Irish was compared to the other people in the class.

Once I finished the course, I decided not to sign up again the next term. I told myself that I was too busy to keep it up, and on one level, that was true. Aside from coursework, I was playing rugby with UCC, and I had also gotten a job working evenings and weekends. But I think the fact that I wasn't doing great in the voluntary course also had a subconscious influence to step away from it. That being said, I hadn't abandoned Irish. If anything, my desire to become fluent in the language was growing, but I wasn't sure how to go about achieving this, so I was waiting around for inspiration. I was working at a newsagent on Patrick Street, and one of my coworkers, Áine Aherne, had a pretty good standard of Irish. I used to nag her to speak to me in Irish every now and again, or have her teach me some bits and pieces while we were working. I also used to regularly drop in to An Seomra Caidrimh, a small Irish-language café in UCC. I was just fascinated to sit there and listen to others speak Irish, hoping that one day I would be just as confident a speaker as the people I saw in there.

Meanwhile, for my final year of college, my work schedule changed, meaning I couldn't play rugby, so I decided to find some other club or society to join. I heard about An Cumann Drámaíochta, the Irish language drama group, in UCC. I was interested in acting, and combining that with Irish made it sound like a great idea to join. It had been well over a year since I had stopped attending the weekly course, and I think I had kind of forgotten how I had struggled a bit in that class. Between the positive memories of how well I had done in the Leaving Cert, and the little bit of speaking in Irish I did with Áine, I felt I would really thrive in An Cumann Drámaíochta. I went along to the first meeting of the term, and reality gave me a hard slap across the face. There were 11 girls attending beside myself, and the entire meeting took place through Irish. But I couldn't understand a word. Even when I had found the voluntary course at UCC a bit tough, I had always been able to get the gist of what was going on. Yet I hadn't a notion of what was being said in this meeting, so I sat there for an hour, didn't say a word, and when the meeting was over, I slipped out and never returned. To be clear, the other people there had tried to be friendly and welcoming, but the fact of the matter was that I didn't have enough Irish to participate. Having convinced myself that I had at least a reasonably good standard of Irish, it was humiliating to realise in a public setting that I didn't. In Cork parlance, I looked like an awful langer going to that meeting.

But little did I know that the foundations for my further improvement in Irish had already been set, albeit in a different language. You see, Irish hadn't been the only language I had struggled with in school. I also studied German, and while I had never felt I was totally useless with that language, I never excelled at it either. But I had been interested in studying Law, and the points for Law and

German were a little lower than just for Law, so I put that course as my first choice on my CAO form. I missed Law and German by five CAO points, and was offered a place in Arts instead. I decided to take German as one of my subjects in Arts, because I had sent my Leaving Cert exams back to be rechecked, and if I was upgraded on any result, I would get into Law and German. Since the German class was the same for both Arts & Law students, it made sense to begin it in Arts while I waited on my rechecks, because if I moved into Law and German, I would not be behind on the German side of things. But when I attended the first German lecture, I had serious doubts. I had barely gotten a high enough score in German in the Leaving Cert to even be eligible to take the class, and listening to the lecturers speak about the expected standard, I felt I was in way over my head. I instantly dropped German for Celtic Civilisation. A couple of weeks later, my appeal results came back, and my geography grade had been upgraded, meaning I was now eligible to take a place in the Law and German course. But since I thought my German wasn't good enough, I declined.

The point of this is that at 18 years old, I believed I was someone who didn't have a natural aptitude for languages, be it Irish, German, or French, in which I had also done poorly during the one year I had to learn it in school. But my opinion of my linguistic abilities changed in my second year of university, when I had to take a module on the Old English language. I had heard horror stories about how difficult Old English was, and how it was hated by most of the students studying English. To my surprise, I actually did really well with Old English. My confidence in my academic capabilities had grown since secondary school, and I realised that if I put in the time and effort, I could master any subject, including archaic languages. Indeed, I enjoyed Old English so much, I began exploring whether I would do a masters or doctoral degree in the subject. But to do this, I needed another language, Latin. I had been under the impression that Latin was the hardest language one could ever try to learn. When I was a first year at Christian Brothers College, the students were divided into two streams. The smarter students studied Latin, while the weaker students did art. By being placed in the weaker class, I had picked up the message that, basically, I wasn't smart enough to study Latin. But after studying Old English, I was optimistic that I could handle it. Vincent Murphy, the Latin teacher at CBC, gave me a Teach Yourself Latin book, and I threw myself into it. After a few months, I found that I had developed reasonably good skills in reading and writing Latin. This realisation that I could learn languages by studying by myself kick-started a craze that, over the next few years, involved me studying Italian, Swedish, Old Norse, Cornish, and Welsh.

Of course, this discovery that I could do a good job of teaching myself languages made me reassess my relationship with Irish. While the meeting with An Cumann Drámaíochta showed me that my Irish was not very good, I now had the confidence that I could do something about it. I bought a *Teach Yourself Irish* book in Easons, and I remember naively thinking that if I could just master that book, then I would automatically have fluent Irish. But I didn't throw myself into studying Irish just yet. By this stage, I was doing a post-graduate diploma in education in order to become a secondary school teacher. I was also playing rugby and still tipping away with the Latin, so I didn't have much time to study Irish as well.

In truth, I bought the book thinking that just possessing it would force me to read it. I glanced at it from time to time, but never built an hour into my day to focus on it as I had done with Latin. Yet while I was not studying much Irish at the time, I was still determined that one day, I would be a fluent speaker. I had gone back to CBC to teach as part of my teacher training, and while there I had an interesting chat with Sean Dunne, my old music teacher. He told me that he had always felt Irish was important, and that as an adult, he had decided to learn it properly and was now fluent. Since this was what I hoped to do myself, it was encouraging to hear of someone else who had summited the mountain.

But an even more important conversation was the one I had with Gillian Scannell, a substitute teacher at CBC. I told her in passing that I was interested in improving my Irish, and she told me about her friend, who was raised in an Irish-speaking home. She said that her friend's father was an Englishman who had gotten a job in an Irish university. He had decided that as he was moving to Ireland, he should learn Irish, and not only did he master the language, he insisted on making it the language of his home. This story blew my mind. To think that someone who wasn't even Irish could come to Ireland and learn the language so successfully that he spoke it as his daily language was humbling but heartening at the same time.

Before, my goal had been to be a fluent Irish speaker, but that had changed. Now, nothing would do other than master Irish and then raise my children through Irish. So, I knew what I wanted to achieve with Irish, and I knew that when I put my mind to it, I could put the time in and improve my Irish. But I was thinking that this was something I would do eventually, not necessarily a process to begin right now. I needed a kick to start putting this plan into action. I would soon get it.

In 2006, I was offered an opportunity to go study in the United States, so I made my way to the University of Delaware, about half-way between New York City and Washington, D.C. I packed my *Teach Yourself Irish* book, which I hoped to browse through, but I also brought a bunch of Latin books, which were still my priority on arriving in the US. A few incidents changed this, however. I quickly befriended two Irish-Americans in Delaware, named Pete Coyle and Dan Corkery. Over conversation, I mentioned that I knew Irish. Pete and Dan said they thought that was cool, and mentioned that they had a flag in their dorm room with a motto in Irish. They said they didn't know what it meant, and they asked me to come over and translate it. No problem, I told them. Sure enough, inside in their dorm room, they had a flag from the 69th New York Infantry, a famous unit that fought in the American Civil War and earned the nickname the "Fighting Sixty-Ninth". The slogan on the flag said "Riamh Nár Dhruid Ó Spairn Lann", which translates as "never did shrink from combat". The only problem was that I couldn't translate it in 2006! I wasn't lying when I told Pete and Dan that I knew Irish, in that I could say and understand many things in Irish, but undoubtedly they thought I meant I was a fluent or native speaker. Once again, I was left looking stupid because of my weak Irish. However, I later learned that this particular slogan is what we might generously call grammatically idiosyncratic, and fluent Irish speakers are often stumped by it as well.

About a week after my failure with the flag, I was training with the University of Delaware rugby team when Kyle Niblo, another Irish-American friend, came out wearing a t-shirt with something written in Irish on it. At first, I thought this was great, but I began to panic when I realised that I couldn't translate this either. Kyle came over and asked me what I thought of his t-shirt. I had to admit that I didn't know what it meant, or at least that I could only translate part of it. For the record, the t-shirt said "Más feidir leat é seo a léamh, rachaimid a luí", or "if you can read this, we will go lie (i.e. go to bed together)"! These two episodes got me thinking. I knew I wanted to speak fluent Irish, but clearly I was nowhere near reaching that level. I knew what it took to get there, but instead of working on my Irish, I was spending far more time on Latin. I enjoyed learning Latin, but if I was serious about getting the hang of Irish, I was going to have to make sacrifices.

Other factors were also encouraging me to dive into Irish. I had joined a foreign student club at Delaware. The club operated through English of course, but you quickly became conscious that these students from all over the world also spoke their native language in addition to English. Indeed, like a lot of Irish people, I found that living overseas was making me think more deeply about the role of the Irish language in my own identity. The incidents with the flag and the t-shirt also helped me realise that whatever Irish I had learned in school was starting to slip away. If I ever wanted to speak Irish to my children, like that Englishman I had heard about, then I needed to start working before I lost the Irish I had. I felt it was now or never. Within a few weeks of arriving in the US, I had committed myself to becoming a fluent Irish speaker.

By this time, as a result of exploring different languages, I had gained some important insights into how to learn a second language. A lot of people think of learning a language as being akin to downloading something from the internet. In this analogy, the key to learning the language is to have the right "internet connection" to facilitate the download, equivalent to finding the "right" teacher, or some new methodology, or the "best" book. This mindset makes the learner passive, and puts the responsibility for learning the language on the "internet connection". If the learner fails to "download" the language, it can be explained as the "internet connection" being faulty.

Rosetta Stone, the language learning software, caters directly to this mindset in how it markets its product, insisting that those who have tried and failed to learn a language in the past simply need the right "connection". Indeed, most of the Irish population has a similar explanation as to why we as a society fail to speak Irish despite extensive schooling in the subject. The answer given is almost always that "it is the way Irish is taught" or "I had bad teachers". The download analogy doesn't stop with how we learn a language either. A lot of people assume that once you have learned it, it stays with you permanently, in the same way that an entire movie remains on your computer once you have successfully downloaded it.

But this is not how language learning works. In fact, it is much more like trying to get physically fit or to build muscle. The key is simply dedicating time on a regular basis to the goal you are pursuing. In both cases, certain exercises will work your target muscles harder than others, but just as there is no ab exercise that will give you a flat stomach if performed once a week, there is no approach to learning a language that will allow you to be fluent if you only attend one weekly class. If you want to run a marathon, you have to find a way to build several runs into your weekly schedule, and the same thing is true for learning a language. This isn't to say that one needs to work on learning their desired language for hours at a time, but rather that dedicating 20 minutes a day to the task will help the learner far more than one two-hour session a week. The longer your regular sessions are, the more improvement you will see, but the key in terms of time dedication is multiple sessions on a weekly basis, not total number of hours a week.

The physical training analogy doesn't hold in all aspects, however. If one is training to run a race or to lift weights, it is possible to over-train, damage muscles, and therefore become less effective in what one was trying to improve. But this isn't the case with language learning. Certainly, you can become tired of doing an activity or even come to feel that you don't want to dedicate the time anymore, but so long as you engage with the language, you will continuously improve. We see this when it comes to speaking our first language. Imagine it as a muscle. How often do you "work it out" or use it? All day, every day, which is why its use is effortless. But people who go a long time without speaking their first language can find that it takes time to get back into the swing of speaking it.

Thus, my guiding principle when it came to seriously learning Irish was that I needed to find ways to use my Irish language "muscles" as often as possible. The most obvious way to do this with any language is to immerse yourself completely in an environment where it is spoken. Of course, a lot of people don't have the time, money or opportunity to do this, so they have to find ways to bring their target language into their normal routine. For me, in the beginning, this meant setting aside an hour in the evening, four or five times a week, and tackling the *Teach Yourself Irish* book. Even on those days when I hadn't built Irish into my schedule, or days when my plans changed and I no longer had an hour to spare for Irish, I made sure I at least spent some time with that book. Usually, this meant abandoning whatever novel I was reading in English, and bringing *Teach Yourself Irish* into the bathroom with me instead.

I found this book to be very useful, and went through it a couple of times. Even today I still pick it up for a browse from time to time. The book was helpful in that it had much more of a focus on day-to-day conversation than what I studied in school. For the first time, I was learning things like how to ask someone if they would like a drink, or how to introduce someone in a conversation. One of the most fascinating chapters was the one that covered the "modh coinníollach", or the conditional verb tense. I don't know if my class never learned the modh coinníollach because my teachers thought it was too advanced for us, or if I somehow just missed it, but I have no recollection of ever studying it in school. The modh coinníollach has a formidable reputation for being the most incredibly complicated part of learning Irish, so I was surprised to find that it was actually not a difficult concept to grasp at all. There certainly are some challenging aspects of Irish grammar, but I don't think the modh coinníollach is one of them.

Once I felt I had a firm grasp of everything in the *Teach Yourself Irish* book, I looked for ways to read, write and listen to Irish as often as possible, and make it part of my daily routine. Every morning while eating breakfast, I read the news in Irish online. At first, I found this level of Irish to be very advanced, but with the help of a dictionary, I soon had broadened my vocabulary extensively. One of my daily treats had been reading the sports pages of Irish newspapers (in English) while eating lunch, but eventually I began to look at this forty minutes as another opportunity to practice my Irish. Although I didn't really want to cut out reading the sports page, I reminded myself that if I was serious about becoming fluent, sacrifices would have to be made.

As I was already practicing reading Irish at other times of the day, I saw this as a chance to listen to some Irish instead. At first, I tried watching documentaries on TG4. The problem with doing this, as other Irish learners have discovered, is that it is very hard to focus on the spoken Irish when English subtitles appear on the screen. Although you pick up some words in Irish, most learners find themselves reading the subtitles and tuning out the Irish language. I switched to listening to Raidió na Gaeltachta instead. This obviously cured the problem of subtitles, but as understanding spoken Irish had always been the weakest part of my Irish repertoire, I found the speed of speech, and certain dialect differences, made it very difficult for me to follow. Finally, I settled on watching Nuacht, TG4's news show. This programme didn't run with any subtitles, and while the spoken word was still tough to follow at first, the images always gave you the gist of what was being said, and in that sense it was easier to learn from than just listening to a radio broadcast.

There were other spaces in my day that I discovered could be filled with Irish. I usually watched TV while eating dinner, so some evenings I substituted this with watching TG4 on my laptop. The subtitles remained an issue, but I figured that since dinner was a time to relax anyway, only practicing a little Irish was better than nothing at all. I also had a longstanding habit of reading in the bathroom and in bed before I went to sleep, and I switched from reading English books to Irish ones. This was an exceptionally tough change to make, because devouring books in English had been something I had done since I was a young boy. Obviously, the range of books available in English is far more extensive than in Irish, and it was also frustrating to go from reading 40 or 50 pages in one go, to five or six. But I persevered at this, and took great satisfaction in seeing my pace of reading and depth of comprehension improve as time went on.

One of the books that I came across was the infamous *Peig*. This book, an autobiography of a woman who was one of the last inhabitants of the Irish-speaking Blasket Islands, is renowned as the book that killed off any interest most Irish people might have had in Irish. Peig Sayers' life was so miserable and depressing, so the popular legend goes, that being forced to read about it in school drove people in their thousands away from the language. I had not read *Peig* in school, and I was apprehensive about tackling it, but I enjoyed reading it. No one would ever confuse it with *The Da Vinci Code*, but I didn't find the story of mind-numbing boredom and misery I had been conditioned to expect. As with the modh coinníollach, I think the opinion of most Irish people towards *Peig* is formed before they ever even encounter it, and suggests that at least some of the negativity towards the Irish language is based on biases that people pick up, rather than lived experience. It is interesting to note that the English translation of *Peig* has high ratings on Amazon's website. It seems that most of these readers are foreigners and that, without the baggage that Irish people bring to reading the book, they mostly read *Peig* in a positive light.

Another way I discovered that I could improve my own Irish was to teach it to others. I came across some Americans who were interested in learning, so I began teaching a small class. In particular, this helped improve my own pronunciation. As I mentioned earlier, for a long time I mispronounced words in Irish because I didn't know how to pronounce them based on Irish spelling, but it wasn't until I started teaching Irish that I realised how inconsistent my pronunciation was. As my students began asking questions about how certain combinations of letters were pronounced, I realised that my own understanding of this was hazy, and it forced me to go figure it out properly for myself so I could teach them.

Of course, there was one weakness in my plan to become a fluent speaker of Irish, namely that while I could listen to Irish and read Irish every day, I rarely had a chance to speak it in Delaware. Daltaí na Gaeilge is an organisation that promotes the Irish language in the United States, and they hold several immersion weekends throughout the year, so I began attending those. It was certainly a humbling experience meeting Americans whose Irish was far better than my own. I also encountered many Irish people at these events, and almost all of them said that it was moving to the United States that provided the catalyst for their own efforts to try and learn Irish.

But a couple of weekends a year was still not enough practice speaking Irish. So I started talking to myself in Irish! That obviously will sound crazy to some people, but I found it was a very effective way of practicing. If I was going for a walk, or just puttering around the house, I always tried to run my thoughts through my head in Irish rather than English. Although I sometimes actually spoke these words, mostly I just thought them. Oftentimes I would think of something that I was unsure of how to phrase in Irish, which prompted me to look it up, and hence my spoken Irish improved even though I usually wasn't speaking to anybody.

I don't know exactly when the moment came that I passed from being a learner of Irish to someone who "had" Irish. I think this happened quickly enough, maybe five or six months after I began studying in earnest. But at the time I probably didn't realise it, because I felt there was still so much of the language I had left to learn. It was only later on that I appreciated that there is no ending point for learning a language, as there are always new words or idioms to discover, even in your first language. Fluency is often the target language learners set themselves, but people who only speak one language often don't know just how broad and vague a concept like "fluency" is. It is only when you speak two or more languages that you understand that there are degrees of fluency, and that a person who can have an extensive conversation about sports might struggle to fully express themselves in a discussion of philosophy in the same language.

So, I think I would not have been wrong to call myself "fluent" in Irish after six months or a year of studying, but by consistently working on my Irish, I am a much stronger speaker now than I was back then. But there were two changes in my life that helped improve my Irish further. Firstly, I got a job at Drew University in New Jersey, and this was particularly fortunate because Drew received an Irish language teacher through the Fulbright program every year. This gave me a chance to speak in Irish several times a week with someone who had a degree in the Irish language, and was certainly a better way to enhance my Irish than talking to myself!

Probably the most important change for my language development (and my life generally!) came about when my daughter, Aisling, was born in 2015. Ever since I had heard about the Englishman who had raised his family through Irish, I had decided that I would do the same thing. However, it was going to be even more than a challenge than it might have been, since I was living in the United States. Furthermore, my wife, Kathy, is American, and while she has picked up some bits and pieces of Irish from me, she didn't really speak it. The idea of speaking Irish to Aisling was a bit daunting, but I was determined to do it.

I quickly learned, however, that doing so was hugely beneficial to me in terms of pushing my ability in Irish further along. Aisling was born with long eyelashes, and on the day of her birth, I realised I didn't know the Irish word for "eyelashes". So, if I wanted to speak to her in Irish and tell her what pretty eyelashes she had, I needed to find out what it was (*fabhraí*). As Kathy and I settled into daily life with Aisling, I found a huge number of words that I needed to learn like bellybutton (*imleacán*), vomit (*múisc*), nappy (*cluidín*), bib (*bráidín*), and diarrhea (*buinneach*)! Once I learned these words and used them a few times, they naturally fitted into our day-to-day lives. Furthermore, with online Irish dictionaries available on a smart phone, you can look up any word at any time, and a sound file on how to pronounce a given word is often available as well.

As most of my work needed to be done during the evening, I was largely responsible for taking care of Aisling during the day while my wife was at work. We spent a lot of this time watching cartoons on TG4. I had never considered watching cartoons in Irish before Aisling came along, but I realised they are an excellent tool for someone to improve their Irish. Not only does TG4 not put subtitles on its cartoons (so you have to concentrate on the spoken Irish), the conversations within them are much closer to natural spoken Irish than someone reading the news. My wife obviously spoke English to Aisling, but hearing so much Irish in the house, she found that her ability to understand the language, and to even speak it a little, quickly improved as well.

So that is it, the story of how I went from being someone who struggled terribly with Irish in school to someone who is a daily speaker of Irish. I hope that if anyone wants to become an Irish speaker but isn't sure how to go about doing it, my journey can offer a template for what to do. There are a couple of final tips I would like to give. Firstly, as noted above, the most important thing you can do (assuming you can't go live in the Gaeltacht for an extensive period of time) is to put in the time to learn it. There is no magic book or computer program that offers a shortcut to learning a language. Shorter interactions with Irish several times a week are more beneficial than one block period of time set aside weekly.

Most importantly, don't lose heart if you felt you were making great progress with Irish, and then hear a native speaker rattle something off that you find incomprehensible. Most people don't appreciate that there are not three dialects of Irish (Ulster, Connacht and Munster), but in fact four, with the fourth one largely based on the Irish learned in schools outside of the Gaeltacht. This might be called *Caighdean* (standard) Irish, or sometimes it is dismissively referred to as "school" Irish. Some people claim that this is a kind of fake Irish, as it is too heavily influenced by English pronunciation and idiom, and therefore is not authentic Irish like that spoken in the Gaeltacht. One can make that argument if they wish, but it is likely that this *Caighdean* Irish has more speakers than the three traditional dialects combined, possibly even among people who speak Irish in their home. If you are learning your Irish outside the Gaeltacht (but within Ireland), chances are you are falling into the *Caighdean* dialect as a result of the Irish you learned at school, although undoubtedly one of the traditional dialects will also have a strong influence on the kind of Irish you speak. Keep this in mind if you find a speaker of a particular dialect harder to comprehend. You will eventually have a grasp on all the dialects through experience, but some will be naturally easier for you to understand than others.

The final piece of advice to learners would be not to get discouraged when you find that you have to relearn some words. This is something every learner of any language experiences. I once heard that a learner has to encounter a word 25 times before it sticks permanently, and to me, that sounds about right. To give one example, I was out walking with Aisling one day in the autumn, and she picked up a pinecone. I didn't know the Irish for pinecone, so I had to look it up (*buircín*). But then winter came and I didn't take Aisling outside walking for a while. One day in the spring, we went out and she picked up a pinecone again. Since I hadn't used the word in a while, I had forgotten it and had to look it up again. Don't fret when this happens to you, as it is part of the process.

So now that we have covered the things an individual can do to burnish their Irish, let's explore what can be done to improve the position of Irish within society as a whole.

CHAPTER 2

WHY DON'T WE SPEAK IRISH?

Why don't Irish people speak Irish?

It is a simple question, but one without an easy answer. If a foreigner asked it, he or she would likely be looking to Irish history. Irish was spoken by all the people of Ireland for centuries. What happened to change that? In order to consider the problem of whether Irish could be revived, it is important to offer some answers to this question.

Irish has been spoken on the island of Ireland for thousands of years, although for how long exactly is unclear. The problem is that the spoken word leaves no permanent record (at least before recording technology came along) and therefore it is impossible to say when people starting speaking Irish. Linguists have been left to rely on archeology, models of language evolution, and more recently, genetics, to figure out when the Irish language arrived in Ireland. Estimates range from over 4000 years ago to about 3000 years ago.

The question of how long Irish has been in Ireland is not just a minor academic quibble. Its answer helps shape debates about the Irish language today. One journalist, Victoria White, has taken issue with Irish language activists who claim that "Irish is the national historic language of Ireland." White believes that this is not a fact, and that "we don't know what sounds were uttered by the worshippers at Newgrange." In relation to what language these pagan tomb builders spoke, White is correct, but she implies that Irish was not the language spoken at Newgrange, which we simply can't say one way or the other. Meanwhile, at a meeting of Belfast City Council in

2015, Ruth Patterson, a DUP representative, claimed that the Celts (and we assume, the Irish language) arrived in Ireland as recently as 250 BC. Patterson lamented the fact that schoolchildren were not taught how these "warlike" Celts invaded an island populated by "my people". By her "people", Patterson seemed to be referring to the Cruithin, a group who some scholars claim to have inhabited Ireland before, or alongside, the Irish-speaking inhabitants of pre-historic Ireland. Ulster unionists in particular have been attracted to the idea of the existence of the Cruithin, as its suggests that their ancestors and their non-Gaelic language formed the basis of the original people and culture of Ireland, before Irish-speaking Celts invaded.

The antiquity of the Irish language, or more specifically, the question of whether it was the first dominant language in Ireland, plays an important role in the debate about whether Irish should be preserved or revived. For revivalists, the belief that Irish has been spoken in Ireland for almost as long as people have lived on the island means that the language is the centerpiece of Irish identity across time. As a result, efforts to support the language and encourage its wider use are justified from this point of view. However, those on the other side of the debate often claim that Irish is one of several languages that have held sway over the island at one time or another in its history. They argue that Irish replaced some other language or languages before the birth of Christ, and now it is being replaced by English. In addition, they point out that other languages have formed part of Ireland's linguistic history, from Norse and Norman French in medieval times, to Polish and Chinese today. By stressing the fact that Irish replaced some earlier, unknown language, the anti-revivalists simultaneously deny that Irish was the original language of Ireland, as well as stressing the fact that language change is natural and ultimately should not be resisted.

At any rate, everyone can agree that Irish dominated all aspects of Irish life and society in the centuries leading up to the Norman invasion in 1169. The arrival of the Normans is an important moment in the history of Irish because, in bringing parts of Ireland under the direct rule of the English state, it set in motion the eventual replacement of Irish by English as the main language of Ireland.

Irish continued to be spoken by the vast majority of people living on the island for centuries after 1169. However, the 17th Century saw the linguistic balance of power in Ireland shift sharply in favour of English as a result of political developments. Firstly, the Battle of Kinsale in 1601 marked the end of the independent Gaelic lordships and the Irish-speaking political elite that had held sway over the island since the beginning of recorded history. The Cromwellian campaign of the 1650s and the Williamite Wars later in the century brought about a massive land transfer from people descended from the Gaelic aristocracy to settlers from England and Scotland. The Irish who managed to keep their lands found it wise to copy the settlers in terms of their dress, religion, manners, and above all, language. Put simply, in 1600, Irish was still the first language of some people with significant political, economic and social clout, but by 1700, it was not.

This had significant consequences for the future of Irish. While it is safe to assume that a clear majority of the Irish population were monoglot Irish speakers in 1700, this would not be enough to prevent its demise. As Aidan Doyle has pointed out "what is important for language maintenance is not so much absolute numbers as the social status of speakers."[2] It would be a mistake to assume that all Irish speakers lived in miserable poverty. Nicholas Wolf has shown that reasonably well-off Irish monoglot farmers survived into the 19th Century.[3] But the poorest people in Ireland in the 18th Century

2 Aidan Doyle, *A History of the Irish Language: From the Norman Invasion to Independence,* Oxford: Oxford University Press, 2015.

3 Nicholas Wolf, *An Irish-Speaking Island: State, Religion, Community and the Linguistic Landscape, 1770 – 1870,* Wisconsin: University of Wisconsin Press, 2014.

were Irish speakers, while the people with wealth, political power and social influence were English speakers. This could not but cause Irish speakers to reflect upon their language and to think about what linguistic arrangement would be most beneficial for their children.

Research has suggested that by 1750, a majority of people at least understood English, marking the beginning point of a significant shift in language use from Irish to English in Ireland. The return of the organised presence of the Catholic Church at the end of the 18th Century, after a century of banishment owing to the penal laws, added further emphasis to the importance of English. The clerical hierarchy was unsurprisingly drawn from the wealthier Catholic classes, which were almost exclusively English speaking. Thus, not only were politicians, businessmen and landowners all English speakers, but so too were priests and bishops. The message was clear. If one wanted to have any kind of influence, power or wealth in Irish society, they had to speak English.

It is difficult to track exactly the historical decline of Irish. The British government did not begin taking censuses until 1801, and these did not collect information about language use until 1851. Estimates for how many people spoke Irish as a first language in 1800 vary, but somewhere between 45% and 55% of the population seems likely. The majority of these Irish speakers probably had some command of English as well, as it has been suggested that only 15% of the population were monoglot Irish speakers by this time. One scholar has estimated that by the 1830s, only 28% of Irish children were being raised through Irish, showing the extent of the language's decline. However, while the proportion of the Irish population who spoke Irish was falling, the number of people who spoke Irish was rising, in line with the dramatic growth of the Irish population as a whole. Seán de Fréine has suggested that five million Irish people either spoke Irish or had parents who spoke Irish on the eve of the famine[4], with Gearóid Ó Tuathaigh calculating that there were three million Irish speakers.[5] Paradoxically, 1845 simultaneously marked the weakest point Irish had declined to in its history (up until that point) and the greatest number of speakers it ever had at one time.

The Great Famine was a devastating blow to Irish as a community language in large parts of Ireland. The worst impact of the disaster was felt in the poorest parts of the island, which was precisely where Irish remained strongest. The Great Famine is often cited as the primary reason for the decline of Irish, but as the figures above show, language shift was already well under way before the potato blight wreaked havoc. Nevertheless, it certainly was, in Ó Tuathaigh's words "a violent accelerator" of the language's decline.[6] He estimates that by 1851, the number of Irish speakers had fallen to 2.13 million. In other words, within 6 years, one third of the Irish speaking world had vanished, these speakers either dead or living overseas.

The psychological impact of this on Irish speakers must obviously have been traumatic. Even before the famine, Irish was seen as a language for people with no prospects, but the 1840s led to the association of Irish with death, despair and perpetual misery. Parents believed that only English offered any future for their children, and the switch from Irish to English picked up pace. By 1891, only 14.5% of the population (about 680,000) spoke Irish according to the census. This decline amongst communities who speak Irish has continued into the 21st Century, slowing occasionally, but never stopping.

Of course, languages do come and go, and many people in Ireland will point out that the story of the decline of Irish echoes the story of other languages from all corners of the world. But it is worth pointing out that the dramatic drop in use of the Irish language stands out

4 Seán De Fréine, *The Great Silence: The Study of a Relationship Between Language and Nationality,* Dublin: Mercier Press, 1978.

5 Gearóid Ó Tuathaigh, *I mBéal an Bháis: The Great Famine and the Language Shift in Nineteenth Century Ireland,* Conneticut: Quinnipiac University Press/ Ireland's Great Hunger Museum, 2015.

6 Ibid.

in comparison to other tales of linguistic decline. Ó Tuathaigh notes that the shift from Irish to English was "by European standards, a remarkable historical event."[7] Seán de Fréine writes "before the Famine, Irish ranked, in number of speakers, probably comfortably within the first hundred of the world's 5000 or so living languages". Its demise therefore was "an event the like of which has not befallen any other European nation in a thousand years."[8]

It is not just the size of the language community and the speed with which it disappeared that makes the history of Irish anomalous. It is also the fact that the Irish nation derives its sense of historical uniqueness from a language it no longer speaks. In other words, Irish is a rare example of a national language, as opposed to a regional language, to have suffered such a dramatic collapse. The only other nation-state that I can think of that is comparable to Ireland in this regard is Egypt. The people of Ireland and Egypt imagine that they are direct descendants from the ancient people who once occupied their land. They believe they share a common "Irishness" and "Egyptianness" with these distant ancestors, even though the language these people spoke has all but vanished. However, for a variety of reasons, the sense of loss Irish people feel regarding Irish is not something Egyptians feel in the same way.

This is what I am getting at when I use the term "national language". I am defining it as the language that was spoken, or at least is imagined to have been spoken, by most or all of the members of a nation for most of its recorded history. Critics will point out that as "nation" is something of a loose concept and ultimately an imagined social construct, defining something as a "national language" is meaningless. I would largely agree, up to a point. I am not trying to create an objective, linguistically and scientifically foolproof term when I call Irish a "national language". Indeed, Irish

---

7 Ibid.
8 Seán De Fréine, *The Great Silence*, op. cit.

mostly collapsed when Ireland was a part of the nation-state of the United Kingdom. As such, Irish was a regional language in relation to the state within which it was contained. Had history followed a different course, it is not impossible that most Irish people today would have no difficulty in imagining themselves as part of a wider British nation, and as a result, be less perturbed by the gradual disappearance of Irish.

But the fact that Ireland did emerge as an independent nation-state has added a greater sense of retrospective significance to Irish's demise from the perspective of today. Nor is this solely due to the fact that the leaders of that independence movement were supporters of reviving Irish. Imagine if Ireland had somehow acquired full independence in 1922 under the leadership of the old Home Rule party, which did not have the cultural nationalist agenda of Sinn Féin. This "Home Rule" state would still have had to reckon with the Irish language in some form or another. Remember, nation-states (especially in Europe) claim the right to exist based on the existence of their ancient nation. Irish was the language of the Irish nation for almost all of its recorded history, and for that reason, could never have been ignored by any independent Irish state. Indeed, it is largely for similar ideological reasons that the Scottish Nationalist Party, which had been indifferent toward Scots Gaelic for much of its existence, found itself engaged in mild promotion of that language once a Scottish parliament was actually established and the party acquired control of it. The fact that the claim of Scots Gaelic to be the national language of Scotland is far more debatable (in terms of for how long and how geographically extensive it was spoken in Scotland) compared to that of Irish in Ireland underlines the point I am trying to make (while not forgetting that for most of its history, Scots Gaelic was simply viewed as Irish).

In other words, the relationship between Irish and the Irish nation-state is almost unique in comparison to the linguistic history of the other nation-states of the world. In Europe, there is no other independent nation-state in which the national language has been reduced to a minority language community. It is worth bearing in mind that in some cases, these "national languages" are as much an act of historical imagination as anything else. In the not-so-distant past, large parts of France did not speak French, but this does not prevent the large majority of French people from seeing French as the language of their nation. Of course, not every nation in Europe speaks a unique language. There is no Belgian, Austrian or Swiss language, for example. But unlike Ireland, there never was a language in these countries that formed the basis of their historic identity, or, as Seán de Fréine puts it "they speak, not foreign tongues which have infiltrated their culture, but their own native languages."[9]

Ireland is a part of the English-speaking world, and the point is often made that the United States or Australia don't have their own national languages and embrace English as their language. This is true, but again, the history of these countries is very different from Ireland. These nations developed initially as settler colonies, with the original inhabitants and their languages driven to the margins of society, if not entirely obliterated. The beginning point of the history of these nations, at least in the popular imagination, was precisely when English-speaking settlers showed up. Obviously, there were many English settlers in Ireland as well, but the Gaelic population that existed before this did not disappear, and still forms the largest genetic component of the modern Irish population.

Perhaps even more importantly, the written records of this Gaelic society have also survived, meaning Ireland's ancient history cannot be ignored or written out of the "national history" as has happened to the ancient indigenous history of places like Australia or the United States. The point of all this is not to claim that the decline of the Irish language is somehow more tragic than that of

9 Seán De Fréine, *The Great Silence*, op. cit.

any other language, but rather that the relationship between language and identity is more complex in Ireland than almost anywhere else. Irish people are in a historical and cultural trap. Members of a nation imagine themselves to be part of a group whose essential identity has not changed across time. But knowledge of the language shift that took place means an awareness of an enormous rupture in the historic continuity of the Irish nation, threatening to undermine both an individual and collective Irish identity. This has complicated consequences for how Irish people view the Irish language, and we will return to this in a later chapter.

We have already noted that the importance of English in many fields of Irish life, compared to the unimportance of Irish, was a significant "push" factor in the dropping of Irish in favour of English. But it is worth bearing in mind that major changes in western society generally in the 18th and 19th Century also played a key role. After all, medieval England was conquered by French-speaking Normans. From the arrival of William the Conqueror in 1066 to the ascension of Henry IV in 1399, French was the first language of the English monarch and many of England's aristocrats. Despite French having such an advantageous position for over 300 years, English remained the language of most of the people of England. Why did English not suffer the same decline as Irish? The main difference is that the modern state engages with its population far more regularly than the medieval state did, and the language choice of the state can mean speakers of a non-state language feel pressure to switch.

Allow me to demonstrate what I mean. Tomorrow, you might make a trip to the post office to post a letter. On the way home, you might then be pulled over by a Garda and issued with a speeding ticket. When you get home, you might get a call from your child's school asking you to come and speak with his or her teacher. Wishing to avoid another speeding ticket, you might decide to take the bus instead. When you get back from the school, you might decide to turn on the TV and watch the news on RTÉ. While watching the news, you might catch sight of Mick Wallace sitting in the Dáil wearing an AC/DC t-shirt, and this might prompt you to write an email to your local TD complaining about the lack of a dress-code in the Dáil. In the course of this single day, you have had six interactions with different employees of the state, and you almost certainly have had all of them in the language of the state: English. The English-speaking peasants in 12th Century England would rarely, if ever, have to deal with their Norman government, and therefore would not have felt any particular pressure to adopt the French language. But over the centuries, governments increased their role in society and interactions with their populations became much more common. An Irish-speaking peasant in the 19th Century would regularly meet officials of the state, be they policemen, or court officers, or teachers, while the expansion of state bureaucracy meant more jobs were available for English speakers than ever before.

Nor was the growing role of the government the only change in modern society. The Industrial Revolution and the growth of the scale and size of businesses that accompanied it utterly changed how people worked and lived. Prior to the Industrial Revolution, most people lived rurally and worked in agriculture. Aside from occasional trips to markets or fairs, the language one spoke within one's immediate vicinity would suffice for almost everything. But the gradual shift from employment on the land to employment in the urban world of factories and businesses (the latter often requiring literacy) meant that one's local language might no longer be enough to get by. While Ireland did not see extensive industrialisation, the parts of Ulster that did certainly drew Irish-speakers into their orbit, while the importance of English as the language of business only grew throughout the 19th Century.

Nicholas Wolf notes that after the foundation of Maynooth in 1795, the Catholic Church, like the British state, became more involved in the daily lives of the people of Ireland.[10] While some priests, bishops and even cardinals spoke Irish, the language of the Irish Catholic Church was unambiguously English. Where once mass was said to small groups, the removal of the penal laws allowed for larger, chapel-style gatherings. In administering to bigger flocks, often with a range of abilities in Irish or English, priests found it easier to default to English in giving sermons or reading the Bible. The Catholic Church was certainly more accommodating of the needs of Irish speakers than the British state, but as an institution it had no great desire to preserve the language, and as such it added to the pressure Irish-speakers felt to adopt the English language.

We have established the reasons why Irish speakers would want to speak English. But this doesn't explain *how* the general population of Ireland switched languages. The short answer, basically, is that Irish speakers learned as much English as they could pick up, and then used English as their home language when raising their children. Where did they learn English? At work was one place. Irish speakers employed as servants or farm hands for English speaking land owners would have been well-placed to pick up English. People who regularly visited towns for markets, fairs or any other business would have had to learn English out of necessity. Service in the army, once it relaxed its restrictions on recruiting Catholics, would have been another place for the Irish to learn English. And, of course, English was also learned in schools.

The hedge schools of the 18th Century have earned a reputation as heroic defenders of the Catholic faith, providing an education for the poor masses shunned by the state because of their religion. But more often than not, the education provided at these schools was through English, often at the insistence of Irish-speaking parents. When a national primary school system was established in Ireland in 1831, this increased the availability of English-language education

10 Nicholas Wolf, *An Irish-Speaking Island*, op. cit.

for Irish-speaking children. These primary schools were later seen by some as the main driving force behind the language shift. In some areas, they undoubtedly played a crucial role, but as the figures noted earlier showed, the retreat of the Irish language was already taking place with great speed before these schools were created. Thus, the pattern of language shift was that Irish speakers learned English as a second language. They then raised their children through English, with these children often being able to understand Irish from hearing it at home, but not speak it. In turn, these English-speaking children raised their own English-speaking children, who could neither speak nor understand Irish, and the language disappeared from most parts of the country. This didn't happen everywhere simultaneously, but began in the east in the 18th Century and spread west, with Irish only spoken in small corners of the western seaboard by the end of the 19th Century.

When it comes to the Irish language debate in Ireland today, the entire argument turns on the issue of "choice". We will unpack this idea of "choice" more fully later on, but for now it is worth reflecting for a few moments on the role of "choice" in the great Irish language shift. I have heard the argument put forward that the Irish people of the past chose to stop speaking Irish, and therefore the language question in Ireland has been permanently settled, making efforts to revive Irish pointless. Firstly, the idea that when Irish people of the past make a choice, it can't be revisited in the future, is stupid. After all, we decided to legalise divorce in a referendum in 1995 a mere nine years after the Irish people voted to uphold the constitutional ban on divorce in 1986. But more importantly, to what extent did Irish speakers choose to start speaking English? One popular idea in Ireland is that the British government killed off Irish. In one sense this is true, in that the colonisation of Ireland created the conditions that destroyed the utilitarian value of Irish. But the British government never forced parents to only speak English to their children.

In that sense, this switch from Irish to English could be seen as a "choice". But the linguist James McCloskey writes:

> Almost all instances of language-loss, I believe, can be traced back ultimately to...acts of coercion, to violations of the basic human freedom to speak as one chooses to...It is true that, in the face of...pressures, members of a community can decide that it would be a rational and sensible thing to give up the targeted language and the cultural baggage that goes along with it. In every case I know about, though, that 'choice' was circumscribed by enormous external pressures towards conformity.[11]

Along similar lines, Gearóid Ó Tuathaigh notes that "in describing such a complex issue as language shift as starkly as 'pragmatic,' without reference to the structures of power and influence within which the shift took place, one runs the risk of seeing it as responding to an almost impersonal force of nature. The cultural 'climate change' in modern Ireland, to which the adaptive response was a change in the vernacular, was ideological and political, and had identifiable human agency."[12] One can only imagine that this "choice" would have been traumatic for many of the parents that made it. Ó Tuathaigh observes that "the emotional impact on a family or household of suppressing or expelling a language and replacing it with another – the inter-generational ruptures involved – must have been sharply disruptive, however rational the motivation for the change."[13]

The "choice" to switch from Irish to English in many households was an act of love and sacrifice. Love in that parents wanted the best possible future for their children, but sacrifice because it imposed a

11　James McCloskey, *Voices Silenced- Guthanna in Éag: Has Irish A Future- An Mhairfidh Gaeilge Beo?*, Dublin: Cois Life Teoranta, 2001.

12　Gearóid Ó Tuathaigh, *I mBéal an Bháis*, op. cit.

13　Ibid.

terrible burden on the parents. It must be remembered that for them English was a second language, and undoubtedly many would have had only a limited command of it. Imagine trying to raise your children by only speaking to them in the French, or German, or Spanish you learned in school. This would obviously have placed great restraints on the conversations parents could have with their children, to say nothing of the sorrow they must have felt in deciding not to replicate the sounds, idioms and expressions of their own youth. Such a commitment must have been physically and mentally exhausting, but one can easily understand the determination of parents to give their children opportunities that they themselves never had.

While the desire to learn English is easily understood, it might be wondered why Irish had to fall by the wayside at the same time? The answer appears to be twofold. Firstly, in the 21st Century, there is a general appreciation for the benefits of bilingualism and an awareness that human beings can operate effectively in more than one language. But this was not always the case, and it seems likely that parents would have viewed any acquisition of Irish as interfering with their children's learning of English. Furthermore, the association of Irish with poverty made its retention unattractive. Anecdotal evidence suggests that many Irish peasants believed they were poor because they spoke Irish, and therefore worried that passing Irish onto their children would mire them in economic misery as well. In this sense, it needs to be remembered that while parents made a "choice" to speak English over Irish in their homes, they left these children without a "choice" regarding language use. The use of the bata scóir, or tally stick, to punish children who spoke Irish in school has been remembered as an example of how the state repressed Irish, but little attention is given to the fact that parents were often willing and eager participants in this system. The consequences of this approach are evident in the recollections of Douglas Hyde in his wanderings through Irish speaking areas in the late 19th Century:

I met a young man on the road…I saluted him in Irish and he answered me in English. 'Don't you speak Irish," said I. "Well, I declare to God sir," he said, "my father and mother hasn't a word of English, but still, I don't speak Irish". This was absolutely true for him. There are thousands upon thousands of households all over Ireland where the old people invariably use Irish in addressing the children, and the children as invariably answer in English, the children understanding Irish, but not speaking it, the parents understanding their children's English but unable to use it themselves.

In a great many cases, I should say most, the children are not conscious of the existence of two languages. I remember asking a *gossoon* [youth]… some questions in Irish, and he answered them in English. At last I said to him "Nach labhrann tú Gaeilge? [Don't you speak Irish?] and his answer was "And isn't it Irish I am speaking?" "No, *a chuisle,*" said I, "It's not Irish you are speaking but English." "Well then," he said "that's how I spoke it ever!" He was quite unconscious that I was addressing him in one language and he was answering in another.

On a different occasion, I spoke Irish to a little girl while waiting for a train [in Sligo]. The girl answered me in Irish until her brother came in. "Arrah now, Mary," said he, in what was intended to be a most bitter sneer; "and isn't it a credit to you." And poor Mary – whom I had with difficulty persuaded to begin- immediately hung her head and changed to English.[14]

This gives us an insight into what was going on in some of these homes. Parents spoke English to their children and insisted that they

14 Douglas Hyde in *An Irish Literature Reader: Poetry, Prose, Drama,* ed. James MacKillop, New York: Syracuse University Press, 2006.

spoke English back to them. However, because these children were also surrounded by Irish (with some children later telling stories of overhearing their parents speaking in Irish after they had gone to bed), they learned to understand it, and in some cases, speak it. But when the first of the two young men mentioned above had children, English would have been the sole language of the household, and the "choice" made by their grandparents meant the grandchildren had no choice about what language they spoke.

The collapse of Irish amongst the native speaking population attracted the attention of many native English speakers in Ireland, and by the end of the 19th Century, various groups had been formed to try and at least preserve the language. The most famous of these was the Gaelic League, established by Douglas Hyde and Eoin Mac-Neill in 1893. This has often marked as the beginning point of the Irish revivalist movement, but what is striking is that from the beginning, there was some ambiguity about the exact aim of the movement, at least in terms of reviving Irish.

In a speech Hyde made to the Gaelic Society in Niagara in 1891, he declared "I do not for a moment advocate making Irish the language of the country at large, or of the National Parliament...What I wish to see is Irish established as a living language, for all time, among the million or half a million who still speak it along the West coast, and to insure the language will hold a favourable place in teaching institutions and government examinations." In a pamphlet on its objects and means, published in 1896, the Gaelic League said that its primary aim was "the preservation of Irish as the National language of Ireland, and the extension of its use as a spoken tongue." Thus, from the beginning, this "revivalist" movement was actually focused on preserving Irish where it was already spoken. Clearly there was also an intent to spread its use in English-speaking areas, but what did that actually mean? That all people would have some capability in Irish as a second language? That Irish would eventually replace

WHY DON'T WE SPEAK IRISH?

English as the daily language in every part of Ireland? Or simply that more opportunities would be provided to those who wished to learn it as a hobby? From the time the Gaelic League was formed, the idea that Irish could be "revived" has been bandied about, but it has never been clear what exactly this involves. This ambiguity has lingered around efforts to promote Irish to this very day (and we will try to address this in a later chapter).

The Gaelic League was unable to prevent the continuing decline of Irish in the Gaeltacht, but its spread across Ireland and campaigns for greater recognition dramatically changed attitudes towards the language. Many Irish people, especially those who had grown up only speaking English, took considerable pride in the existence of the language and saw it as the premier marker of a distinct and independent Irish nation. Not surprisingly, many of the men and women who participated in the Irish Revolution had been involved with the Gaelic League. Michael Collins wrote in 1923 "Irish history will recognise in the birth of the Gaelic League in 1893 the most important event of the 19th Century. I may go further and say, not only the 19th Century, but in the whole history of our nation. It checked the peaceful penetrations and once and for all turned the minds of the Irish people back to their own country". When a 26 county independent Irish state emerged in 1922, Irish was destined to have a pride of place that it never had under British rule. But what would this mean for the future of the language? Could the enthusiasm that many Irish people had shown for Irish in the decades leading up to independence be channeled into preserving, or increasing, the number of speakers?

It is generally acknowledged that the new Irish state tried, and failed, to revive Irish. In *The Guardian* Fintan O'Toole writes "Most of those who led the Irish revolution believed passionately that Irish independence simply wouldn't be worth having if it did not lead to a revival of the Gaelic language as the vernacular in Ireland. The state they created made Gaelic compulsory and insisted that it must be the 'first official language'. The project failed completely". Is this accurate, though? As stated already, there was always ambiguity about what a revival entailed, and without a clear goal, it is difficult to achieve something concrete. Undoubtedly there were people in Ireland, even within the government, who wanted to have Irish replace English as the main language spoken Ireland. But was any Irish government ever fully dedicated to that goal? That is debatable.

Speaking of the revolutionary period, Aidan Doyle observes that "most Irish people, even members of Sinn Féin, the nationalist party, were not really serious about replacing English with Irish."[15] Tomás Mac Síomóin is more critical of the state's intentions towards Irish, writing "Irish 'revivalism' never seriously contemplated strategies to replace Irish with English as the common vernacular of a modern state. Instead...official revivalism collaborates with a State language policy that is, in effect, little more than a continuation of British linguistic policy in Ireland."[16] How do we resolve such differing views as those put forward by O'Toole and Mac Síomóin? It is possible that, in a sense, they are both correct. Proof of this can be found in a quote from Walter Cole, elected to the third Dáil. Speaking in 1922, Cole declared "We want to make the Irish population in the future an Irish speaking population". In other words, he supported a revival of Irish, but it was one that would take place in the future, not today. This probably reflected the attitude of most members of the Irish government, then and now. At the core of this idea was the belief that the only thing preventing Irish from being spoken by everyone was a lack of knowledge of the language. Thus, the government's commitment to the revival of Irish was mostly focused on creating conditions that would allow the Irish men and women of the future to do the reviving.

15 Aidan Doyle, *A History of the Irish Language*, op. cit.
16 Tomás Mac Síomóin, *The Broken Harp: Identity and Language in Modern Ireland*, Dublin: Nuascéalta, 2014.

Of course, Irish schools were identified as the best way to enable the Irish population to learn the language, and the introduction of compulsory Irish became, and remains, the centerpiece of the Irish "revival" effort. This isn't to say that the need for incentive was not recognised, and from 1926, applicants for jobs within the Irish civil service had to pass both written and oral Irish exams. Reg Hindley writes that it "was assumed that to make it officially essential for employment under the state would have similar effects on the speaking habits of the Irish public as has the unofficial everyday need to use English". However, while school children and civil servants were required to demonstrate a competency in Irish "there was never any suggestion that eligibility for election to the legislature should be made dependent on a command of Irish".

The Irish government wanted others to revive Irish, but there was no desire to take that commitment upon themselves. Indeed, Aidan Doyle remarks that one of the ironies of the Irish Revolution is that the attainment of statehood served to weaken, rather than strengthen, the building momentum for the promotion of Irish. "For many the language movement had been merely one of the ways in which they could work for independence. Now that independence had been achieved, there was not the same impetus to keep supporting Irish."[17] In a similar vein, Reg Hindley comments that once the Irish state emerged as the protector of Irish, voluntary activity in the Gaelic League no longer seemed necessary.[18] So, for those to whom Irish language activism prior to 1922 was merely a tool to strengthen the cause of political independence, or those who wanted institutional protection for the language, the birth of the Free State seemed to solve all problems. The failure of the "revival" project might be summed up as follows: the government thought the people would revive it, the people thought the government would revive it, and in the end, no one revived it.

17   Aidan Doyle, *A History of the Irish Language,* op. cit.

18   Reg Hindley, *The Death of the Irish Language: A Qualified Obituary,* Oxford: Routledge, 1990.

The clearest evidence of the state's commitment to "reviving" Irish lay with the schools. As Adrian Kelly has observed however, this effort was doomed from the start because it was "was founded on the incorrect assumption that if English had replaced Irish as the language of the country primarily because of the anglicised education system, then the reverse could be brought about by a native government."[19] As we have seen, education did play a considerable role in spreading knowledge of the English language around Ireland, and it must be stated once more that it was the hedge schools, with the approval of parents, which began this trend, not the government established national schools.

But the decision parents made to switch from Irish to English was influenced by larger economic, social and political factors than simply what they learned in school. As no similar motives existed to switch from English to Irish in the 20th Century, no reversal of this language switch took place. What passive supporters of an Irish "revival" did not appreciate was that in order for a language switch to take place, there had to be a generation willing to "take one for the team" and endure the difficulties of living through their second language in order to make its use painless for their children. This, after all, is how Irish speakers raised their children as English speakers in the first place. Despite the best intentions of Walter Cole and those like him, no future generation would ever switch to speaking Irish at home simply because they obtained a working knowledge of it at school. Yet confidence that the nationalistic pride of Irish youth, combined with the teaching of Irish, could restore Irish remained high. Timothy Corcoran, the first professor of education at UCD, declared "the popular schools... can restore our native language. They can do it without positive aid from the home."

What role did Irish play in the new national education system? In

....

19   Adrian Kelly, *Compulsory Irish: Language and Education in Ireland, 1870s – 1970s*, Dublin: Irish Academic Press, 2002.

1922, it was introduced as a subject in all primary schools. The problem, as Adrian Kelly observes, is that many primary school teachers simply had little or no Irish, and were not in a position to teach it. This had been addressed by the 1930s, but there may be merit in Kelly's argument that the difficulties this imposed on children in the 1920s may have created a disdain for the position of Irish within the education system that has survived to this day. The study of Irish became a mandatory subject of study for the old Inter Cert in 1927 and the Leaving Cert in 1934, although this was only of concern for the minority of students who progressed to second level education. Starting in the 1930s, the first two infant classes of primary school were taught entirely through Irish, despite the advice of teachers and educational experts alike that teaching young children in a language they didn't know could harm their educational development.

Kelly shows the practical consequences of this policy by highlighting how sixth class children in the 1940s were using the fourth class English books of the 1920s, as they were basically two years behind in terms of their English language literacy owing to the focus on Irish in their infant years. Ironically, even the use of Irish language schools in the Gaeltacht did as much harm as good in trying to revive Irish. Reg Hindley records that many parents in the Gaeltacht made English rather than Irish their home language, as they were afraid their children would not learn enough English in the Irish medium schools being provided by the state.[20] Starting in the 1960s, some of the efforts to promote Irish through compulsion were relaxed. Infant classes were taught through English once more from the early 1960s onwards. The requirement that an Irish exam must be passed in order to attain a Leaving Certificate or to be employed in the civil service was dropped in 1974, and the number of hours dedicated to Irish in the primary school dropped from five hours to three and a half hours in the 1980s.

---

20   Reg Hindley, *The Death of the Irish Language,* op. cit.

One of the main complaints about the state's Irish language policy is that the language is not taught correctly in schools, which usually means that there is too much of a focus on reading and writing Irish, and not on learning to speak it. Adrian Kelly demonstrates that this complaint was regularly made by school inspectors and government ministers from the 1920s onwards. Yet why did it persist? The culprit seems to have been the Primary Certificate exam. This was introduced in 1929 and became mandatory in 1943, before being abolished in 1967. In brief, this exam was entirely a written one, and teachers seemed to have prioritised Irish reading and writing skills over speaking skills to prepare them for the Irish part of the Primary Certificate. Indeed, the relationship between the Irish language and examinations has been one of the most criticised aspects of the revival effort. Adrian Kelly writes "the decision to make the passing of Irish a qualifying requisite for the passing of certificate examinations which were the keys to future education, career and lifestyle, a signal of the language revivalists triumphalism, was perhaps the most repugnant element of the revival campaign and the most damaging to the perception and status of Irish."[21]

Kelly suggests that there was an element of spite in the decision to make the passing of Irish exams necessary to obtain an educational qualification. Perhaps there was, but to see this essentially as an act of pettiness is to ignore what those behind this policy were hoping for. Kelly himself has observed that "economics was not recognised as an agent of linguistic change by the Free State government."[22] But by connecting knowledge of the Irish language to educational achievement, revivalists were precisely, in this limited way at least, trying to use economics as "an agent of linguistic change". They believed that knowledge of Irish alone would create Irish speakers, and by creating an economic incentive to learn Irish (in order to pass

21 Adrian Kelly, *Compulsory Irish*, op. cit.
22 Ibid.

the exam and obtain a certificate of education), they assumed people would then be able to speak Irish and be thankful they had learned it. Nor was Irish the only subject that had to be passed in order to get a Leaving Certificate. Kelly shows that in 1961, more than twice as many people did not obtain their Leaving Cert due to failing the English exam than failing the Irish one. To only view the necessity of passing Irish solely as vindictiveness seems harsh.

In recap then, the history of the Irish language is a tale of steep decline from the 18th Century onward, followed by a "revival" effort from the turn of the 20th Century. Many people believe this attempt to revive Irish has been a dismal failure, which contributes to the negative attitude held by a lot of Irish people towards the language today. Certainly, the number of people speaking Irish has declined throughout the history of the Irish state, while only a very modest number of people have adopted Irish as their daily language in the Galltacht. If the benchmark for an Irish "revival" is everyone in Ireland speaking it as their first language, then it has been a colossal failure.

As noted earlier, however, this concept of an Irish "revival" is one that every Irish government has theoretically supported, but without any of them ever making it a priority. That the "revival" never reached a level that very few people were committed to anyway shouldn't detract from the notable achievements attained in increasing the presence of Irish in English speaking areas. This is particularly obvious when we consider Irish language literacy. The poet Tadhg Ó Donnchadha estimated that by 1880, only 50 people could read and write in the Irish language. One of the primary achievements of the modern Irish movement has been the development of a modern, written Irish language. Today, it is estimated that there are 3,000 Irish language books available to purchase at any one time. This is a tiny number compared to the number of books published in English, but remarkable when one considers a written form of the language was all but non-existent at the end of the 19th Century. As Seán de Fréine has observed: "More people are able to read and write Irish than ever before."[23] On top of this, the introduction of Irish into the national school system has created speakers of the Irish language that otherwise would not exist. In the next couple of chapters, we will try to figure out what being an "Irish speaker" actually means and whether schools could do a better job of producing Irish speakers. However, there are thousands of people, outside the Gaeltacht, speaking Irish on a daily basis thanks to the efforts of Irish language activists and the Irish state.

James McCloskey makes the case that assessments of the Irish "revival" should not be all doom and gloom. He writes:

> What is remarkable about [the Irish] situation, and what is unique as far as I know, has been the creation of a community of people who have learned Irish as a second language, who speak and write with a degree of fluency, and who use the language regularly and seriously. Some have produced fine literature, and some pass the language on to their children. This is immensely different from the tokenism that marks most revival movements that I know of.... it is a very substantial and very unusual achievement indeed (unique, in fact, as far as I know). It is something to be celebrated. Celebrated soberly, with a clear and unflinching view of what a delicate and shifting foundation it all rests on, with the clear understanding that it could all be swept away in a decade or two, but celebrated nevertheless.[24]

McCloskey points out that many language revivalists around the world are envious of the position attained by Irish, which thousands

23 Seán De Fréine, *The Great Silence,* op. cit.
24 James McCloskey, *Voices Silenced,* op. cit.

of students study every year as part of a national curriculum, which has its own TV and radio stations and a vibrant online presence. They find this to be "extraordinary", and McCloskey calls on us to see it in a similar light. We should.

CHAPTER 3

WHERE IS IRISH TODAY?

So what is the position of Irish today?

The short answer is that it is difficult to say. The obvious way to tackle that question is to find out how many people speak Irish. But getting an exact figure for that is not as straightforward as it might appear. Depending on the parameters of what is meant by "speaking Irish", estimates have ranged from about 10,000 people to 1.7 million.

Irish is spoken by a small number of people as their first language, and is learned by most school children throughout the entirety of their primary and secondary education. As a result, most of the population has some familiarity with the Irish language, but saying anything beyond that with some degree of precision is tough. We know there are some people who speak Irish as competently as they speak English, and other people whose first language is English but who are also fluent in Irish, and people who are English speakers but can say some things in Irish, and people who know a couple of words in Irish but no more than that. The problem is that providing even approximate numbers for any of the above groups is very challenging.

According to the 2016 census, 1,761,420 people, or 39.8% of the Irish population, answered yes to the question "do you speak Irish?". Of course, this raises the question of what exactly it means to speak Irish. For me, to say you speak a language means that you are fluent in that language. I have studied several languages over the years and can say little bits and pieces in them, but I would only ever say I "speak" English and Irish. So, if to "speak" Irish is to have a fluent command of it, then we would all agree that the idea that 1.7 million people speak Irish is a great exaggeration.

But if our standard for "speaking" a language is lower than fluency, then that figure becomes a little more plausible. When I first moved to the United States, I made friends with a guy called Alan. In one of our earlier conversations, Alan told me that he was a fluent Spanish speaker, and also had "conversational Portuguese". Not long after, I was out with Alan when we ran into another friend of mine, Ana, who was from Portugal. Naturally, I thought it there was no better way to introduce Ana to Alan than by pointing out that Alan had "conversational Portuguese".

Ana and I very quickly found out that Alan's "conversational Portuguese" was limited to being able to say "Hello, my name is Alan" in that language. Technically, I suppose, that would be enough for one very short conversation, but it certainly was not what I thought he meant by "conversational". I don't think Alan was lying when he said he had "conversational Portuguese", but more that he had a much more generous definition of what that involved than I did. The exact same issue arises when you ask people whether they "speak" Irish, in that "speak" can be broadly interpreted. If Alan's "conversational Portuguese" standard is applied, then we can say that the figure of 1.7 million probably underestimates how many people "speak" Irish.

The problem in trying to assess how many people speak Irish is that both overestimations and underestimations of one's ability in Irish are common. I have seen the 1.7 million figure referred to online as "propaganda of North Korean proportions", and certainly this isn't an unfair assessment if all of these people were claiming to be fluent Irish speakers. But on the other hand, there are also thousands of people who study Irish for thirteen years and claim not to speak "a word" of Irish or not to be able "to string a sentence" together. These claims are often taken at face value in order to condemn the standard of teaching of Irish in schools. We will address that issue in the next chapter, but for now it should simply be stated that most of these statements are exaggerations, often put forward by people who want to argue for an end to Irish lessons in schools. I have often thought it would be an interesting idea to find people who studied Irish up until the Leaving Certificate and claim they don't speak "a word" of Irish. Then they could be offered €10 for every Irish word they could remember. I imagine most of them would remember one hundred words without much difficulty!

It seems reasonable to assume that everyone who studied Irish up until the Leaving Cert has at least a limited vocabulary of Irish words. Even the foundation level Leaving Cert paper, taken by about 7.5% of students and undeniably aimed at students with very weak Irish language skills, still requires students to write a couple of short passages of 50 to 90 words. Given that, how many people might be said to understand at least a little bit of Irish? Well we can make a rough (and somewhat arbitrary) estimate. In 2015, 90% of the students who enter the Irish education system go on to sit Leaving Cert. This figure has been climbing in recent years however, so for balance we will use the 1998 figure (83%) as an estimation of the percentage of students who remain in school until the end of sixth year. We will then deduct the number of people foreign nationals living in Ireland (11.8%) from the population in total in 2016. Then we can use the 83% figure to estimate how many people in Ireland sat (or will sit) the Leaving Cert, and then deduct the percentage of people exempt from studying Irish in the Leaving Cert (6%) and the percentage of people who fail the foundation level Irish paper (0.25%). This would give us a figure of 3.2 million people in Ireland who are capable of saying something, anything, in Irish.

The point of calculating this figure isn't to create a wild overestimate of the number of Irish speakers to serve as propaganda for Irish language activist groups. I am trying to say that when it comes to the question of "do you speak Irish?", it isn't simply a yes or no answer. Instead, we should think of Irish-language ability as being a spectrum upon which most (although certainly not all) Irish people fall. This would range from fluent speakers of Irish who use the language every day at one end, to people who left school decades ago and now just remember a couple of words and phrases at the other, with a variety of levels of ability falling in between. To many people, this might seem like an incredibly small return on the investment the state has made promoting Irish. Perhaps. But it is also worth remembering that this modest spread of Irish stands in contrast to the late 19th Century when much of the English-speaking population of Ireland was entirely ignorant of the language.

If most Irish people have at least a few words of Irish, then how many are fluent speakers? Once more, this is not easily answered and depends on who is doing the asking. Tomás Mac Síomóin has claimed that only "0.02%" of Irish people speak Irish.[25] This would only amount to 915 people and, even acknowledging that Mac Síomóin believes that the percentage of the Irish population who speak Irish is "putatively miniscule", is surely an error. If we adjust this to 0.2%, we are left with a figure of about 10,000 people which is also the number of people Mac Síomóin claims speak Irish every day in the Gaeltacht. These figures from Mac Síomóin are revealing as, if I have corrected his figure properly, it suggests that he only sees daily Gaeltacht Irish users as "real" speakers of Irish, despite the fact that he acknowledges that another 60,000 people outside the Gaeltacht claim to speak Irish every day.

Nor would Mac Síomóin be alone in holding such views. This reflects a fault line that exists within the Irish language community, with speakers inside and outside the Gaeltacht sometimes claiming to have a greater authority over the other in regard to what "true" Irish is. We will return to that point at the end of the chapter, but it

25 Tomás Mac Síomóin, *The Broken Harp*, op. cit.

is worth noting that even if one uses Mac Síomóin's own measure for how to count Irish speakers, his figure seems a touch pessimistic. According to the 2016 census, there are 20,586 people in the Gaeltacht who speak Irish on a daily basis. Of course, this is entirely based on self-assessment, so whether this figure only includes people who speak almost nothing but Irish in their home, or extends to people who might throw an occasional Irish phrase into the English they speak almost exclusively is difficult to say.

About 96,000 people live in the Gaeltacht. Over 66% of the Gaeltacht population reports that it can speak Irish, but only 21.4% speak it daily. These bare figures reveal a lot about the Gaeltacht. In comparison to the rest of the country the proportion of people who can and/or do speak Irish is quite high, but even within the Gaeltacht boundaries Irish is very much a minority language. Indeed, when one considers that the number of Irish speakers recorded as living in the Gaeltacht in 1926 was 246,811, the decline under the watch of the independent Irish state has been staggering.

However, Reg Hindley has pointed out that the Irish government has found itself in a catch-22 situation in trying to preserve the Gaeltacht. Irish survived in these areas for longer than anywhere else precisely because they were so poor and therefore less exposed to the English-speaking, modern economy. To do nothing meant Irish would decline as parents switched to English to give their children a chance to escape the poor locality they were raised in. But once the government tried to promote industry in the Gaeltacht, starting in the 1970s, they discovered that emigrants returned with English-monoglot spouses and children, further eroding the position of Irish there. To say this is not to absolve Irish governments of any blame for the decline of the Gaeltacht, but to recognise that even with the sincerest commitment, Dublin would have struggled to stop the rot.

Returning to the present day, Irish speakers are not limited to the Gaeltacht. Of the 73,808 people (1.7% of the population) recorded as daily speakers of Irish in the census, the majority (53,271) live in the rest of Ireland, or the Galltacht. This is worth reflecting on for a second. There is a tendency in Ireland to think of Irish only existing as a living language (if people agree it is living at all) in the Gaeltacht. This figure suggests there are probably more Irish speaking homes outside the Gaeltacht than within it. But the Galltacht Irish speakers are often ignored in assessments of the strength of the Irish speaking population. For some people, like Mac Síomóin, there is a tendency to ignore the Galltacht Irish speakers because there is a sense that they are not speaking "real" Irish. This issue will be discussed in more detail at the end of the chapter.

But those who oppose efforts to revive Irish also often only concentrate on the number of Gaeltacht speakers. Their motives for doing so are simple: by diminishing the number of people counted as Irish speakers, they seek to justify cuts to Irish language budgets and the denial of services to Irish speakers. For example, in a 2017 article in the *Belfast Newsletter*, Robin Bury (an admitted opponent of the state's support of Irish), wrote that "less than 20,000 people are native speakers."

Thus, he completely ignored the 50,000 or so people outside the Gaeltacht who speak Irish daily, at least some of whom, by any definition, are "native" speakers. Indeed, if the Irish government's policies towards the Gaeltacht since the foundation of the state have been a disaster, the growth of daily Irish speakers in the Galltacht can be claimed as a victory of some sort. In addition to the daily speakers noted in the census, a figure of 111,473 is given for the number of people who speak Irish on a weekly basis. As I mentioned earlier, the key to fluency in a language, especially a second language, is regularity of use. Given that (and not turning a blind eye to the fact that self-reported figures are problematic), combining the weekly and daily speakers gives us a figure of 185,281, which we might cautiously accept as the number of people who speak Irish fluently. This would amount to 4.2% of the Irish population.

Another source that offers hints as to how many people speak Irish is a survey carried out by the Economic and Social Research Institute in 2015, entitled "Attitudes Towards Irish on the Island of Ireland". This survey involved 1215 respondents in the Irish Republic. While the authors felt the survey accurately represented the age and gender breakdown of the broader Irish population, the fact that it used unweighted data means that certain segments of the Irish population could have been over or under represented.

What were the findings of the survey? Firstly, 57% of the respondents said they had basic fluency in the Irish language, with basic fluency being defined as the ability to say a few simple sentences. 14% of those surveyed said they had advanced fluency, meaning they could participate in most conversations in Irish, with 3% identifying themselves as having native-like proficiency. 6% of the respondents said they spoke Irish every day, and 7% said they spoke it weekly. If we apply these numbers to the Irish population generally (based on the 2016 census), we get 2.7 million people with basic fluency in Irish, and 666,116 people who can understand most conversations in Irish. This would also mean that there are 142,739 people in Ireland who have native-like proficiency. This data suggests we have 285,478 daily speakers and 333,058 weekly speakers of Irish.

The latter four figures in particular seem suspiciously high in my opinion, and suggest that the overrepresentation of certain groups may have skewed the study. If we focus just on daily speakers of Irish, which we might see as the group most representative of Irish as a living language, the discrepancy is striking. The last three censuses have consistently reported about 74,000 daily speakers of Irish. But the figure from the ESRI survey is almost four times that. It should be noted that 32% of the advanced fluency group (which included daily speakers) said they were not recorded as Irish speakers at all in the census. This suggests that the number of Irish speakers may be underreported in the census, although no explanation is offered for why such a large number of Irish speakers are not counted (correspondingly, only 3% of non-Irish speakers said they were recorded as Irish speakers). Yet even this figure would not account for why the census and the ERSI survey have such different numbers for the number of daily speakers.

A third source to help us gauge how many people speak Irish is a survey entitled "The Irish Language and the Irish People," published by Micheál Mac Gréil and Fergal Rhatigan in 2009. The authors surveyed 1015 people, with 7.8% of them describing themselves as "fluent or very fluent". Extrapolating this number to the Irish population in general would give us 371,122 fluent Irish speakers. This would represent twice as many fluent speakers as reported by the census (when counting all daily and weekly speakers as fluent), but only about 56% of the number of people who said they can "understand most conversations" according to the ESRI survey.

9.3% of those surveyed by Mac Gréil and Rhatigan said they spoke Irish weekly or more often. As a percentage of the Irish population, this would represent 442,491 people, far more than the 185,281 daily or weekly speakers recorded by the census, but less than the 618,536 suggested by the ESRI survey. It is also interesting to note that Mac Gréil and Rhatigan's figures would suggest that about 71,000 people speak Irish once a week or more despite not viewing themselves as fluent in Irish. 19% of the Irish born respondents in Mac Gréil and Rhatigan's survey said they spoke Irish at home, while 19% (presumably the same people) also said they spoke Irish with Irish speaking friends. Again, that figure seems suspiciously high compared to the Irish population in general, and may include people who use the odd word or phrase in Irish, as opposed to people who converse entirely through Irish.

The problem with all three sources is that they are based on self-assessment. Therefore, we are left floundering on the fact that people are likely to have different interpretations of what it means to be "fluent", to "understand most conversations" or to be a "daily speaker". If we want to get an accurate measure of how well people can speak Irish, our primary source of information are the results obtained by students in the Leaving Certificate exam. Certainly, there are limitations on what this can tell us about people's ability in Irish, but as an objective assessment, it is the best we have. Let's say we want to figure out how many people leave school with fluent Irish. For the purpose of this exercise, I have (somewhat arbitrarily) decided that the cut-off for fluency is a B1 or higher in honours Irish. This isn't a perfect measure, although I think it is fair to say that anyone who gets this grade or above has a reasonable command of the language.

In 2016, approximately 5024 students obtained an A1, A2 or B1 in Leaving Cert honours Irish. Factoring in the total number of students who sat the Leaving Cert, and accounting for early school leavers, this figure suggests that 8% of Irish people leave school with a reasonable level of fluency in the language. Again, this figure can only suggest so much. Firstly, just because this group can speak Irish well does not mean they will ever speak it again once they leave school. We cannot use this figure to say that 8% of the Irish population has fluent Irish, because as time passes without the person actually using Irish, their ability to speak it decreases. Nor should a level of fluency based on the score one attains on the Leaving Cert be confused with native-like proficiency. While these students could probably cope with conversations on a wide range of topics, it is easy to imagine that there are many areas (like philosophy, economics, sex) where a lot of the students wouldn't have the vocabulary to express themselves as readily as in English. So, the Leaving Cert results are helpful, but don't provide a clear answer on the position of Irish today.

This is the dilemma of trying to evaluate the position of Irish. We know people speak it, but how many speak it, how well they speak it and how often they speak it is unclear. Of course, for those in the anti-Irish lobby, these figures are irrelevant. They point out that Irish is almost never heard in public in any part of Ireland outside the Gaeltacht, and question whether anyone really speaks it at all. In an article in the *Irish Independent* in 2016, Donal Lynch, even while acknowledging the number of daily users of Irish recorded in the census, wrote "nobody really speaks it". This is fairly typical of the logic of those holding a grudge against Irish. They claim nobody speaks Irish and then when it is pointed out that there are indeed people, thousands of them, who speak Irish every day, they claim those people don't count. If 73,000 people died on Irish roads in the last 20 years, would anyone say "nobody really died on Irish roads"? No, they wouldn't. If 73,000 people claimed they were molested as children, or that they identified as gay or transgender, would a journalist feel comfortable saying "nobody really suffered sexual abuse as a child", or "nobody really is gay"? Of course not. But opinions that are insultingly dismissive of the very existence of Irish speakers are commonplace.

The defense for this mindset is always "if people speak Irish, how come I never hear them"? The simple answer is given by Douglas Hyde. Writing in 1884, Hyde recalled his youth in Roscommon and noted "Often I saw if there were anyone in the parish without Irish, everyone would speak English when they were in their presence, but if there was a man who only spoke Irish there, they would often speak English even in his presence". There is a long-standing tradition in Ireland that it is "bad manners" to speak Irish in the presence of English speakers. Indeed, throughout the English-speaking world, there can be a deep resentment towards people having the audacity to speak another language when it is known (or assumed) they speak English. More often than not, what is going on here is not any real interest in civility or manners, but a defensive response to maintain the dominant position of English.

Such an attitude played an important role in Irish being pushed to the margins of society in the first place. I was once in a pub in Donegal, sitting on a couch and chatting to a few people, mostly tourists, in English. I was sharing a hotel room with a friend, Shane O'Rorke, who was sitting at another table. After a while, Shane came over to our table, stood behind me and tapped me on the shoulder. He asked in Irish (because we only ever speak Irish to each other) if he could have the key to the room because he was retiring for the night. I told him no problem, gave him the key, and asked him to just leave the door open so I could get into the room myself later on. My friend left, but the woman sitting beside me (an American) turned to me and told me it was very rude to speak in another language around people who didn't understand it. Frankly, I thought this took unbelievable arrogance on her part to say this. The conversation between my friend and I took place to the side of the main conversation at the table. It only lasted a couple of seconds, and had nothing to do with her. I wasn't long telling her this either.

But the problem is that a lot of people in Ireland would completely take the American's side in this instance. Not all of them might be brave enough to say the same thing if they were in her position, but they absolutely would think she was in the right in what she said. For this reason, Irish speakers usually only speak Irish if they are only around other Irish speakers. Since most Irish speakers probably have more friends who only speak English than speak Irish as well, this doesn't happen regularly. I have often been in a situation where there are five or six Irish speakers in a group who would have the entire conversation in Irish except for the fact that there is one person there who doesn't speak Irish. On top of this, Irish speakers are aware that even if they are speaking Irish amongst themselves in public, there is a chance that some disgruntled stranger will make a snarky comment towards them.

Another issue is that Irish speakers usually assume someone they are meeting for the first time only speaks English and wouldn't even think to ask whether the person spoke Irish. I was once staying with some friends in south Dublin. One morning, I headed into the city centre by myself and of course, being a culchie, I got lost in trying to make my way back to the house! I saw a woman walking her dog, and decided to ask her for directions. We started talking (in English) when her dog suddenly took off, trying to escape his leash. She started running after the dog, trying to bring it under control, but I noticed that when she was talking to her dog, she was doing so in Irish. When she came back with the dog, I spoke to her in Irish and she responded in the same language. She was able to give me the directions as Gaeilge, and I made it safely back.

The point here, however, is that here were two total strangers who were more than happy to communicate in Irish, but who resorted to English because social norms in Ireland dictate that this is the language you always speak with strangers. If it hadn't been for the fact that she was walking her dog, neither of us would have known the other spoke Irish. So just because Irish is rarely heard in public does not mean there aren't people who can speak it and indeed want to speak it.

Of course, the idea of people wanting to speak Irish brings us back to the role of choice in the Irish language debate. The trump card in the anti-Irish arsenal is the belief that people don't speak Irish because they don't want to. To those who believe this, the point is inarguable. People learn Irish in school for years they say, but despite that, we never hear people speak it. Clearly the people have chosen English over Irish. Indeed, they see people who refuse to speak Irish as heroic resistors to the state's efforts to spread the language. In his book, Tom Garvin notes that the desire to revive Irish was "never an authentic or widely held belief.... the masses continued to speak English and quietly resisted language change in their private lives."[26] Similarly, Adrian Kelly, speaking about the Irish people in the decades after independence, commented that they were "a population which chose ignorance of its national language over knowledge of it."[27]

Undeniably there were people, then as now, who see any effort to promote Irish as stupid and took pride in defying the "authoritarian" desire of the state to have them speak another language. But to claim that everyone who speaks only English does so as a free choice is ridiculous. That there are many people in Ireland who would like to be fluent in Irish but aren't is undeniable. Yet all of these people are counted as opponents of the promotion and revival of Irish. Indeed, it has struck me that for all the surveys taken about the Irish language, the obvious question almost never asked is "would you like to speak Irish fluently?"

In April 2017, the online news website *The Journal* ran a poll asking people "would you like to speak more Irish?" Almost 25,000 people took part. 70% said they would indeed like to speak more Irish, with another 6% saying they already spoke Irish fluently. Only 21% of responders said they did not want to speak more Irish. They organised a second poll asking the same question in February 2018. This time fewer people took part (about 13,500) but the numbers were almost identical to the previous poll. 70% of the people said they would like to speak more Irish, 7% said they were already fluent, and 21% said they had no desire to speak more Irish (in the first poll, 1% said they did not know, but this option was not available on the second poll). Obviously, one has to be careful about taking online polls at face value, but these may be evidence that a majority of Irish people wish they spoke Irish fluently. Meanwhile, a 2018 survey undertaken by Kantar Millward Brown for Conradh na Gaeilge revealed that about 40% of Irish people wanted more

---

26 Tom Garvin, *Preventing The Future: Why Was Ireland So Poor For So Long?* Dublin: Gill and MacMillan, 2004.

27 Adrian Kelly, *Compulsory Irish*, op. cit.

opportunities to both speak and learn Irish. While this suggests that a majority of Irish people do not have a great desire to speak Irish, it reinforces the fact that hundreds of thousands of Irish citizens wish they spoke more Irish.

"Well why don't they speak it so", is the inevitable retort. It is complicated, isn't it? We can all agree that just because people may want something very badly, does not mean they are in a position to get it. Most of us would like to be millionaires, after all, but it isn't simply a case of choosing to be one. A growing number of Irish people are now overweight, and one can be sure that most of them would very much like to change that state of affairs. So why don't they just do it and get the washboard stomach that society tells us we should all have? You are probably looking at similar factors to those that prevent adults from learning Irish, such as a lack of confidence that they can do it, a lack of information about how it can actually be done, not having enough money to pay for dedicated classes or professional help, and a belief that the pressures of work and life mean they don't have the time to dedicate to the cause.

Some statistics from the ESRI survey on attitudes towards Irish are interesting in this regard. Firstly, it noted that 67% of people surveyed were either strongly, or somewhat, "in favour" of Irish. It also showed that 5% of people said they had once tried to improve their Irish, and 10% of people had tried several times. It seems a reasonable assumption that most people who have a favourable view of the Irish language would like to speak it fluently themselves, although these figures suggest that just over a fifth of those people will actually make an effort to improve their Irish. This doesn't mean that people who say they would like to speak Irish are insincere. Instead, we might guess that for most of them they feel there is no point on trying, because they won't succeed.

This leads us to reflect on what exactly is choice and free will? For those of us who live in the western democratic world, these are the foundation stones upon which our society is built. However, because these concepts are so central to how we identify as a society, they are powerful tools that can be deployed against almost any proposal and make opposition to it seem reasonable under the illusion of choice. Thus, for example, any suggestion to provide relief for people in poverty might be countered by the claim that people, through their choices, have allowed themselves fall into a situation where they need assistance, and to provide help will only encourage more people to make the "wrong choice" in future.

Along similar lines, "choice" is often a weapon to be wielded against the Irish language, making efforts to encourage its use appear undemocratic. When can we say that people have an actual choice? Well if you have a red t-shirt and a blue t-shirt in your wardrobe, we can say you have a free choice in which one you wear (even though a whole host of factors might make one choice much more attractive than the other). A second level of choice might lie between being an omnivore, and a vegan. Certainly, one can choose to be a vegan, but in doing so one knows this provides many more challenges than the other, like limiting (and possibly raising the total cost of) your shopping options, limiting your choice of meal when at a restaurant, and forcing you to be cautious about eating food prepared by friends or family.

And then there is the "choice" we make when it comes to speaking Irish (in addition to English). I think the best analogy to this "choice" of speaking Irish can be made with the idea of drinking a cup of tea. To speak only English in Ireland is to make a cup of tea in your own home. It is effortless, follows a clear routine and most of the time you probably aren't even conscious you are doing it at all. For someone who speaks Irish fluently, the decision to speak Irish is like driving ten miles into town to your favourite café to get your cup of tea. It isn't that difficult to do, but it does require a little effort and planning and some days you really wish it could be as easy as making tea in your own home. To not speak Irish but to choose to speak it fluently is to decide to go to Tokyo for your cup of tea. It absolutely can be done, but it requires a considerable amount of money, time and effort on your part, and a lot of people will think you are stone mad for doing it. This is what we have to keep in mind when we talk about people "choosing" not to speak Irish in Ireland.

A related argument in the matter of choice refers to the English language in Ireland. Journalist Victoria White has written "English is now ours and we use it because we want to". I have no argument that the vast majority of people in Ireland, including most Irish speakers and aspiring Irish speakers, are content to speak English as their first language. But to suggest that the linguistic situation that exists in Ireland today does so because people "want" it is ridiculous. Think back to the young men Douglas Hyde encountered who didn't even realise they weren't speaking Irish. This might have been what their parents wanted, but they, like almost everyone in Ireland today, were not in a position to execute any kind of free choice in the matter. I grew up in an English-speaking area, raised by English speaking parents. I went to primary and secondary schools that taught exclusively through the medium of English, and all of my friends spoke nothing but English. At what stage exactly did I "want" English to be my language?

Could someone in Ireland today decide they didn't "want" to speak English? One could probably establish a circle of friends and find a partner only speaking Irish, although your pool for both would be limited. To speak only Irish would mean one is all but unemployable aside from a few select jobs, like teaching in a Gaelscoil or working for the Irish language media. Despite rhetoric to the contrary, an Irish speaker would almost certainly be compelled to interact with the state through English, and in engaging with businesses and services around Ireland, there would be no option but to speak English. To say we speak English "because we want to" is laughable because it implies there is some kind of alternative. As Tomás Mac Síomóin notes "English is compulsory for all; Irish is only an optional extra."[28] When it comes to choosing a language in Ireland, it is Hobson's choice, and nothing more.

Another complex part of the Irish language puzzle is the attitude of people towards the language in general. Broadly speaking, most surveys and polls show that a large majority of the Irish people have a favourable view of Irish. This is not to say such an attitude is universal. There certainly are vocal opponents of Irish, and it seems to me at least that a disproportionate number of journalists, broadcasters and columnists in the Irish media wish to stop state support for the language. But the general population appears to be more supportive. In June 2017, the *Irish Times* ran a poll asking whether people believed the Taoiseach should speak Irish, and 71% answered yes. This figure, almost identical to the number of people from the two *Journal* polls who said they would like to speak Irish, might reasonably be said to equate to the percentage of the Irish population who are supportive, in some sense, of Irish.

But what kind of future does this segment of the population want for the language? The ESRI and Mac Gréil and Rhatigan surveys offer some answers to that question. There was very little support for the idea of Irish replacing English as the main language of Ireland, with only 1% (ESRI) and 3.7% (Mac Gréil, et al.) of respondents in favour. The numbers were slightly higher for people who wanted to see Ireland as a bilingual nation, but with Irish as the more prominent language, between 4.7% (Mac Gréil) and 5% (ESRI). A much higher proportion of people were in favour of a bilingual Ireland with English as the more prominent language, between 32.5% (Mac Gréil) and 43% (ESRI). Most of the rest of the respondents supported preserving Irish, as either a spoken language in the Gaeltacht or some other form of preservation, from 42% (ESRI) to 52.5% (Mac Gréil).

---

28 Tomás Mac Síomóin, *The Broken Harp*, op. cit.

The number of people who wanted Irish forgotten was small, ranging from 6.6% (Mac Gréil) to 1% (ERSI), although it should be noted that the latter survey also offered a "don't know" answer to those surveyed, which 8% opted for.

The Mac Gréil and Rhatigan survey also broke down these attitudes based on factors like education level and gender. They showed that men were both more likely to want Irish revived (43.2%) and to see it discarded (8.9%). Such polarised opinions were also found amongst people reared in Dublin, who were both most likely to support a revival (45.9%) and most likely to support abandonment (10.8%). Not surprisingly, young people, especially people under 40, were more in favour of reviving Irish and less likely to support it being abandoned. In terms of education level, support for revival was highest amongst people who had gone on to third level education (47.5%) while those who had never advanced beyond primary education were the most likely to want Irish forgotten (16.8%). In terms of employment, professional or executive workers were most likely to support reviving Irish (55%), with people in positions of supervision most supportive of discarding (6.6%) Irish. Compiled together, we might say that the average person in favour of reviving Irish is male, under 40, raised in Dublin, received a third level education and is employed in a professional or executive capacity.

So what we have learned is that most Irish people view Irish in a positive light, with even a large minority wanting it to be revived in some fashion, but this does not seem to have prompted most people into taking action to preserve or revive the language. The exception to this has been the rise of Irish-medium schools, or Gaelscoileanna, in the last four decades. In 1972, there were only 11 primary schools and five secondary schools outside the Gaeltacht using Irish as the language of instruction. Between 1985 and 2002, the percentage of Irish primary school children educated through Irish rose from 1.1% to 5%. That has risen to 6% today, with 145 Gaelscoileanna outside the Gaeltacht, as well as 29 Gaelcholáistí (secondary schools) and 13 Aonaid (Irish-language units within English speaking secondary schools) in the 26 counties. The demand for Irish medium education has continued to grow, and many Gaelscoileanna are having to turn away applicants every year.

The reason for this growing demand has been the source of some controversy. The most obvious answer is that with their smaller class sizes and high success rate in terms of student academic achievement, the Gaelscoileanna and Gaelcholáistí are often the most attractive option available to parents. Another factor, at least for the parents I have spoken to who sent their children to these schools, was that they wanted their kids to have fluent Irish, something that they themselves had never been able to acquire. Given the fact that all available information suggests that most Irish people would like to speak Irish to a high level, this makes sense.

For some people, however, the desire to provide an educational advantage for their children or to do something positive for the Irish language can't explain why parents would send their offspring to these schools. Other, darker forces are seen to be at play, namely, racism and elitism. If racism is the cause of the rise of the Gaelscoil, then how does one explain the fact that many of the Irish language schools were built in the 1970s and 1980s, before immigration brought ethnic diversity to Ireland? Even if racism was the main motivating factor for parents, how would we know this? Do parents waiting outside the Gaelscoil to collect their kids at the end of the day say things like "Feck it, this place is great! Not a black in sight!"? Racism is an easy smear to make against the Gaelscoileanna, without any real way of disproving it.

As for elitism, whenever I hear someone say that explains the interest in the Gaelscoileanna, I am always struck by three thoughts. Firstly, hasn't the Irish language come a long way from the days when it was dismissed as a *patois* spoken by dirty peasants to a marker of being elite?

Secondly, that since the rise of mass democracy in the west at the end of the 19th Century, "elitism" has become an insult thrown around with impunity, to the point that it is essentially meaningless. Follow any political debate in the western world, and you will see the charge of "elitism" lobbed by all sides against one another. There is no better way of saying that your policies, or your way of life, are authentic and genuine than by saying those of the other side are "elite".

And the third thing I think when I hear the Gaelscoileanna being accused of elitism is "Good!" Language shift in Ireland happened precisely because English was the language of the elite. Nothing could improve its position more than if Irish actually were the language of our political and economic elites. Of course, the language of the "elite" in Ireland is still unmistakably English, but that fact has never prevented the slur being hurled at Gaelscoileanna. Indeed, what I find remarkable is that whenever a newspaper article is written about Irish language schools, the writers always seem to accept the "elitism" as a given truth, and put the onus on Gaelscoileanna representatives to disprove it. This would be the equivalent of interviewing people from Pavee Point to see if in fact all Travellers are thieves and liars, as large segments of the Irish population believe. But negative myths and untruths about the Irish language have a way of largely going unchallenged by some sections of the Irish media.

It should be noted that not all criticism of the Gaelscoileanna has come from people outside the Irish language community. There have been murmurs that while the Irish language schools are producing more people who can (although not necessarily do) speak fluent Irish, the kind of Irish these students are speaking is not the real thing. This reflects something of a split amongst Irish speakers that has emerged from the efforts to revive Irish beginning in the late 19th Century.

On the one hand, we have speakers of Gaeltacht Irish, whose Irish more closely resembles the language spoken by monoglot communities in the 19th Century, although it certainly has continued to evolve and change. On the other hand, we have the dialect of Irish spoken by people who learned their Irish as a second language. This dialect of Irish has been given several names. In chapter one, I called it the *Caighdean* or standard dialect, but it is known by a variety of other labels such as "school" Irish, "Dublin" Irish, "Nua Ghaeilge", "Gaeilge B'l' Áth" or, most dismissively, "Géarla". There certainly are significant differences between the Irish of the Gaeltacht and that of the Galltacht. To someone who has learned their Irish in school, the pronunciation and rhythm of Gaeltacht Irish, especially as spoken by older speakers, can be indecipherable. People in the Gaeltacht can usually understand what "Nua Ghaeilge" speakers are saying, but to them the language often seems fake and clumsy.

The reason for this difference is that *Caighdean* Irish developed amongst people who spoke English as their first language, and therefore English had a considerable influence on the pronunciation, idiom and syntax of this form of Irish. In many ways, it was a reversal of the process that created "Hiberno-English" in Ireland, when people whose first language was Irish began using English as their main language. A related phenomenon in this regard has been the development of "Béarlachas", which refers to an obvious borrowing from English into Irish, often in place of a word or phrase that already exists in Irish. An example of this is the use of "tá fáilte romhat". In Irish, this means "you are welcome" in the sense that you are welcoming someone to a place, as it literally translates as "there is a welcome before you". But "you are welcome" has another purpose in English besides welcoming someone to a place. It is also an acknowledgment when someone thanks you for something. "Tá fáilte romhat" has now also acquired that second meaning in Irish as well. It should be noted that "Béarlachas" is not confined to people who speak "Dublin" Irish. It is common today for native Gaeltacht speakers to say "tá fáilte romhat" in response to "go raibh maith agat".

At the heart of this split within Irish is the question of authenticity, with people both inside and outside the Gaeltacht dismissing *Caighdean* Irish as fake. In 1972 the Irish Communist Party described "Dublin" Irish as "a jargon of the middle class… it is also largely incomprehensible to the native Irish-speaking community. It was developed by Free State civil servants whose native language was English". Victoria White has written that "what passes for Irish" in the Belfast Gaeltacht is "an English necklace threaded with beads of Irish". Tomás Mac Síomóin has referred to the Irish learned at the Gaelscoileanna as a "teanga easnamhach" or "deficient language", a halfway house between English and Irish. He is also critical of the Irish spoken by the youth of the Gaeltacht, labelling it "Géarla", and saying it is a "syntactical, lexicographical and phonetic mixture of Irish and English that would be well-nigh incomprehensible to monoglot native speakers of only 40 years ago."[29]

By criticising the Irish spoken by young people in the Gaeltacht, Mac Síomóin shows that criticism about the authenticity of the language does not just flow in one direction. *Caighdean* speakers are often baffled by the amount of English loanwords in modern Gaeltacht Irish, which annoys Gaeltacht speakers who find questions about the quality of their Irish by people from the Galltacht to be arrogant. What happens to create this divide is that when a "Dublin" speaker of Irish doesn't have the word they need in Irish, they go look it up in a dictionary, whereas a Gaeltacht speaker in the same situation is content to use an English word instead. As Michael McCaughan writes in his book *Coming Home* "It has been said that you can tell a Dublin Irish speaker from a Connemara native because the Dubs have an Irish word for everything."[30]

This has also raised questions about what words are genuinely part of the language. Some people argue that if the word does not

29 Tomás Mac Síomóin, *The Broken Harp*, op. cit.

30 Michael McCaughan, *Coming Home: One Man's Return to the Irish Language*, Dublin: Gill Books, 2017.

develop organically amongst Gaeltacht speakers, then it is not "really" Irish. On the other hand, Foras na Gaeilge has coined many new words for Irish in recent years, amongst them "féinphic" for "selfie". This is not as odd as it might sound to an English speaker, as most major world languages have language academies that perform this exact role. Although I can understand the arguments on both sides, I think dismissing *Caighdean* speakers with their use of dictionaries is misplaced. The more sources of inspiration and innovation for a language, the better. The call for a purer form of Irish based only on how it was spoken by native speakers a century ago seems pointless, because most people, including, it seems, young people in the Gaeltacht, have no way of reaching that standard anyway. Furthermore, the fact that we have native *Caighdean* speakers, who learn *Caighdean* Irish as their home language, makes the idea that there is only one authentic form of Irish more problematic.

What is the future of Irish then, as things currently stand? Within the Gaeltacht at least, there seems to be grave concern for the language's future. Some estimates suggest that it will disappear as a community language within as little as ten years, to say nothing of the fact that the type of Irish being spoken by young people in the Gaeltacht is markedly different from that spoken by their parents or grandparents. What about outside the Gaeltacht? Mike Krauss, a linguist, had suggested that the two most important things for the future of any language is (1) the number of speakers and (2) the support of a nation-state.

Many Irish language activists question just how sincere the state's commitment to Irish is, but compared to the poverty of resources available to most languages in decline, Irish is very well-supported. The use of state money to provide a TV station, radio stations and dictionaries are all vital to helping some people retain their Irish and other people to acquire it. The position of Irish within the school system exposes most of the population to the language, and based on Leaving Cert results, we can say it produces about 5000 fluent speakers of the language each year (that is people who could, but not necessarily do, speak Irish fluently).

Tomás Mac Síomóin has claimed it is a "cop-out" to think that the Gaelscoileanna are compensating for the collapse of the Gaeltacht in terms of creating speakers with the equivalent richness of language and regularity of use. He is right. The Gaelscoileanna will produce people who can speak Irish fluently, but not necessarily people who will speak it, and after a time, their fluency will fade. Conor McGregor, for example, received his entire primary and secondary education through Irish, doing his Leaving Cert in 2006. But by 2015, in an interview with Máire Treasa Ní Cheallaigh, he acknowledged that while he could understand everything she said to him in Irish, he found it difficult to reply in Irish. What will happen to Irish? In the *Dublin Review of Books*, Joe Mac Donnacha writes "it is reasonable to conclude that it will continue to exist into the far distant future in some form or other... as long as the state deigns to support the language through the various levels of the education system, there will always be small groups who will be able to speak the language to a competent level of ability... But this does not mean it will be a living language – at least not in any sociolinguistic sense."

We should do something about that, then.

CHAPTER FOUR

WHY CAN'T WE TEACH IRISH PROPERLY?

We began chapter two by asking why Irish people don't speak Irish. In that sense, we were asking, from a historical point of view, why the majority of Irish people don't speak the language.

But if an Irish person asked another Irish person "why don't we speak Irish?", they wouldn't be asking for a history lesson. Instead, they would be looking for an answer to a different question, namely why, despite learning the language for 13 years in school, most Irish people can't, or don't, speak Irish.

Of course, everyone knows the answer: "It's the way it is taught."

Or at least, that is what everyone will tell you. I'm going to argue in this chapter that how the language is taught actually hasn't got much to do with why people don't speak it. But it is worth reflecting for a moment just how deeply ingrained this idea is.

I gave a talk in Donegal once about Irish language myths. My lecture mostly focused on exaggerated claims about how much the Irish state spent on the Irish language. I never said anything about the role of Irish within schools. But once the floor was opened for comments and questions, all anyone wanted to talk about was how badly the language was taught. I tried to point out that if we compare the achievements of Irish students in other subjects besides Irish, it is difficult to conclude that they are learning these subjects markedly better than Irish. No one was buying it. An American colleague of mine, Bill Rogers, interjected and pointed out that despite considerable exposure to Spanish in school, most American students never learned that language either. This didn't alter any opinions. These people already knew what the problem was, and no amount of fancy talk from so-called "academics" was going to change their mind!

Why is everyone so convinced that the teachers are to blame? I think at some stage, every Irish man and woman pauses to reflect why they don't speak Irish. After all, they spent so long studying it at school, why didn't any of it stick? Someone must be to blame, we think, and our choice of a scapegoat is either ourselves, for not being clever enough to learn Irish, or our teachers, for teaching it so poorly. No prizes for guessing who most people decide to pin the blame on.

However, the reality is that neither the teachers nor the students are to blame. I will return to the teachers in a moment, but I have met some people who talk about having a sense of shame and guilt for not speaking Irish. I always feel desperately sad when I hear people say this, because the fact that they don't speak Irish isn't their fault. The problem is that our expectation for what could and should be achieved by teaching Irish as a school subject in primary and secondary school is totally out of line with what can practically be expected given the circumstances. The things we learn best in school are the very things that we put into practice most outside of school. We don't use Irish outside of school, so what we learn of the language is never put to use. The best teachers in the world can't fix that. There is no mystery about the matter.

Teachers have been unfairly blamed for our failure to speak Irish. Journalist Eoin Butler has pointed out just how illogical it is to say that Irish needs to be "taught better", as if there was some secret way to teach Irish perfectly that most of the Irish population is aware of, but somehow has eluded professionally trained teachers and the employees of the Department of Education.

But we teach Irish for 13 years? How can people not pick it up? Well let's look at exactly how much time is spent on Irish and what kind of learning is taking place. 13 years sounds like a huge amount of time, and it is, but it isn't as if this entire time is dedicated to learning just Irish. For a start, Irish primary school students only spend half the year (183 days) in school, and secondary school pupils spend even less (167 days). So in terms of days spent learning something, we are really talking about six and a half years.

OK, then how much time of the school day is dedicated to Irish? I have seen people claim that one third of primary school time and one fifth of secondary school time is dedicated to teaching Irish, but wild exaggerations such as these are usually put forward by people looking to reduce the place of Irish in our schools. The Irish National Teacher Organisation allocates three and a half hours a week for Irish primary school children, which works out to about 40 minutes a day. When I was a Leaving Cert student, I had five 40 minute classes a week in Irish, which I think is fair to assume is standard for secondary school students. Therefore, both primary and secondary school pupils learn Irish for 40 minutes a day in class, and if we assume an average of about 20 minutes homework, we can say Irish students study Irish for about an hour each school day.

Now learning something for an hour a day for half the year over 13 years still sounds like it should be enough time for people to learn something fully. It might be, but we need to look a bit more closely at what is happening in the classroom, and whether this "learning under-achievement" is unique to just the teaching of Irish. It seems fair to say that, for a motivated learner, spending an hour of study a day over a long period of time would eventually lead to fluency in a language. Indeed, based on my own experience, I have found this to be the case. But what usually takes place in primary or secondary school classrooms is passive, rather than active, learning. What I mean by passive learning is that the student picks up some things by sitting in class, but during that 40 minutes, the lesson usually isn't his or her main focus. In other words, the student isn't putting their maximum effort and attention into what is going on in class, but is spending much of the time thinking about the million other things that young people usually think about.

This is true for all subjects, not just Irish, but it is also worth bearing in mind that (at least in my experience) most of the teaching of Irish is done through English. This is often out of necessity, but the point should be made that when we are talking about students learning Irish for 40 minutes, they are not immersed in Irish for that time period. Therefore, what really should be our expectation for how much students will learn when they themselves are not particularly motivated about learning?

"Hold on", I hear you say, "Isn't it the teachers' job to motivate students? By saying that the students are not motivated, are we not just saying that, ultimately, it is still the fault of the teachers that students don't learn Irish?" The short answer is no. I think people who have never taught often have incredibly unrealistic expectations for what teachers are capable of. Some people seem to feel that a teacher has failed in their duty if they don't create a deep and unending passion within each student for the subject, and if there is ever even a moment's boredom in the classroom.

We obviously want every teacher to make a subject accessible and interesting for students, but learning and motivation is a two-way street. Students also take some of the responsibility for their learning, and if a student isn't concerned one way or another about a subject, there is only so much a teacher can do. In the case of Irish especially, some students come into class having being told by their parents or peers that it is a dead language and a waste of time, and reversing that mindset is often exceptionally difficult. But, as already noted, I am not claiming that passive learning only takes place in Irish. It happens in all subjects. Something akin to it also takes place when, as adults, we enter the working world. We all know that just because you are sitting at a desk doesn't mean that you are really working. Just as you drift from actively working to passively working, so students do the same thing with learning.

There is an article by the historian E.P. Thompson called "Time,

Work-Discipline and Industrial Capitalism". His basic argument is that for most of human history, people spent much of their time idly, interspersed with short periods of frenetic work, usually around harvest time. But this rhythm of work was unsuited for the day-in, day-out grind needed for the factory life that came with the advent of the Industrial Revolution. The idea of showing up every day on time and working for 12 or 14 hours in a shift had to be drilled into people. The point is that, in evolutionary terms, we are not conditioned to exerting maximum effort all day every day in task work, which is why we slack off on a fairly regular basis. And as hard as it is for adults to adjust themselves to the discipline of the workplace, common sense says it is much more difficult for children when in school. So even with the most inspiring and creative teacher, a considerable amount of passive learning in schools, for all subjects, is inevitable.

After reading this, you might wonder how anyone ever learns anything at school. As I said, the things we learn best in school are the things that we are also either using or continuing to learn outside of school. If I may give myself as an example, the two subjects I excelled at in school were English and history. But a major reason for this was that I was a vociferous reader of both novels and history books in my own time. If the learning of a subject is only confined to what is done in the classroom, then for most people, achievement in that subject will always be limited. So to think that fluency in Irish is possible for everyone so long as teachers "teach properly" is to expect too much.

For proof of this, let's compare how well we learn Irish with how well we learn maths. Most Irish students spend about as much time learning maths as they do Irish. But do maths teachers do a better job than their Irish counterparts? Do we really learn more maths than Irish? On first consideration, many Irish people might say yes. Most people who have completed their Leaving Cert can probably add, subtract, multiply and divide, calculate percentages and figure out basic fractions. In contrast, the average Irish person (apparently) hasn't "a word of Irish". A clear win for the maths teachers?

Perhaps not. Even if we take the idea that everyone has some mathematical ability but most people have no Irish language ability at face value, there is an obvious explanation. Most of the basic math skills mentioned above are ones that we use in our day to day lives. They stick with us because we use them regularly, not because they have been taught any better. It is also worth keeping in mind that we learn all of those skills in primary school. The secondary school maths curriculum includes algebra, trigonometry, geometry, and calculus. We learn this kind of mathematics for five or six years, but is our grasp of algebra any better than our understanding of the modh coinníollach once we leave school? I don't think so. Indeed, in 2016, 5024 Leaving Cert students received an A1, A2 or B1 in honours Irish, but only 2750 people attained those marks in honours maths. Based on this at least, it is hard make the argument that Irish teachers are somehow doing substandard work compared to their peers teaching maths. The teachers of both subjects are facing the same problem: if you teach students content or skills that they never use outside of school, they won't retain it for long. The classroom alone will not create a nation of fluent Irish speakers.

A lot of this is obvious on reflection, but yet people persist on blaming teachers, because they feel ultimately someone is at fault for their inability to speak Irish. Let me give you an example. Ian McKinley was a young man from Dublin who was forced to retire from professional rugby in 2011 due to an eye injury. He wound up coaching rugby in Italy where, thanks to the use of protective googles, he was able to return to playing professionally. In interviews with the Irish media, McKinley noted he spoke fluent Italian after living there for two years. He commented that "it makes a mockery of learning Irish for 13 years and you can't speak a word of it."

I had to wonder whether McKinley (who acknowledges that he was "horrendous at languages" in school) understood the enormous gulf in learning that takes place between learning a language in a classroom for 40 minutes a day, and being completed immersed in it for a couple of years? Yet, despite the fact that the vast majority of Irish people are completely immersed in English their entire lives, there seems to be a deluded notion that teachers should somehow be able to produce people who are completely bilingual in both Irish and English.

Let's get some numbers for how misguided that is. Our average 15 year old learns Irish for an hour each school day. As he or she spends 167 days in school, that is 167 hours of learning Irish each year. That sounds like a lot, but how much time is this student spending engaging with the English language? If we assume the student sleeps seven hours each night, and that they spend most of their waking moments speaking or thinking in English, we can estimate that they are exposed to English for 6038 hours a year. Compared to that, 167 hours looks pretty small, and it is. Based on these numbers, an Irish teenager spends 2.6% of their time engaging with Irish, and well over 90% of their time operating through English. How could we ever expect our education system to provide some kind of equivalent capability in Irish and English on that basis?

Perhaps a metaphor will best explain why our education system falls short of our expectations for teaching Irish. Imagine if we took our school children out of class and had them walk to the school field. Once there, we ask them to run one single lap of the field. We have our students run this lap three times a week, for 13 years. Then at the end of their schooling, we turn around and say "how come the children can't run a marathon? Sure haven't they been doing running training for 13 years?" That is effectively what we are doing when it comes to teaching Irish. The question shouldn't be why Irish people can't speak Irish despite learning it for 13 years, but rather why would anyone ever think that doing things the way we have been doing them would create some kind of bilingual population?

Something else we should keep in mind is that it isn't just Irish that our students struggle to master, but other languages as well. Some people would disagree with this. Indeed, I have often heard people say that their German or French is much better than their Irish, which is usually put forward as proof that there is something wrong with how Irish is being taught. I certainly know where they are coming from. For most of my secondary school experience, I was much more confident in my German than Irish ability. But in my case, I think one reason I did better at German was that I began it with a blank slate when I entered secondary school. I didn't have the hang-ups and baggage that I brought to learning Irish from primary school, and I think for a lot of people that "fresh start" goes a long way to explaining why they feel they are more successful at learning a continental language rather than Irish.

But the scores from the Leaving Cert don't bear out the idea that we are teaching foreign languages any better than Irish. If we take my (arbitrary) cut-off point for fluency based on one's score in the Leaving Cert, more students got a B1 or higher in honours Irish (5024) than honours French or German combined (4396) in 2016, despite the fact that four hundred more students took either the French or German paper than took the Irish one. This difference might be accounted for the fact that some students doing well in Irish have attended Irish immersion schools at some point, with French and German immersion options in the Irish school system being much more limited. Yet the point stands that it seems difficult to make the case that Irish students learn European languages better than Irish.

But, the argument goes, Europeans learn foreign languages much better than we do. If this is true, then they must be using better teaching methods than we are. There is no arguing the fact that, anecdotally speaking at least, it seems that continental Europeans are much more likely to speak two or three languages, while we are stuck with just one. However, if one digs a little deeper, some differences outside of the classroom offer clues as to why this is so. Firstly, many Europeans live in areas, especially border areas, that are mixed language zones. Given that these people have a practical need to pick up another language in this environment, it is not surprising that they do.

Yet the most common second language amongst continental Europeans is English. This obviously has nothing to do with sharing a border with English speakers, but it isn't necessarily proof of better classroom learning. Put simply, European students are much more self-motivated when it comes to learning English than our students are when learning French or German. English is a global language, the language of preference in business, in diplomacy, in international politics, in science and in entertainment. English is cool, English is sexy and English is important. When a student in, say, Germany, leaves the classroom, he or she is far more likely to go home and watch a TV show, or movie, or listen to music in English than an Irish counterpart ever would in German.

To say this isn't to claim that teaching methods and practices are irrelevant when it comes to learning languages. Indeed, there are considerable differences in English-language proficiency among second-level students from different countries. Speaking anecdotally, Scandinavian and German students seem to be much better at learning English than Spanish or Italian students. But the point I am trying to make is that it is impossible to draw comparisons between Irish students learning French and French students learning English, because the motivation to learn on the part of these students can vary dramatically. A native French or German speaking student knows there is another language that, in global terms, is much more important than his or her own, and therefore many of them are hungry to learn it, no matter how good or bad their teacher is. But for English speakers, while learning other languages is viewed as important, there simply isn't another language that is more essential for success than the one they already speak. Therefore, if we want to assess whether we are doing a good job teaching foreign languages, we need to compare ourselves to other English-speaking countries. The evidence suggests that we are about as successful as the rest of the Anglophone world when it comes to our students learning other languages, in that we aren't very successful at all. Motivation seems to be the key difference.

Well if we English speakers struggle to learn other languages anyway, should we bother learning Irish in schools at all? Indeed, the most hotly contested debate when it comes to the Irish language is whether it should be compulsory to learn it all the way through school, and if not, when should it become an optional subject instead? One of the criticisms of "compulsory Irish" is that it creates hostility towards the language. This is often accompanied by the claim that if it were made optional, students would be more likely to develop a positive attitude towards it and want to study it. The idea that making the subject optional would somehow create hordes of students more eager to learn the language is nonsense. In 2004, the British government made learning a foreign language optional for GSCE (approximate to the Junior Cert) exams. The result? By 2011, only 40% of GSCE students were studying a foreign language. "Fair enough", the response might be "but since making Irish compulsory causes people to hate it, at least by making it optional, you are reducing the animosity towards the language."

Well that is just it. I don't believe that compulsory Irish is the root cause of animosity towards the language. To say this is to fly in the face of all accepted wisdom in Ireland, and to disagree with the thousands of people who would undoubtedly say that having to learn Irish in school is precisely the reason they hate the language. I will examine the hostility towards Irish in much more detail in the next chapter, but for now I will say that there is far more going on than simple resentment at having to learn it in school.

The obvious proof of this comes when we compare Irish to maths. Maths is just as compulsory as Irish in the school system, and it is studied for the same amount of time. But why doesn't maths produce the same anger and revulsion that Irish produces, if compulsion is the sole cause? Where are all the people writing into newspapers complaining about maths being forced down their throats for 13 years? It isn't as if mathematics is a barrel of laughs either. In polls in other countries, it is often picked by students as the subject they hate the most. Some might argue that maths is more "useful" or "practical" than Irish and therefore is not as despised. That argument doesn't hold water either. Certainly a strong understanding of maths has many potential career leads, but only a small minority ever pursue them. Put simply, the average Irish person uses Leaving Cert mathematics about as much as they use Irish – never. So whatever else about the advantages or disadvantages of compulsory Irish, the idea that it is solely responsible for making people hate the language doesn't stand up.

One of the issues about the compulsory Irish project is precisely the fact that it is referred to as "compulsory Irish". Technically, Irish is the only subject that is mandatory for the Leaving Cert, while English and maths are "core subjects" that are, in theory, optional. Of course, the reality is that all schools insist that their students take English and maths, so they are de facto compulsory subjects as well. The irony is that even though Irish is the only compulsory subject, thousands of students are able to get an exemption from studying it, while one imagines that the number of students who can opt out of studying English or maths is tiny. Irish then is the only subject stuck with the "compulsory" label, which adds to the sense in many peoples' minds that there is something oppressive about having to study it. In an article about whether cookery classes should be mandatory for all Irish students, Ian O'Doherty wrote "If you make cookery classes compulsory, it will attract the same resistance anything with the word 'compulsory' attracts." He is completely correct, which is one reason that the teaching of Irish in schools attracts far more criticism than that of, say, maths. People have pointed out for decades that it is unfair to only tar Irish with the compulsory brush, when English and maths hold an identical position in our schools.

In his book *Compulsory Irish*, Adrian Kelly has responded to this argument by saying "English and mathematics formed part of the essential, practical led curriculum; Irish was part of the culture led curriculum."[31] I disagree with Kelly here. Firstly, I don't see how that changes the fact that English and maths are as compulsory as Irish. Kelly seems to be saying that their compulsory nature is justified on "essential, practical" grounds, while Irish's status is not, because it is more of a "culture" thing. Well a considerable amount of the English curriculum, with its focus on creative writing and literature, is clearly more in the "cultural" than "practical" side of things. I can't imagine there are too many Leaving Cert students who think studying Irish is a waste of time but are enthralled with the practical value of reading Shakespeare and studying poetry.

Similarly, as noted earlier, it is hard to argue that the mathematics we study at secondary school is practical or essential for everyone, given that the vast majority of us never use it again once we leave school. When it comes to what students study in school, "practicality" is subjective. I didn't know when I was 17 that I would one day be a historian and that the ability to read primary sources in Irish would be an essential part of my job. Nor had I any idea that being able to speak Irish would be invaluable in helping me learn Welsh, which my research eventually required that I be able to read. It turns out that learning Irish was of far more "practical" value to my career than algebra or trigonometry. I understand that I would be very much in the minority in that regard, but the point is that it is only with the benefit of hindsight that we can figure out what subjects will be "essential" for students.

31   Adrian Kelly, *Compulsory Irish*, op. cit.

Of course, the argument over compulsory Irish brings us back once again to the idea of "choice". It is not surprising that many of the people who think that the Irish people of the past simply "chose" to stop speaking Irish, and that the Irish people of today "choose" to speak English, see the lack of "choice" regarding the study of Irish as an abomination. We live in a democratic society and people are entitled to make choices, they argue, including what subjects they pick to study in school. I think there is much to admire in anyone who lives by the principle that we, as a society, should facilitate "free choice" as much as possible.

My concern, however, is that many of those people who call for an end to compulsory Irish only have a commitment to "choice" that is skin deep. In particular, I don't think these "choice warriors" are nearly as committed to "choice" when it comes to people "choosing" to speak Irish. A good example of this was seen on a debate about the Irish language on TV3's *Tonight Show* in June 2018. Radio presenter Niall Boylan argued that students should be allowed choose whether they study Irish in school (making the comparison that students in the United States and Australia are not compelled to study the indigenous languages of their respective countries). Yet at the same time, he berated Bláthnaid Ní Chofaigh and Pearse Doherty (who were also taking part in the debate) for choosing to speak Irish together before the cameras started rolling. Boylan also called for the Irish state to stop wasting money on TG4, the Irish language channel. In other words, Boylan was a champion for those who want to choose not to study Irish in school, but opposed people choosing to watch TV in Irish or to speak Irish whenever they like. Such hypocrisy is common among Ireland's language "choice warriors".

It is worth asking how serious these people are when it comes to language choice. Do they support Irish speakers who exercise their constitutional right to interact with the state through Irish? Were they horrified when a man was arrested in Dublin in 2013 for speaking to a Garda in Irish, a choice he is legally entitled to make? Would they support the creation of an Irish language university to allow people to choose to receive as much of their education as possible through Irish? In most cases, I imagine not. The case for ending compulsory Irish because of the right to choose only has merit if it isn't being made from a hypocritical, selective understanding of who gets to choose what language and when.

All information points to the fact that most Irish people support Irish students learning some Irish in school. An ESRI survey on the Irish language found that only 12% of people felt that Irish should not be taught in schools at all, with 82% believed that it should be. However, a survey carried out by Amárach Research in 2017 found that 53% of people think Irish should be optional in school, while 42% think it should not be. Anecdotally speaking, there seems to be a lot of support for students learning Irish up until they complete the Junior Cert, but with a majority of people believing it should be optional after that.

There are probably a couple of different reasons why people hold this point of view. One would likely be that, after studying the subject for ten years already, if people have not picked up a passion for Irish by then, they never will. Others have made the argument that all subjects should be optional after the Junior Cert, with Irish being no exception in that regard. The latter point raises the question about how much choice students should have when it comes to picking their school subjects in general. Some people feel that students should have complete freedom to choose their subjects at second level, while others think that some subjects should be compulsory up until Junior Cert. However, my own educational philosophy is that compulsory subjects are a good thing, despite the negative association with the word "compulsory". Indeed, if it were up to me, not only would I keep English, Irish and maths as mandatory up until the Leaving Cert, I would also make a science subject compulsory as well.

You see, what is often forgotten in our aversion to the idea of compulsion is why we make something compulsory in the first place. The reason, paradoxically, is to give people a choice. Let me give an example. I hated science in secondary school, and when it came to picking my subjects for the Leaving Cert, I avoided physics, chemistry and biology like the plague. But when I reached sixth year and was looking at various college courses, I found that some were off-limits because I didn't meet the requirement of studying one science subject for the Leaving Cert. So the choice I made as a 15 year old ended up limiting my choices as an 18 year old. Had that choice been taken out of my hands at 15, then I would have had a greater range of choice at 18.

This is why compulsory subjects are important, because we simply don't know what content we will wish we had learned once we finish school. Take English for example. On one level, this seems the subject that should most obviously be mandatory. But the argument could be made that the subject of English, as it exists within the Irish curriculum, isn't of vital importance to most students, since it focuses on creative writing and literature. Improving our students' ability to read well and write clearly is essential, but that happens in most school subjects and is not dependent on one studying the subject of English. Yet allowing students to opt out of English would alter the future for some people who otherwise would have gone on to be excellent writers, or to develop a life-long love of English literature.

As someone who has had no use for the maths I learned in school, I have absolutely no regrets about being made to study it in school, as I know that it could have allowed me to pursue a wide range of careers. Similarly, I am glad that I was made to study foreign languages, studying German for six years. Indeed, were it not for one marking blip when I did my Leaving Cert, I would have studied Law and German, which would have meant spending at least one year in

Germany. Who knows, I could today be living in Germany as a fluent German speaker had life followed that course, and I certainly would have been most grateful for learning German then. And so it is with Irish. We require people to study it precisely so they can choose to speak it once they leave school.

"Hang on", you might say "but surely making Irish compulsory all the way to the Leaving Cert is not depriving people of that choice if it is still compulsory for the Junior Cert?" That is a fair point, to which I say that the longer we have people learn Irish, the more likely they are to pick up enough Irish that they have the choice of using it. I offer my own history with the language as a case in point. I would definitely have dropped Irish after the Junior Cert had I been allowed. But it was having to study it for the Leaving Cert that put me on the road to fluency, and enabled me to choose to raise my daughter through Irish. I understand that what happened to me with Irish in my later school years doesn't happen to most people, but it remains true that my not having the choice to drop Irish at 15 means I can choose to speak it today.

Indeed, our main problem as far as Irish goes isn't that too many people are upset at having to learn it at school, but rather that too many people regret not learning enough of it. Given that apparently 10% of Irish people try to relearn Irish as adults, studying the subject all the way to the Leaving Cert only gives them a stronger base to build from. Indeed, I have often thought that if we were to reduce the amount of time students have to study Irish in schools, cutting it out of their last few years of education is to prune the subject at the wrong end. There are two reasons for this. One is that as teenagers get older, they begin to think independently, and, as such, it is probably the first time that some of them start looking on the Irish language as something more than a school subject.

Secondly, when we say that students learn Irish for 13 years, it is often overlooked that it is only for the last five or six years, i.e. when they are in secondary school, that they are being taught by someone with a degree in Irish. In primary school, on the other hand, the competency in Irish amongst teachers can be mixed indeed. A 2006 report by Dr. John Harris of Trinity College found that a quarter of primary school teachers rated their own Irish as "weak". Speaking broadly, it seems fair to say that since most secondary school teachers have a degree in Irish, they are more likely to have a greater enthusiasm and knowledge of the subject than their primary school counterparts. Reducing the years that people will spend studying Irish under teachers with stronger Irish skills certainly won't help improve wider proficiency in the language.

For some people, it isn't Irish being compulsory that is the problem so much as the idea that Irish is taking up valuable time that could be filled by some other subject that is more "useful". This is to return to Adrian Kelly's argument that only "practical" and not "cultural" subjects should be a mandatory part of the curriculum. Firstly, is making a "cultural" subject a central part of our school experience such a terrible thing? I have encountered many foreigners who think it is admirable that we insist on teaching Irish and seemingly aren't beholden to focusing only on subjects because of their perceived economic value.

This opinion is not so widely held in Ireland itself. In 2016, Rosita Boland penned a column in the *Irish Times*, wishing her effort learning Irish had been put to use on something else. She wrote "I have spent many months travelling in Central and South America. I often found myself wishing the time I had spent trying to grapple with the compulsory text of Peig had been spent voluntarily in Spanish classes instead - something useful." It seems odd that Boland thinks that Irish alone was the subject that should have made way for her to study Spanish instead. Why not geography, for example? Could the time she spent trying to grapple with the compulsory text of *Busy At Maths* been used more wisely? I assume she also learned either French or German in school –could these classes not have been replaced by Spanish ones? On top of that, what stopped her learning Spanish "voluntarily" on her own time?

Nevertheless, Boland's argument is one that many people make, namely that the time dedicated to Irish should be spent on something else, usually another language. This is bolstered by the belief that mastering international languages will be essential to our economic future. However, Dr. Kevin Williams, the former president of the Educational Studies of Ireland, has spent much of his career challenging this assumption. Williams has written in *Studies: An Irish Quarterly Review* that "it cannot be said that for most occupations in the English-speaking world, knowledge of a second language is necessary. And even if it were established that most school pupils would need knowledge of a foreign language, it would be almost impossible to predict in advance which foreign languages they would need". Rosita Boland, take note!

Kevin Williams isn't against the teaching of foreign languages, far from it, but he states, in the *Irish Independent,* that it is time "to cease the exaggeration of the necessity for us to know other languages to get by in a world that is dominated by English." In this regard, Williams observes that if "the case against the inclusion of Irish on the school curriculum is based on claims of its relative lack of usefulness in the spheres of commerce and trade in comparison with foreign languages, this case cannot be said to be compelling as foreign languages cannot be said to be conspicuously useful either." In other words, and as we discussed earlier in this chapter, there is no language more useful to learn than the one we already speak. Indeed, because we already speak the language that most of the students around the world are trying to learn, we can afford some space in our curriculum to follow more "cultural" pursuits.

To be clear, as someone with a passion for languages myself, I am certainly not saying that we shouldn't give people the chance to learn foreign languages in school. But many of these calls for increased foreign language teaching are nothing more than a smokescreen to attack the position of Irish within our schools. There is no practical thinking behind these demands. For example, in 2014, the *Irish Times* ran an article that noted a debate that took place in Loreto Bray amongst transition year students about whether it would be better to learn Irish or Chinese. This builds upon a suggestion I have seen put forward regularly online, that we should take Irish out of our school system, and replace it with Chinese. But such an idea is badly misconceived and can only be put forward by someone who has not considered the incredible practical difficulties this would involve.

For a start, where would we get all the Chinese teachers from and how much would they cost? Even if we could pull a magical lever and make all of our teachers Chinese scholars tomorrow, why would anyone think our students would succeed in Chinese any more than they would at Irish? Although many people find Irish to be a difficult language (more on that later!), it is distantly related to English, and in terms of its alphabet and some of its vocabulary, there are at least enough similarities that an English speaker to begin to make headway with it. This is not at all true of Mandarin Chinese. With a writing system, sound system and a use of tones that are all completely alien to English, Chinese would simply be much harder for students to learn than Irish. If you think we have underachieved with our Irish teaching, wait until you see what kind of Chinese speakers we produce (the one student at the Loreto Bray debate who had studied both languages commented "I'm learning Chinese and trust me, Irish is way easier).

But even if we could create Chinese speakers as competent as the Irish, French and German speakers that currently come out of our school system, what would be the point? In teaching a relatively small number of American college students over the last six or seven years, I have encountered about 20 Chinese students. In that same time period, how many Irish students have enrolled in Chinese universities, or at least have developed strong enough Chinese skills that they could hold their own with third level Chinese students? I'm guessing very few. In 2016, it was reported that there are 300,000 Chinese students attending American colleges, and that number is growing. In short, more Chinese people will always speak better English than we will ever manage with Chinese. This isn't to say that students shouldn't have the chance to learn Chinese, but the idea that we will reap some major economic boon by replacing Chinese with Irish in our school system is deluded.

Another argument against compulsory Irish is that making anything compulsory guarantees that people won't learn it. Indeed, people have half-seriously suggested that maybe the best way to promote Irish is to ban its use. Of course, even if its use could be banned, there is no way that would do anything to help the language. But are we so sure making things compulsory in school isn't an effective way of having people learn? Ian O'Doherty, an outspoken critic of the state's support for Irish, doesn't think so. In that article he wrote about making cooking part of our school curriculum, O'Doherty commented "Frankly, if we force kids to learn how to cook in a classroom, we'll end up with a society that can cook only as well as it can speak Irish and that's a pretty horrifying thought - in anyone's language." But contrary to what many people think, compulsory learning, in the right circumstances, is actually very effective. And I can prove it, with two simple questions.

One, can you read and write? As you are reading this book, I will assume the answer is yes.

And two, did you choose to become literate? For most people, the honest answer is no.

Literacy is the most compulsory thing in our school system. What students do all day, every day, in every subject, is practice their reading and writing skills. Indeed, the main reason that nation-states developed national education systems was to create populations who could read and write. Because we live in an age when almost everyone is fully literate, we don't understand what an extraordinary achievement mass literacy is. In his famous book *Orality and Literacy*, Walter Ong pointed out that literacy and the technology of writing revolutionised how humans viewed the world, while also reminding readers what a laborious process it is to learn to read and write. For most of our time on the planet, humans have not been able to write, and it is only in the last 150 years or so that it became more common for people in the western world to be literate than not. In the past, literacy was only possessed by a small fragment of the population, akin, perhaps, to computer programming today. Indeed, over the course of human history, the ability to speak multiple languages was far less rare than the ability to read or write in one language.

The point is that literacy is an incredibly difficult skill to master, but we achieve almost one hundred percent success teaching it in our schools. Why is this? The first reason is the volume at which we teach it. Nearly every school subject we teach also functions as a literacy class, and our students spent almost the entirety of each day reading and writing. The second reason comes from parental support. While some parents are better than others at encouraging their children to read, all parents at least have a positive attitude towards their children learning to read, something that would not be true of Irish for example. And the third reason goes back to what I said earlier about successful learning being dependent upon how often content or a skill is required outside the classroom. Even the most uninterested school student needs literacy to read their friends' texts or tweets. Compulsion then isn't the problem for Irish, but rather the lack of need for it outside of school hours.

Therefore, if we are to try and revive Irish, the one thing we should understand by now is that it is not simply a question of trying to "fix" how Irish is taught. Nevertheless, maintaining the position Irish currently holds in our schools is important to maximise the opportunity for people to learn the language, even if it is only to create a stronger foundation for people who decide to take up the language once again as adults. I know for a lot of people that is not a strong enough reason to keep teaching children Irish, but as discussed in this chapter, I don't find the arguments against it to be compelling either. In fact, a major concern for me is that were Irish to be made optional for the Leaving Cert, the campaign to make it optional for the Junior Cert would begin immediately, and so on it would continue until Irish was driven entirely from the school system. Indeed, the only decent case I have heard put forward against compulsory Irish is that it is a dead language. Not that Irish actually is a dead language – you would have to be a moron to think that. Rather, my concern is that if, after 13 years, our school system is producing English speakers with such a poor grasp of basic words like "dead", then maybe we do need to stop teaching Irish to concentrate on remedial English instead.

CHAPTER FIVE

THE HATE THAT HAS NO NAME

A few years ago, I noticed that an online commentator called Mortimer O'Faherty, or certain variations on that name, kept appearing under many of the articles I was reading. In particular, it seemed there wasn't an article written about the Irish language that didn't compel Mortimer to pipe up and say something. His contributions about Irish were always negative. He especially resented the idea that Irish should be called the "native" language of Ireland, and went to great lengths to argue why it was wrong to do so, even if the author of the article he was commenting on never used that phrase. It didn't matter if I was reading the *Irish Times, Irish Independent, The Journal* or any other Irish website where users could leave comments, I was sure to find Mortimer waging war on the Irish language. Over time, he began to remind me of Captain Ahab in *Moby Dick*, trawling the internet looking to harpoon the great Gaelic whale. The regularity of his comments seemed maniacal. As someone who is a passionate supporter of Irish and who regularly defends it online, I couldn't figure out where this guy was finding the time or energy to make all the comments he was making. In the end, I realised that if my efforts to defend Irish were motivated by love, then Mortimer's were being fueled by an equally powerful force: hate.

There is a vicious hate in Ireland towards the Irish language and the people who speak it and promote it. Many people in Ireland are blissfully unaware of it, but anyone who speaks Irish or takes an interest in it is well aware of its existence. Bláthnaid Ní Chofaigh has said that she feels "At times, it's racist. Nobody ever calls it that but no other culture would tolerate it." Racism is the wrong word for it perhaps, but in terms of the bile and bigotry that is directed towards the Irish language, it is certainly something akin to it. At a time when society is becoming far less tolerant of hatred towards people based on their skin colour, their faith, their ethnic background or their sexual orientation, hatred towards Irish goes largely unchallenged and, indeed, is tacitly endorsed by certain segments of the Irish media. It is the hate we don't see and yet the hate that is all around us. The hate that has no name.

Where does this hatred come from? Foreigners who visit Ireland or who read our online discussions are always surprised at the vitriol towards Irish. They can understand that circumstances have meant that most Irish people don't speak the language fluently, but why are some so hostile in their opinions of Irish? As discussed in the previous chapter, the common response is that having to learn Irish in schools turns people against the language.

Irish is one of three subjects that students have to learn throughout their schooling, alongside English and maths. For a variety of obvious reasons, comparing attitudes towards Irish and English wouldn't make sense, but certainly we can draw parallels between Irish and maths. In terms of the difficulty of the subject, the regularity of use outside of the classroom, and the long term practical value to the average person, Irish and maths are on a similar footing. All other things being equal, we would expect comparable enough attitudes to exist amongst people towards the two subjects. But maths doesn't attract anything like the loathing that Irish gets.

There is another way we can show that the teaching of Irish has very little to do with attitudes towards it. And that is by casting an eye to the northeast, to Scotland. The Scots Gaelic language, (which Scots pronounce "Gallic"), is very similar to Irish. Indeed, for much of their history, they were considered the same language. The big difference is that most Scottish people do not learn Gaelic in school.

Indeed, for most, the option of studying it doesn't exist even if they want to learn it.

So logically, we would expect the attitudes towards Gaelic to be more positive in Scotland than Ireland, wouldn't we? But is that what we find? NO! If anything, I would say the hatred for Gaelic in Scotland is more widespread and vicious than what we find in Ireland (more on this a little later on). This obviously undermines the idea that learning Irish is creating a hostility toward the language that otherwise would not exist.

Something else is going on. Let me give you an example. At the first ever dinner held by the Irish Association of Accountants, a speech was made that called for the end of compulsory Irish in schools because "it hindered trade and commerce" and called for "energy and finances to be directed elsewhere". A considerable number of people in Ireland would agree with these opinions and they are regularly expressed today. But here is the catch: that dinner was held in 1927. Irish had only been made compulsory in primary schools five years previously and was not yet a mandatory part of the secondary school curriculum. How could anyone say that the introduction of Irish into schools five years earlier was already "hindering trade and commerce". This wasn't a statement made based on experience or objective analysis, but rather preexisting bias. The point is that there was a hostility towards Irish at the very moment it was introduced to schools, indeed long before, and that this legacy of hatred plays a much bigger role in the animosity that exists towards Irish today than simply our collective experience as school children.

Well if this negative view of Irish doesn't come from having to learn it in school, where does it come from? As Tomás Mac Síomóin puts it, the fact that the Irish language "presses obviously on the raw nerve of a significant number of Irish people must have some psychological significance. If so, what could that significance possibly be?"[32] Explaining a powerful emotion like hatred is complicated, because a variety of personal and social factors come into play. But it is possible to tease out three separate strands that come together to form the foundation upon which the hostility towards Irish is built.

The first is our colonial legacy. Throughout the period of English, then British colonisation of Ireland, the native culture was denigrated at every turn, with this mindset eventually accepted by many Irish people. Although Ireland became independent in 1922, these attitudes didn't magically disappear and are still with us today. The second, somewhat related, factor is our position as an English-speaking country. Like the rest of the Anglophone world, we share a tendency to ridicule other languages and to be suspicious of people who speak them. The third factor is the identity crisis, both on the level of the individual and of society, that is provoked by the existence of Irish. Put simply, Irish people are aware that Irish (contrary to what many of the anti-Irish brigade would say) is a central part of Irish identity and resent not being able to speak it. This resentment turns into a hatred of the language itself and a wish that it never existed at all, which would resolve the identity crisis.

In his book *The Broken Harp: Identity and Language in Modern Ireland*, Tomás Mac Síomóin writes that, owing to the selective way Irish history is taught in schools, "the vast majority of Irish people remain totally unaware that their ancestors were colonised."[33] I would disagree with Mac Síomóin on this point. In my experience at least, most Irish people are very aware of the fact that Ireland was once a British colony, although whether they fully appreciate the implications of this for their own day and age is perhaps another matter.

But before we examine the legacy of colonisation for the Irish language, it is worth pointing out that there certainly are people who

32 Tomás Mac Síomóin, *The Broken Harp,* op. cit.
33 Ibid.

deny Ireland was a colony at all, or at least for the later part of its history. Speaking of the 18th Century, the historian S.J. Connolly has written that Ireland "was not in any real sense a colony" because it was "neither a physically distant nor a racially separate possession". Regarding physical distance, one wonders how far away something needs to be to qualify for colonial status. Was Gaul not a colony of Rome because it was too close to Italy? Was Poland not a Nazi colony because it shared a border with Germany? Race is undoubtedly a more complicated matter, but there seems to be ample evidence that people living in Ireland were tarred with the brush of "racial and cultural inferiority" that Connolly deems a feature of the 'real' colonisation that took place outside of Europe.

Other people claim that Ireland was a colony up until 1801, but once it officially became part of the United Kingdom, then its status as a colony ended. I must confess I have never understood the logic of this position. After all, isn't the end goal of colonisation the complete absorption of a colony into a state, with all distinction obliterated? Were the Native Americans really not colonised now that their lands form the United States? Furthermore, there is plenty to suggest that Ireland wasn't quite the integral part of the British state, treated no different from the rest of the United Kingdom, that some people imagine.

Firstly, during the Great Famine, the British government insisted that all relief efforts would have to be borne by Irish taxpayers alone, and thousands of famine refugees were deported from Britain back to Ireland in the midst of the crisis. If a famine broke out in Donegal next year, would we insist that only money from Donegal could be used to tackle the crisis and that people from Donegal had no right to escape south for relief? Another hint that Ireland was still viewed through a colonial lens is seen by the decision to bombard Dublin city centre during the Easter Rising, with little regard for the ordinary people of Dublin who, it should not be forgotten, were British citizens. The historian Fearghal McGarry writes that "it is difficult to envision the same tactics being deployed so readily in a British city." Certainly, one can make the argument that Ireland was unusual in comparison to other colonies (being in Europe, its people being white, some of whom helped subjugate other peoples), but it takes an act of mental gymnastics to claim Ireland wasn't a colony at all.

So, Ireland was a colony then. For some people, no further explanation is required then to understand why English, later British, settlers in Ireland would insist on the superiority of their own culture and the wretched barbarity of Gaelic society. But we might wonder a little more at why cultural colonisation had to accompany political colonization.

An insight can be gained if we look at the writings of Barbara Jeanne Fields, an American historian. Fields' research, especially her famous article 'Ideology and Race in American History', is focused on the history of racism in the US, but some of her ideas could certainly apply in Ireland as well. Fields argues that, contrary to what one might think, African slavery came before the existence of racism. In other words, Europeans didn't see Africans for the first time in the 15th Century, automatically view them as inferior and decide to enslave them immediately. Instead, these Europeans took Africans as slaves, but only over time did they come to view black people as inherently inferior. Once they believed this, they could justify permanent, transgenerational slavery and also convince themselves that in fact they were doing what was best for these "child-like" people. Fields notes that the ideology of racism arose because white people could not ignore that on a basic, human level, enslavement was wrong, and therefore had to create an ideology that justified it, one which denied that black people were human in the same way white people were.

It is not difficult to see how some of these principles also could apply in the colonisation of Ireland. Anglo-Norman culture had a sophisticated understanding of property rights before Norman adventurers arrived in Ireland in 1169. On top of that, Christian thinking was and is pretty clear on the question of theft. Therefore, these colonisers would have understood on several levels that seizing land from someone else was morally problematic. But by insisting that Gaelic culture was inferior and backwards, not only did this justify taking land from "uncivilised" people who couldn't use it "properly" anyway, it also meant that the destruction of the Gaelic way of life was viewed as a blessing for the people because they were being improved though civilisation. Attacks on Irish culture were not an accidental by-product of colonisation then, but rather provided the ideological framework to justify it.

It is worth a brief examination of some of the attitudes expressed about Irish culture and society by those who came to conquer the island. Gerald of Wales accompanied the future English king, John, in his expedition to Ireland in 1185. Describing the Irish people, Gerald wrote "Thus this people is a barbarous, a truly barbarous one: because it is most rude, not only in its barbarous mode of dressing, but also in its abundant hairdos and beards...all their customs are most barbarous." Henry VIII noted that nothing did more to keep the people of Ireland "in a certain savage and wild kind and manner of living, than the diversity that is between them in tongue, language, order and habitat". The renowned poet Edmund Spenser was an Elizabethan settler in Ireland, and he believed the English difficulties in ruling Ireland were due to the existence of Irish, because "the speech being Irish, the heart must needs be Irish, for out of the abundance of the heart, the tongue speaks." Irish culture needed to be destroyed in order to make the Gael "in a short time to forget his Irish nation", while Spenser even called for "all the "O"s and "Mac"s which the heads of clans have taken to their names to be utterly forbidden and extinguished for that...will much enfeeble them."

John Dunton, a London publisher, travelled to Ireland in 1698, and described Connemara as "a wild mountainous country in which the old barbarities of the Irish are so many and so common." Writing in the 18th Century, Jonathan Swift commented that "'It would be a noble achievement to abolish the Irish language in this kingdom... This would, in a great measure civilise the most barbarous of them." William Shaw Mason was an Irish statistician educated at Trinity College. In 1822 he declared "the common Irish are naturally shrew, but very ignorant and deficient in mental culture: from the barbarous tongue in which they converse which operates as an effectual bar to any literary attainment." In an 1899 debate about whether Irish should be offered as an optional school subject for secondary school children, three Trinity College professors opposed the idea. Edward Gwynn, a scholar of Early Irish literature, said that "Modern Irish has little to recommend it; its syntax is monotonous and underdeveloped." John Mahaffy was the professor of ancient history, and he said that Irish had no educational value, that he would not lament its death and that literature in the Irish language was either "silly or indecent". Robert Atkinson taught both Romance languages and Sanskrit at Trinity. He declared that Irish was merely a "patois" an "imbroglio, mélangie, an omnium gatherum", and that someone could not read Irish literature "without feeling that he had been absolutely degraded by contact with it".

The purpose of these quotations is to demonstrate how, across the centuries, Irish culture and especially the Irish language were synonymous with backwardness and were to be despised. Just because Ireland became an independent state did not mean that these beliefs ceased to exist. Instead, they continue to be passed across generations by people who, in all other regards, probably consider themselves to be proud Irish men and women. They are still evident today. For example, the televised debate about the Irish language in 2018, when radio presenter Niall Boylan accused his fellow panelists Bláthnaid Ní Chofaigh and Pearse Doherty of being "rude" for speaking Irish before going on-air. Although the justifications have changed, the criticisms remain identical: speaking Irish is barbarous and uncivilised.

No one should be in any doubt about the powerful influence that these colonial attitudes continue to have, even long after the colonisers themselves have disappeared. According to one study from the University of Cape Town, about one third of South African women bleach their skin to make it lighter in colour. The World Health Organisation claims that 77% of Nigerian women use some kind of product to lighten their skin tone. The fact that millions of African women in the 21st Century feel that there is something wrong with the colour of their own skin is proof enough of the long-lasting and damaging legacy that empire and colonisation has wrought on the world.

Tomás Mac Síomóin believes that the Irish people, as a result of the country's past, suffer from what he describes as "Super-Colonised Irishness Syndrome". He describes the process through which this develops: "The Irish colonised subject understood from his English master that he was of a lower order of being, gormless, but sly, humorous and sometimes charming. The quintessential Paddy was scatterbrained and childlike, thus inherently incapable of governing himself or his own kind... Paddy internalised this self-demeaning myth, simultaneously displacing his preexisting Gaelic mythic self as this false consciousness, and the understanding of his true place in the overall colonial dispensation, was taking hold."[34] Mac Síomóin believes that the Irish nation suffers from a collective Post-Traumatic Stress Disorder in the wake of colonisation. He cites evidence to suggest that the trauma of colonisation may be passed on genetically across generations, pointing out that Irish people share high levels of dysfunctionality with other groups around the world like Native Americans, Maori and Australian Aborigines.

34 Tomás Mac Síomóin, *The Broken Harp*, op. cit.

Although I don't necessarily agree with Mac Síomóin on the bio-logical side of his argument, I think he is completely correct in high-lighting how colonial hang-ups still play a role in the way we view ourselves as a people today. He writes that "distaste for Irish speak-ers and their language, often masquerading as indifference towards them, may be none other than an aspect of the dissimulated self-ha-tred of the colonised subject, a symptom of a complex condition described as...the Super-Colonised Irish Syndrome."[35] Mac Síomóin is astute in observing that contempt for the Irish language often hides behind feigned indifference. How often do we hear people say that they "have no problem with the language itself", but just resent having to learn it in school, or dislike sanctimonious Gaelgeoirí, or fear too much money is being wasted on it? No doubt our friend Mortimer O'Faherty would describe himself as "indifferent" toward the language, even as he hunts for another article about it to lament that people insist on calling it the "native" tongue.

There is a long history in Ireland of ridiculing or shaming people who speak Irish. We remember from a previous chapter Douglas Hyde's story about a little girl called Mary who stopped speaking Irish because her brother told her he was making a show of herself. Another story, apparently also told by Hyde and reproduced in the newspaper *Fáinne an Lae* in 1898, went as follows. "A farmer in Eng-land had a work team harvesting his corn for him. One time, the farmer came upon this group speaking Irish, and he started laugh-ing at the way they spoke. What would you suppose these Irishmen did? They became ashamed at speaking their native language, and switched immediately to English."

Such attitudes are still alive and well in Ireland in the 21st Cen-tury. In 2016, a dispute over language choice at the work place gained national attention. Cormac Ó Bruic was a native Irish speaker from Kerry, working part time in the Flying Enterprise pub in Cork City.

35 Ibid.

According to Ó Bruic, he spoke Irish from time to time with another bar man who was also from the Gaeltacht, as well as with some customers who wished to speak Irish. One day, however, the owner of the pub, Finbarr O'Shea, requested that Ó Bruic only speak English while working. Apparently, this escalated into a row, with Ó Bruic saying that O'Shea "was shouting at me and banging on the table, because I stood up to him and told him I wasn't going to stop." Ó Bruic eventually decided to leave his job, feeling he couldn't work for a business that would forbid him to speak Irish.

Although Ó Bruic received a lot of support when the story gained attention, there were certainly people online who thought O'Shea was completely in the right, with several comments I saw saying that Ó Bruic was being "rude" by speaking Irish. Others felt that as O'Shea was the employer, then he could decide the rules of the business. It seems to me however that people are willing to give the power and privileges of a feudal lord to a business owner over his employees when his or her worldview matches their own. One wonders would those same people have been equally sympathetic had it been the management of the Conradh na Gaeilge pub on Harcourt Street ordering employees speaking English amongst themselves to stop. It is difficult to see how the choice of language used by some staff members to make small talk during a lull in work was causing a problem to the business.

Indeed, it seemed some customers got considerable satisfaction out of it. Ó Bruic claimed that it was only after he had decided to leave the business that he was told that there had been customers complaining that they couldn't understand what was being said, something he doubted since he said he spoke to every customer in English apart from those who asked to speak in Irish. I have worked in enough small businesses to know that "customer complaints" are often a convenient cover for managers to stop something when they themselves have an issue with it. But it doesn't matter – clearly someone had a problem with Irish being spoken.

The response of the Flying Enterprise was also interesting. O'Shea said that the business employed 70 people from six different countries and that "they respect that while at work the most sensible and practical language to speak is English", adding that "we're all Europeans after all." This is typical of the Irelandshire nationalism that I mentioned in the introduction, always seeing its own position as sensible, enlightened and cosmopolitan and those of people on the other side as backwards and illogical. No one would deny that English would be the "practical" language of the business, but whether it was the "practical" language for a couple of guys chatting amongst themselves is a different thing entirely. Interestingly, in *Coming Home,* Michael McCaughan recalls how one of his friends believed that Ó Bruic had been fired for insisting on speaking Irish to customers and staff and refusing to use English! No doubt many people believed in, and took great pleasure from, the idea of "another Gaelnazi" getting "his comeuppance".

Nor was this the only case to catch the public eye in 2016 where Irish speakers were ridiculed. Another one involved people tweeting in Irish. Before explaining what happened, it is interesting to note the changes that social media has brought about for the visibility of the Irish language. As discussed in the previous chapter, a lot of Irish speakers are reluctant to speak Irish publicly, and as a result thousands of conversations take place in Irish every day out of hearing of the general public. But with social media, these utterances in Irish are permanent and can be seen by many people long after they are made. People might say they never hear people speaking Irish, but I can't imagine too many Irish people have never seen people using it on Facebook or Twitter.

Therein lies the problem. A furore erupted on Twitter when Gráinne Maguire, an Irish comedian living in England, apparently annoyed by someone she considered to be a "try hard" for tweeting in Irish, tweeted "Irish people who tweet in Irish creep me out. Like, we get it. WELL DONE YOU! We GET it." Not surprisingly, a lot of people were annoyed at Maguire's comments. Maguire insisted that this was just a joke, that she had only being trying to use her "comedy brain to poke fun at all things Irish" and that as soon as she tweeted it she thought "what a silly stupid thing to say...no one will take it at face value". Humour is a difficult thing to get right all the time, and I am sure we have all had moments where something we said with the intention of being funny was taken the wrong way.

But the problem with Maguire's use of the "humour" defense is that behind every joke there is often more than a kernel of truth. In an article she penned for the *Irish Times*, Maguire (who wrote that she "hated Irish in school") said her tweet was inspired by someone she genuinely believed to be trying too hard by tweeting in Irish. What exactly is the line a person tweeting in Irish has to cross before they become a "try hard", I wonder? Furthermore, Maguire's response the morning after her tweet suggested she stood by her comment. When asked by another Twitter user "why does it creep you out tho? Are they not just allowed sometimes speak Irish no?", her response was "I just find it a bit try hard and pretentious...", while bemoaning the fact that some people couldn't "handle some piss taking at how seriously Irish speakers take themselves."

Maguire is obviously entitled to make a joke about whatever she wants. She is a comedian after all. But she can't complain that people don't find her joke funny when they see that behind it, she means exactly what she is saying. For example, if I made a comment that I believe a woman's place is in the kitchen, I cannot explain away the comment as a "joke" if I really believe that a woman's place is in the kitchen! In other words, Maguire is bothered by people who tweet in Irish. She thinks they are a "bit try hard", that they are creepy and weird and take themselves too seriously. As someone who works in the comedy business, she would be lying if she claimed that humour isn't sometimes a convenient mask for bigotry and prejudice. In ideological terms, there is no difference between Maguire and that English farmer in Douglas Hyde's story. Both used the idea of something being funny to get their real message across: "Irish speakers, shut the fuck up."

Nor is Maguire the only person willing to pass judgement on people who use Irish on social media. I actually have personal experience of this myself. I got a Facebook account around the same time that I decided to commit to learning Irish. From the very beginning then, I used Irish on Facebook. I didn't post updates often, but when I did, they were almost always in Irish. I remember visiting home one time and a friend in passing said I was "putting him to shame" by posting as Gaeilge. He didn't mean that comment in a judgmental way at all, but I felt bad when I heard him say it. The last thing I was trying to do was to make people feel guilty about not speaking Irish.

I suppose I was posting in Irish because I wanted to practice, because I wanted to show people that it wasn't a dead language, and, beyond anything, because I just wanted to. Anyway, one day I noticed that someone had left a comment on my status in Irish. It was a childhood friend of mine, but someone I hadn't spoken to for over ten years. I'm not even sure how we became friends on Facebook. Anyway, underneath my status he had written "wats dat boy????". It actually took me a minute to figure out what he was saying. He was being sarcastic. He was making fun of me for speaking Irish. I'm sure he thought I was a "try hard" for doing so and wanted to let me know. I was stunned, especially since I hadn't spoken with him in years, that he felt he had the right to do that.

He had a brother (also a childhood friend of mine) who had died in a tragic accident a few years before. I'm not proud to admit this, but I wanted to respond by joking about how his brother had been killed. If he could make a comment that hurt me so personally like his did, I was going to give it right back to him. I'm sure to some this sounds like another Irish speaker taking himself too seriously, but I felt this was a direct attack on who I was. In the end, I didn't reply at all. But worse than that, I also didn't post in Irish for a long while after. I didn't want to leave myself open to being insulted like that again. Like little Mary or the farm workers in England, I had been shamed into not speaking Irish. That is the catch 22 that modern Irish speakers find themselves in today. We are told all the time that "nobody really" speaks Irish, but then when we do speak it, we are either told to shut up, or are ridiculed for being elitist and pretentious.

Out of interest, I spent an hour online one day looking for comments made about the Irish language. Here are some of the comments I came across, which I think represent opinions widely held in Ireland. This first set of comments were made about the teaching of Irish in school:

"The real question is how can we get rid of the Irish language in our country. Why the fuck does the rest of Ireland have to suffer when only a few tiny areas makes such a big deal of their language. Everyone else in the country uses English and it just makes sense."

"I hated learning Irish, was so happy when I took my last class in it. I understand why we'd need to learn the language but I'd be better served learning Spanish."

"I was so glad to stop learning Irish. I still can't speak it, and no, it shouldn't be mandatory."

"Why would Irish people need more Irish spoken here? I assume the second language here is Mandarin, followed by Polish or Lithuanian."

"Why not learn Latin, it's about as useful in the vast majority of Ireland."

"The point is, why would I learn a language that has no value in my day to day life? While I am fluent in it, I rarely ever use it."

"There is nothing wrong with learning a second language; but, there are some languages that are more important globally than others. Anyone out there who took Latin? Amo, amas, amat, enough!"

"Well, English is actually useful outside of the Gaeltacht and government jobs. Irish, not so much."

"Knowing Irish is pretty much useless in the vast majority of Ireland."

One commenter, apparently still in primary school, wrote the following:

"Today we children, have to go to school and have to learn Irish. The problem I have with this is why should we? We already have to focus on our studies and you're just giving us another pile of stress to carry on our backs... a lot of people don't like studying Irish because it's a burden. We get a pile of homework a week. I would have liked Irish a lot better if I were the one that chose to study it instead of having someone force it on me."

Another commenter, who said he was fluent in Irish, wrote the following:

"Most students who learn Irish in school, (even if they take it all the way through) just a few short years after graduation all they often remember is 'Conas atá tú' and 'Tá mé go maith'. Are we really providing a service to our students by forcing them to learn something that will have little or no application in their daily lives? Sure its nice to be able to travel to the Gaeltacht and ask people how they're doing, and be able to answer back 'I'm fine'. But does it really require a mandatory credit in our educational system? Given the technological nature of the world we live in, wouldn't it be of greater benefit to be teaching a programming language instead? Are we really providing a service to students by loading them down with skills that will have little application in our digital age? I'm not talking about removing Irish from the curriculum entirely, merely about having it as a mandatory subject. Forcing students to learn Irish strikes me as overkill."

Meanwhile, some interesting comments were also made about Gaelscoileanna.

"The popularity of Irish immersion is purely a result of the demand for specialised academic programming. There's little demand for the Irish language itself."

"Incredible waste of money for a fad. There are no educational advantages of Early immersion. None. Zero. Anyone willing to provide a peer reviewed study ......?"

"There's many more practical and useful languages to learn such as Spanish, Mandarin etc. in terms of economic benefit to an individual and Ireland."

"Keep in mind that for many parents, it is not the learning of Irish that is important, but an attempt to keep their children out of the public system."

"The Gaelscoil is the poor man's private school."

One blogger, weighing up the pros and cons of sending his child to a Gaelscoil noted that one criticism was "the elitist nature of Irish language schools. A 2004 report found that Irish immersion students are more likely to come from higher socioeconomic backgrounds and to have parents who have a post-secondary education."

Now most of these arguments are familiar to all of us. English is far more useful and everyone speaks it so why bother with Irish? Irish is more or less useless, the equivalent of Latin. Other languages would be far more useful to learn. People hated learning Irish because they were forced to learn it. Gaelscoileanna are elitist, a fad and parents enroll their children in them to keep them away from the riff-raff, not because they are actually interested in the language.

But, dear readers, I have a confession. The above comments are real, but I doctored them slightly. Go back and read them again, but switch some of the key words. Instead of "Ireland", read "Canada". Instead of "Irish", read "French". Instead of "Gaeltacht", read "Quebec" and instead of "Gaelscoil", read "French immersion school". Instead of "Polish" and "Lithuanian", read "Cantonese" and "Spanish". All of these comments were actually made about the teaching of French in Canada.

What was the point of switching the words? I wanted to show that attitudes towards French in Canada are very similar to those towards Irish in Ireland. However, in both local and global terms, French is in a completely different position to Irish. According to the census taken in Canada in 2011, 7.3 million Canadians, or 22% of the population, speak French as their first language. It is the mother tongue of over 80% of the people who live in Quebec, Canada's largest and second-most populous province. There are 80 million native French speakers around the world, with about 200 million people who speak French as a second language. French is an official language in 29 countries. In other words, French is spoken by lots of people in Canada, and clearly is a valuable world language. And yet, many people in Canada seem to resent having to learn French, or take issue with parents who chose French-immersion schooling, in a way that sounds all too familiar to attitudes towards the studying of Irish.

Indeed, this is not the only similarity between the teaching of languages in Irish and Canadian schools. I was at a friend's stag party in Nashville when we met two girls from Toronto. I had already begun writing this book, so I was curious to ask them about the French language in Canada. I asked them if they spoke any French. Instantly, I could sense they were uncomfortable with the question, probably in the same way that many Irish people are when someone asks them if they speak Irish. "Well, we have to learn it in school", one of them said "but we don't really speak it." Her friend added "It is just taught really badly, so people don't learn it." Now where have we heard that before? Either Irish and Canadian language teachers have both picked up the same horrible teaching methods somehow, or our expectations for what can be achieved by teaching languages in school are unrealistic.

At any rate, the hostile attitudes towards Irish and French suggest that these aren't based on the actual merit or otherwise of the language, but something else. That "something else" is a sense of superiority that English speakers around the world seem to have regarding their language, accompanied with a resentment of other languages, which translates into a desire to see them used as little as possible.

In his book, *Voices Silenced: Has Irish a Future?*, James McCloskey, professor of linguistics at the University of California, Santa Cruz, points out that there is a history amongst English speakers for not tolerating other languages. He writes:

> English, wherever it has gone in the world, has travelled on an ideological wave of great intolerance for bilingual activity and practice. Imperial cultures have probably always demanded that the language of empire be learned and used. Anglo-American colonial ideology has always taken a step further and demanded in addition that local languages be abandoned. Monolingual ability in English has been the result in large areas of the world, along with deeply-held and unquestioned belief that multilingual ability or practice is rare and exotic.[36]

This disdain for speakers of other languages appears to remain today, long after the age of empire has passed. A linguistic study from 2006 sought to investigate parental attitudes towards their children learning a foreign language, based on feedback given by school pupils in Britain, Germany and the Netherlands. The study found that 98% of German parents and 82% of Dutch parents had a positive attitude towards their children learning a foreign language. However, only 48% of British parents had a positive attitude about their children learning a foreign language, with more students believing their parents had a negative view rather than positive view about second language learning. It seems incredible that any parent could have a negative view about their children learning a second language, but this study shows that such attitudes are not uncommon in the English-speaking world.

In many ways, it is not surprising to see the French language in particular scorned by English speakers. Just as Irish provided an obstacle for English imperialism on a local level, the French people and their language were Britain's main imperial rivals on a global

---

36   James McCloskey, *Voices Silenced*, op. cit.

stage. Therefore, there has long been a suspicion of all things French in the English-speaking world. Allow me to give you an example of this from my own research. A Pan-Celtic society was established in Ireland in 1898 by a man named Edmund Edward Fournier d'Albe. Fournier was born and raised in England, but was of French Huguenot descent. His Pan-Celtic group quickly ran into problems with the Gaelic League, who felt it was a rival organisation that might detract from its own efforts to promote Irish. Some Gaelic League members tried to undermine the Pan-Celts by highlighting how they were really a group set up by a foreigner. But what is fascinating is that they didn't highlight the fact that Fournier was English, but insisted on depicting him as a Frenchman as a way to discredit him. Even amongst the Anglophobic element of the Gaelic League, "Frenchness" was more repugnant than "Englishness", which speaks volumes about how deeply ingrained anti-French biases are amongst English speakers.

In an article in the *Financial Times* in 2016, English broadcaster Jeremy Paxman wrote "the real problem with French is that it is a useless language". Paxman's main point was similar to that made by Kevin Williams in the previous chapter, namely that no language is more useful than English for an aspiring "citizen of the world". But to describe the language as "useless" was to succumb to an age-old desire to denigrate all things French. Paxman also wrote that French had never gotten over the loss of its empire and that "promotion of the French language and its supposed values is just another form of imperialism". There might well be merit in what Paxman is saying here, but it seems extraordinary that he does not see how the exact same thing might also be true of the promotion of English. The idea that French is "useless" is not limited to Jeremy Paxman either. In 2011, Chris Bryant, MP, told the House of Commons that Britain needed to ensure that its young people were learning languages "and not just the useless modern languages like French." Bryant felt that Mandarin, Spanish, Portuguese and Arabic were all much more important languages for British students to learn.

Most people would probably acknowledge that Mandarin, with 960 million speakers in the world's most populous country, and with China an economic superpower, is more "valuable" to learn than French. But the other three? They all have more native speakers than French (Spanish with 470 million, Arabic with 270 million and Portuguese with 215 million), but it seems difficult to make the argument that the economic value of any of these languages greatly exceeds that of French. After all, in 2017 France was the sixth largest economy in the world. Only one country that spoke Spanish, Portuguese or Arabic cracked the top ten (Brazil, coming in ninth), while Canada, with a considerable French speaking population, came in tenth.

The point is that Bryant's argument about the usefulness of French compared to other languages doesn't hold water. Instead, it is generally reflective of how many English speakers try to use the mask of logic and reason to express their contempt for other languages (it should be noted that Bryant is a fluent Spanish speaker, so it is not surprising that he sees this language as far more "useful" than French). The proof lies in the fact that there never is a consistent argument about the use of other languages, but rather the goalposts are always moved in a way to suit the individual circumstances of English speakers.

Irish is knocked in Ireland because "nobody" speaks it there and it has no "use" outside of Ireland, but in Canada "nobody" speaks French in "most" areas and "more important" world languages like Mandarin or Spanish should be taught instead. There is a tendency to try any argument against a particular language in order to discourage its use or at least to belittle its speakers. Hence, we get claims that no-one speaks a language, followed by the idea that the language is useless outside of the country, and if this is not true, then the issue is that other languages are even more useful, or that children should have a choice to study it, but if parents choose immersion-education for their children, then they are elitist. It is worth looking at a couple of case studies from around the English speaking world to show that, regardless of the "other" language in question, some issue always seems to be taken with it.

We have already mentioned Scots Gaelic and some of its similarities to Irish. However, the claim of Scots Gaelic to be the "national" language of Scotland is more complex than that of Irish in Ireland. It arrived from Ireland, possibly as late as 500 AD, and this meant that later English speaking populations of Scotland considered it a foreign language, often calling it "Erse" or Irish. While it seems to have been spoken in most of Scotland in medieval times, it was not the dominant language for millennia as Irish was across Ireland.

Furthermore, it is not the only language associated with Scotland. Scots, also known as Lallans, has its own rich history. According to the 2011 census, just under 58,000 people in Scotland, or 1.1% of the population, speak Gaelic. About 3000 pupils receive their primary education through Scots Gaelic, but most Scottish students don't even have the option to study it as a subject in school. In recent years, the Scottish government has taken some steps to promoting the language, such as creating bilingual road signs and outlining plans to make Scots Gaelic an optional subject in all primary schools. Despite the language having a much more reduced place in society compared to Irish, the disdain for Scots Gaelic is every bit as bad, if not worse, than what we find in Ireland.

In 2017, in response to the Moray local council being asked to draw up a Gaelic language plan (as they were legally obliged to do), councillor George Alexander branded Bòrd na Gàidhlig a "Gaelic Gestapo". That same year, one enlightened Twitter user posted the following comments about Bun-sgoil Taobh na Pairc, an Edinburgh Gaelscoil: "Only cunts send their kids tae fucken Gaelic school. Burn it tae the ground. Bonnington Road needs a Starbucks!" Charming.

Meanwhile, a quick look at the comment section of just one article on the Scots Gaelic language reveals some familiar arguments. Here is a sample of what was written:

"Gaelic is irrelevant to the vast majority of people in Scotland. What most Scots get annoyed with is the politicisation of the issue."

"A minority language -nothing against it but, the Gaelic mafia won't like it becoming too popular as they like to keep it private and esoteric... so long as they keep getting the taxpayers' money."

"There is one reason and one reason only the Scottish Nazi Party are forcing local authorities to promote Gaelic...and everyone knows exactly what that reason is."

"Amadan, the point of language is to communicate with each other. Notice how we're all using English. You can use Gaelic as much as you like but only 1% (i.e. nobody) understands what you're saying. What is the point in learning a language hardly anyone understands. May as well go and learn Aramaic."

"I have no issue with anyone wanting to speak Gaelic if they so wish. I do however have issue with tax payers money being squandered on promoting a language which is so poorly supported by the people of Scotland as a whole. Nearly every Gaelic speaker knows English so why waste enormous sums on road signs etc., which are meaningless to the vast majority of native Scots and virtually every overseas visitor. PC gone mad."

Firstly, I have always been amazed by people who say they have no problem with anyone speaking another language as if this was an act of generosity on their part, because taking issue with someone using a language was a reasonable alternative. The complaints made here are identical to those frequently uttered in Ireland, namely that Gaelic speakers (often viewed as "Nazis" or a "mafia") just want to create jobs for themselves, waste money on the language, and force a dead language when they can just speak English anyway. The only difference is the belief that the Scottish National Party is promoting Gaelic as a way of driving a cultural wedge between Scotland and England to boost support for independence. And, as a reminder, all of this animosity is generated despite the fact that no one in Scotland is compelled to study the language.

Scots Gaelic is not the only indigenous language spoken in Britain. Some of the language debates that take place in Ireland and Scotland are also replicated in Wales. The history of Welsh is more like Irish than that of Scots Gaelic, in that it was the language of all of Wales (and beyond) from the beginning of recorded history. The percentage of the Welsh people that spoke Welsh began to drop dramatically in the 19th Century, before stabilising at around 20% in the later 20th Century. As is the case with Irish, getting a grasp for how many people speak Welsh can be a bit difficult. According to the 2011 census, 19% of the Welsh population (566,000 people) can speak Welsh. The Welsh Language Use Survey in 2014 found that 11% of the population (310,600 people) spoke Welsh fluently, with similar numbers (13%) saying they used Welsh every day.

There is no doubt that the Welsh language is much more vibrant that Irish. Any Irish person who passes through the Welsh speaking parts of Wales cannot help but notice how much more widely spoken that language is compared to Irish in the Gaeltacht. Nevertheless, there has been a long history of efforts to discourage the Welsh people from speaking Welsh. A famous editorial in *The Times* in 1866 claimed that "the Welsh language is the curse of Wales...they must forget their isolated language, and learn to speak English and nothing else...for all practical purposes Welsh is a dead language." To put some context to that comment, it should be noted that according to the 1891 census (the first to track usage of Welsh), over 960,000 people spoke Welsh, including over half a million people who spoke nothing but Welsh. Not bad for a dead language!

So, are the complaints made against Welsh similar to those against Irish? Let's check. All responses in italics have been taken directly from various online message boards. Is Welsh a dead language? Yes, according to Welsh writer Roger Lewis who called it a *"moribund monkey language."* Nobody speaks it? *"Even in Wales hardly anyone speaks it and those that do are mostly the older generation."* Check. Is it a useless language? *"I'm learning Welsh. Pretty sure it's useless. Everyone in Wales speaks English, and very few of them speak Welsh."* Check. Is it a waste of money? *"The benefit of Welsh language skills to the GDP is approximately zero, and yet its cost in squandered resources must be huge."* Check. Is it forced down people's throats? *"I personally don't "hate" the Welsh language, but do hate it being shoved down my throat, especially as I pay for its enforcement through taxes and my TV licence."* Check.

Other languages should be taught in its place? *"Wonderful as Welsh maybe as a vehicle for culture and important as it is to preserve diversity of language, I think that perhaps learning Mandarin or Cantonese would be a better bet."* Check. Support of the language is a conspiracy to create jobs for Welsh speakers? *"Couple of extra PCs on the beat. Repairing or replacing the faulty diagnostic equipment at the Royal Gwent. Heck no, let's create a few jobs for the Taffia instead."* Check. People who promote it are fascists? *"I'm Welsh and I must say I think the Welsh language Nazis are comical."* People who speak the language are elitist? *"The crachach got their jobs (inevitably in the BBC, S4C, the Welsh assembly etc.) through nepotism which they are keen to perpetuate, have nice houses in the Welsh-speaking parts of Cardiff or the Bay, and look down on everyone else.*" Check. The anti-Welsh lobby seem much better than their Irish counterparts at creating labels like "Taffia" and "crachach" to belittle those they disagree with. Funny how the criticisms against Welsh are identical to Irish, even though (unlike Irish) the language is widely and openly used in many parts of Wales and it only became a compulsory school subject (up until the age of 16) in 1990.

Of course, similar attitudes can be found in Australia or New Zealand towards the indigenous languages of those countries, even though no one has ever had to study them in schools. But perhaps the most interesting case study of the English speaker's phobia for people speaking another language can be seen in the United States. With 53 million Spanish speakers, including 41 million native speakers, the U.S. has the second largest Spanish speaking population in the world, behind Mexico. Now, as Spanish is one of the most spoken languages in the world, with millions of people in the US who speak it as their primary language, we can expect a much more positive attitude towards it than that shown to Irish and Welsh. Can't we?

Of course not. Instead, what we find are many of the arguments used against Irish in Ireland are reversed against Spanish in the US. Take the "usefulness" of Spanish, for a start. Rosita Boland, Chris Bryant and various Canadian English speakers all agreed that Spanish was a very useful language to learn, certainly far more so than French or Irish. But one American online commenter wrote "Hispanics are obsessed with painting the Spanish language out to be more than what it is. Spanish IS NOT a world language. Sure, there are 400 million plus speakers, but 98% of them are located in the Americas. Spanish has very little, if no presence in Africa and Asia for example."

Well, at least no one disagrees that people actually speak Spanish. Can we assume that the tolerance shown by the anti-Irish lobby, who are generous enough not to object to people speaking Irish, also extends from English speakers towards Spanish speakers? Surely it must, given how free speech is a core American value? Perhaps not. While campaigning for the presidency, Donald Trump declared "This is a country where we speak English, not Spanish." Or as Sarah Palin put it "when you're here, let's speak American." These ideas are sometimes expressed even more crudely on American streets, with many anecdotes shared online about the abuse some people have suffered for speaking Spanish. In 2017, Hector Torres was sitting in an airport in Reno, Nevada, and speaking in Spanish on the phone to his mother. Suddenly, a man in a wheelchair, apparently named Mike, confronted Torres about his choice of language. The encounter lasted over ten minutes, and most of it can be viewed online. Here is just a short snippet from the conversation, to give some sense of how it went:

MIKE: "Fuck you! You are a fucking piece of shit."

HECTOR TORRES: "Incredible. Say it one more time, just for.... say it one more time."

MIKE: "You are a fucking piece of shit, you fucking Spic."

HECTOR: "And explain what I did to you one more time."

MIKE: "Talking that fucking stupid Spanish round here when everybody else is a fucking English-speaking American."

HECTOR: "Incredible."

Where does such hate come from? How can such demands for linguistic conformity be justified? The concept of assimilation is just another convenient use of "rational and logical" thinking to suit an ideological desire.

What about bilingual signage? In Ireland, the argument against them is that everyone can speak English, so there is no point to including Irish as well. With so many monoglot Spanish speakers in the US, however, could anyone object to signs that included Spanish? This comment from an online discussion board seems typical: "I'm not racist or anything, and don't get wrong; Spanish is a beautiful language. BUT, it's very annoying when I read Spanish signs below English in our stores, packages etc. I don't care if nearly 50 million Hispanics speaks Spanish, they should learn English. This is America, an English-speaking country, not a Spanish speaking country."

What about official languages? In Ireland, we are told that making Irish an official language is a pointless and meaningless gesture, because it will not change what language people actually speak. Is this same confidence found in the US, which has no official language? Not at all. 31 individual states have made English their official language, with almost all of them doing so within the last 30 years. There is also a growing demand for English to be made the official language of the country as a whole, with one survey suggesting that 87% of Americans support such a move.

The point of this is simple. All around the world, English speakers have taken issue with any efforts to encourage the use of another language. In each case, these objectors insist that they are only raising "practical" issues, but as demonstrated above, English speakers in one land will make the exact opposite argument of those in another country, depending on which point best suits their agenda. These are not consistent principles being adhered to, but rather an ideological campaign to belittle other languages, and their users, as much as possible. And as Ireland is primarily an English-speaking nation, the prejudices of the Anglophone world are turned against Irish with considerable venom.

The third strand that makes up the rope of hatred encircling Irish comes from the mixed feelings that every Irish person develops within themselves about the language. As a way of demonstrating what I am talking about, let me tell you a story. I was living in Newark, Delaware, when I heard about two Welsh guys who were also living in the town. I was told that they were both 6'8 and had played rugby in Wales. As a member of the local rugby club, I decided to try and recruit them to play for us, so I managed to get hold of one of their telephone numbers. I began exchanging texts with Chris, who said that he and his brother John would love to come and play rugby with us. So I arranged to pick the two of them up and drive them to training.

At this time, I had started learning Welsh myself so I could read Welsh primary sources for my doctoral research, and I was hoping the two lads spoke it. So not long after I picked them up for training, I asked if they spoke Welsh. They both responded defensively, saying it was a "dead" language that no one spoke, that it was "useless" and that they were quite content not speaking it. I let the matter drop. Anyway, John only came to one or two training sessions before he packed in the rugby, but Chris played on and off with us for about a year. One day, maybe six months after that first conversation in the car, we were chatting about something or other when suddenly he said "I really wish I was fluent in Welsh". He had obviously totally forgotten what he had said to me before, so what could explain this change of attitude?

My theory is that nothing had actually changed, but rather what I was seeing was a kind of bipolar attitude that many Welsh (and Irish) people have about their respective languages. In other words, many people simultaneously have a strong desire to speak the language and a resentment towards the language because they can't speak it. The root cause of this identity crisis is nationalism. As noted in the introduction, nationalism is often dismissed as something that only affects people on the fringe of society, but in reality, it influences the thinking of almost every human being alive today. The entire world is divided into nation-states, and at one stage or another, we all must reflect on what it means to be part of "our" nation. Humans are social creatures, and a part of figuring out who we ourselves are is understanding our group identity.

Now we all have multiple groups with which we identify, but one of them is our "nation", which Benedict Anderson aptly labels an "imagined community" because we see ourselves as being part of a group with millions of people that we will never know or meet. But as discussed previously, the Irish language presents a problem in resolving our Irish identity. Nationalism is founded on the idea that a people move together through time, maintaining similar characteristics and markers of identity. One of these national traits is language, but we are aware that, unlike other nations, we have largely lost our language. The natural psychological response is that in order to be part of this nation that has existed for thousands of years, one should be able to speak the language that (we imagine) has always been spoken. That means that an identity crisis is provoked in all of us at some stage about not speaking Irish.

This crisis is resolved in three different ways. For many people, there is a resignation that the ship has sailed and there is nothing they can do to reclaim the language for themselves. This usually is accompanied by a detached, albeit generally positive, view of Irish. Other people end up with a feeling of shame, guilt and a sense of personal failing for not having acquired the language. In some cases, this actually serves as a spur for people to attempt, and sometimes succeed, in learning the language. Even those who do not actually learn the language tend to be quite vocal in their opinions and actions in supporting Irish. But the third group resolves the identity crisis in a different way. Aware that they will never speak Irish, they subconsciously realise (correctly, as it happens) that there would be no identity crisis, and they would be much more secure about their Irishness, if the Irish language had never existed. This ultimately channels itself into a hatred for the language and for any reminder that it is spoken by anybody.

This is what I call "Frank Fitts Syndrome". If you have ever seen *American Beauty*, you will get the reference. Frank Fitts is vehemently homophobic throughout the movie, complaining about his neighbours being "faggots" who "always have to rub it in your face." He is also deeply concerned that his son is involved in a homosexual relationship with his other neighbour, Lester Burnham. Of course, what we learn at the end of the movie is that Fitts is a repressed gay man himself. Just as he expressed a violent hatred of gay people because of his sexual longings, so too we have Irish people hating Irish because they secretly want to possess it.

In 1996, Gráinne Duggan wrote a letter to the *Irish Times* in response to an article the previous week that claimed Ireland was in danger of losing its identity if the Irish language died out. Here is an excerpt from her letter:

> I have neither the opportunity nor, I must confess, a great desire to speak Irish, but that does not make me less of an Irish person that Mr. Ó Gormain. I feel no guilt – regret, maybe, but not guilt – about the fact I do not speak it. A language is a vehicle for communication, and since Irish is only used as such in small areas of the country, it does not have a place in my life.

> I am not arguing for the abandonment of Irish – I am glad I learned it in school, and should I visit a Gaeltacht area, I would use it to communicate. But I, and people like me, are no less Irish for not speaking Irish.

Twice, Duggan asserts that she is no less an Irish person for not speaking Irish. But what is fascinating is that the article she was responding to never made the assertion that speaking Irish made someone "more" Irish than those who didn't. Duggan's comments in this matter are actually pretty common among people who don't speak Irish. What is relevant is exactly what these kinds of statements reveal. I have never, ever, heard an Irish speaker claim they were "more" Irish than people who didn't speak Irish. Perhaps some have, but in my experience at least, that would be extremely rare. However, people who don't speak Irish regularly ask whether their inability to speak Irish somehow dilutes their Irish identity. The question is supposed to come across as a confident dismissal of the need to speak Irish, but in reality, it is a defensive question, revealing an anxiety that not speaking Irish actually might make them less Irish. They thus seek assurance to the contrary, thereby highlighting their dismay at being unable to speak Irish that they are desperate to hide.

In conclusion, then, the roots of the hatred of the Irish language are complex, and have largely not been explored by wider Irish society because there is either a denial that it exists, or it is simply dismissed as being the inevitable consequence of teaching Irish in school. But this unnecessary negativity towards Irish has a mirror image in Ireland, which is uncritical praise for, and misplaced optimism about the benefits of, our island's other language: English.

CHAPTER 6

MAGIC BÉARLA

I once wrote an online article challenging some of the myths about the Irish language that seem to hold sway among Ireland's monoglot English community (more on those in the next chapter). The article had a comment section at the bottom, and one reader wrote "The irony is that you had to write this article in English and not in Irish." Of course, the ultimate irony was that this commenter, much like Alanis Morrissette, didn't have a proper grasp of what irony is. If I was writing in English about why writing in Irish is an effective way to communicate with people, then yes, that would be ironic. But if I want to confront misconceptions and misinformed views about Irish that are held by English speakers, what other language would I use?

Aside from the fact that the reader had a rudimentary grasp of English, the comment also revealed much about the mindset of the anti-Irish sect. Firstly, there was no attempt at all to engage with what I had actually written, which was a factual explanation on why some claims about how much money is spent on Irish are wildly exaggerated. Our friends who like to debate the merits of Irish on "practical and logical" grounds are usually happy enough to ignore facts that don't suit their position. But more importantly, the comment was typical of how those who take issue with an Ghaeilge always try to turn a conversation about some aspect of the Irish language into a comparison of Irish and English generally. The reason for this is simple. In a head-to-head contest based on a variety of factors, English beats Irish, or indeed, any language, hands down. Not surprisingly, the opponents of Irish are always eager to pick a fight on terms they can't lose.

But this is also a classic strawman argument. No Irish language activist is trying to create a situation in Ireland where people must choose between Irish or English. Any effort to promote Irish is not an attack on the English language. Indeed, what revivalists like myself want is for people to be able to speak Irish in addition to English, not instead of English. The fact that some people see the Irish language debate in these terms, or at least pretend to see it in such a light, may reflect, as James McCloskey observed, the English speakers' tendency to assume that humans normally only speak one language. So in writing this book, I am not trying to drive the English language out of Ireland. The English language is an important part of our Irish heritage, and it is of vital importance that all Irish people can speak English for the foreseeable future.

Having said all that, however, there is also a tendency to exaggerate just how important it is for the Irish nation to speak English as its first language. In particular, there is a belief that Ireland would be an incredibly poor country today were it not for the fact that English is the first language of most of our citizens. Had Irish remained the language of most Irish people, so the argument goes, then today Ireland would be an Atlantic Albania, mired in squalor, poverty and backwardness. It isn't surprising that many people believe this. For centuries, the Irish were told by their British betters that only by abandoning Irish and speaking English could they achieve prosperity and civilisation. But to accept this is to buy into the myth of "Magic Béarla", the idea that speaking English as a nation is an automatic road to unending economic success, and that not speaking English means nothing but misery.

It shouldn't require too much reflection to figure out just how flawed the belief in "Magic Béarla" is. For a start, Ireland became a predominantly English-speaking country in the middle of the 19th Century. And yet, with a few good years in more recent times excluded, the economic history of the country in that time has been anything but successful. The most notable feature of the Irish economy, from the 1850s up until today, is the large number of people who leave in order to find employment. This trend has continued regardless of whether the country has been ruled from London, from Dublin, or more recently, in collaboration with (some would still say "from") Brussels. The evidence that speaking English has been our linguistic golden ticket is certainly thin when looking at the last 170 years of our history.

Nor has it proved to be an economic cure-all in other parts of the English-speaking world. One doesn't have to look very hard in the United Kingdom or the United States to find communities or cities that have high rates of unemployment and poverty, despite the fact that everyone there speaks English. Furthermore, a comparison of the economic performance of English-speaking and non-English speaking nation-states shows that speaking English is not a guarantee of anything. In his well-regarded book, *Ireland, 1912-1985,* historian J.J. Lee demonstrated that Ireland had been comprehensively outperformed in economic terms by Denmark and Finland over the course of the 20th Century. Lee's point was that, despite having a similar sized population to these countries, and being largely spared the horrors of the Second World War, Ireland had failed to match the productivity of these two nations. And this was despite the fact that Ireland spoke English as its first language! Ireland's economic position has improved since then. In April 2017, the IMF ranked Denmark 38th in the world for its predicted GDP, Ireland 39th and Finland 46th. Unemployment in Denmark at that time was 4.3%, in Ireland it was 6.4% and in Finland it was 10.2%. Certainly, in comparison with Denmark especially, it seems hard to claim that speaking English has given us a clear economic advantage over similarly sized non-English speaking countries.

Of course, to make simplistic arguments one way or the other about the relationship between language and economic prosperity is foolish, but unfortunately, such childish thinking has a considerable influence on Irish people's perceptions of the English language. I once stumbled upon an argument that two YouTube users were having in the comment section of a video about the respective value of Irish and English. One user, let's call him Spotted Hyena 44, wrote that it was a shame that the Irish language had declined and efforts should be made to encourage its use. Another viewer, whose user name might have been Assassin Kitten, replied that while it was unfortunate that most people didn't speak Irish anymore, the country was economically much better off speaking English. Spotted Hyena 44 didn't take this lying down, and said that there was no reason that Ireland could not be a primarily Irish speaking country and economically successful, pointing to the fact that Scandinavian countries had not been held back by the fact that they didn't speak English as their first language.

Assassin Kitten stuck to his guns, insisting that countries that are predominantly English speaking had an advantage over those that were not. Then Spotted Hyena 44 threw Assassin Kitten a curve ball. He asked whether Germany would be economically better off if all Germans spoke English as their first language. Germany is the 16th largest country on earth in terms of population, but has the world's fourth biggest economy. There isn't really any basis to say that Germany would be a much more successful nation if only it swapped speaking German for speaking English. Assassin Kitten knew this presented a problem for his argument, and weakly responded that while Germany would indeed be better off if it spoke English (has anyone in any internet discussion ever admitted they were wrong?), he conceded that its economic performance would only improve "a little bit".

The question might be asked as to why the myth of "Magic Béarla" remains so persistent when evidence to the contrary is readily available? The answer goes back to the collective trauma our nation suffered, and suffers, from the loss of Irish. Compared to the rest of the world, we know that we are the odd ones out in having a national language that we don't speak. Therefore, we overcompensate for having lost Irish by insisting that we have gained enormous financial benefits for having acquired English in its place. We desperately want to believe that we are way better off for speaking English to ease our angst about not speaking Irish. It was in following that logic to its inevitable conclusion that Assassin Kitten came to believe that even Germany would benefit from speaking English instead of German.

However, the "economic compensation" factor is only one reason that the belief in "Magic Béarla" is so widespread. The second reason is a related myth, that of "Indomitable English". The premise behind this is simple. English will become the first language of the entire globe eventually, and therefore the language shift that took place in Ireland will be replicated everywhere. Therefore, trying to revive Irish is pointless because the tide of English can never be stemmed, and there is no need to feel guilty about losing the language, because that is the inevitable fate of all languages bar one.

A cursory glance at the history of the languages of Britain and Ireland might seem to support that view. Over the last few centuries, English has all but replaced Irish, Welsh, Scots Gaelic, Manx, Cornish and Norn in the respective areas that these tongues once dominated. Its spread around the world has also been impressive. About 60 countries, on every continent, have English as an official language, with hundreds of millions of people outside of these countries speaking it as a second language. Many people are convinced that its use will become even more prevalent. I remember once reading the online comments of an Irishman who had lived in the Netherlands for a couple of years. Not only did he feel that he had no need to learn Dutch (he hadn't even tried) but he insisted that his Dutch friends told him that their language was doomed and was already being replaced by English. Ideas like this have a lot of adherents in the English-speaking world.

It is worth wondering, however, if the march of English is as unstoppable as some think. Even the spread of English across Britain and Ireland was not as straightforward or inevitable as one might assume. As was already discussed in chapter two, the Great Famine played an important role in the decline of the Irish language. The Scots Gaelic community was decimated by the Highland Clearances in the 18th and 19th Centuries. During the clearances, entire communities of Gaelic speaking Scottish highlanders were evicted at once so the land they farmed could be turned over to sheep grazing. These people were usually forced into emigration, with many heading to Canada. Indeed, so extensive were these evictions that Gaelic (in both its Irish and Scottish forms) was the third most spoken language in Canada in the 19th century, behind English and French. The outcome was that the Scottish Gaelic language in Scotland went into steep decline.

Welsh, on the other hand, faced a challenge of a different kind. The mineral wealth of the Welsh coalfields brought an enormous influx of migrants from England to Wales, with the result being that Welsh, the language of almost all Welsh people in 1800, became a minority language by 1900. Therefore, the spread of English was facilitated in each case by significant social and demographic upheaval and change.

Nevertheless, even if none of these events had happened, it is difficult to see how English would not have continued to spread in these countries, albeit possibly with less disastrous consequences for the indigenous languages. But we might ask why, if English is an irresistible force, it has not pushed into the rest of Europe. Only 20 miles separate England from France at the narrowest point of the English Channel. Paris is closer to London than either Dublin or Edinburgh are. Why hasn't English made a beach head in France?

Some might feel such a question is stupid. France is a large coun-try, almost identical in population size to the UK. With 66 million speakers within France's borders, French would be too invaluable for French people to abandon. OK then. But what about Norway. It is only about 300 miles from the British coast. There are only about five million people who speak Norwegian, and let's face it, it is a "useless" language outside of Norway. One estimate suggests that 90% of Norwegians already can speak English. So why don't they just pack in the whole Norwegian language thing and join us Irish as members of the Anglophone world?

Yet Norwegian is in no imminent danger of disappearing, or even declining. Some may feel this is not true, pointing to the fact that English, through loanwords and grammatical influences, is changing the Norwegian language. Indeed, but Norwegian changing and Nor-wegian disappearing are not the same thing, something that our Irish friend living in the Netherlands seems to have misunderstood about the future of Dutch as well. Norwegian, or Dutch, or French, are not under threat because, unlike what took place in Ireland in the 18th and 19th Centuries, parents in these countries are not choosing Eng-lish over their native tongue when it comes to raising their children. We can expect the number of people who speak English as a second language in Europe (and beyond) to increase certainly, but the fate of the Irish language is not what is in store for Norwegian, French or Dutch, at least as things currently stand. Reflecting on why Norwe-gian parents are not switching to English is important, however, as this offers an insight into how exactly Irish can be revived. We will return to this idea later on in the book.

At any rate, I am sure I have got some champions of the English language in Ireland all hot and bothered by implying that English is basically worthless. Relax. That is not at all what I am saying. But what I am trying to say is that when it comes to evaluating how important English is to us, it is important to distinguish between how we Irish benefit as individuals from speaking English, and how much our country or nation benefits from the fact that English is our first language.

Speaking individually, there is no doubt that Irish people are very fortunate to speak English. In a sense, we won the language lottery. We speak the most useful language in the world, and therefore are largely spared the bother of having to learn any others. We can travel to almost any country and be confident that we will find at least a couple of people who speak our language, should we get into difficulty. Our employment prospects are greatly enhanced by the fact that we can move to other Anglophone countries to find a job, especially as four of the ten largest economies in the world are English speaking countries. The biggest movies, the most popular songs and some of the greatest works of literature are all in the language we were born and raised with. As speaking English is of enormous benefit to us as individuals, it is not surprising that some Irish people have done very well for themselves indeed. Bono, Saoirse Ronan, Dara Ó Briain, Enya, and Conor McGregor, to name just a few, have become very wealthy and earned varying degrees of global fame, due in large measure to the fact that they speak English (although the fact that one of this group is a native Irish speaker, and that two more were educated entirely through Irish, shows that speaking Irish is no hindrance to international success).

But the mistake we make is in assuming that because speaking English is good for us as individuals, it must also be hugely advantageous for us as a nation as a whole. That, however, is more debatable. The very reason that English is so useful for us as individuals (it is a global language) is also the reason that there isn't anything especially valuable about all of us speaking English. Around the world, English speakers are a dime a dozen. Estimates vary, but some calculations place the number of English speakers at 1.5 billion people, which would be more than any other language on earth. This was the mistake that Assassin Kitten made when he tried to argue that the German economy would be better off if Germany replaced German with the English language. Undoubtedly, German businesses, especially international ones, have to employ English speakers to succeed. But to fill these vacancies, they simply hire native German speakers who also speak very good English. Assassin Kitten had fallen into the old trap of the monoglot English speaker, in thinking that people by default just speak one language, and failing to understand that Germany already has all the English speakers it needs.

The reason the English language is seen as so vital to the modern Irish economy is it is believed to be central to the fact that we can lure multinational corporations to set up shop in Ireland. English is the language of international business, so it is undeniably seen as a benefit that all Irish people speak English when it comes to attracting companies. But we are fooling ourselves if we think that is the only, or even the main, factor that comes into play when multinationals look at locating in a country. Our low corporate tax rates are certainly a major factor, as is the high level of education attained by our workforce. Yet many people insist on seeing the language factor as being decisive.

When Dell announced in 2009 that it was moving almost 2,000 jobs from Limerick to Poland, I saw several online commenters claim that the reason for this was that Polish people had come to Ireland, learned English, and now were luring business away from us with their new English language skills. The reality that Polish people can learn English in Poland doesn't seem to have entered their thinking. Furthermore, do they really believe that the guy putting the screws in the computer in Warsaw, or the cover on the iPhone in China, is speaking English all day? So long as upper management in these factories can speak English, Apple or Dell don't care what language the grunts on the shop floor speak. In that sense, the fact that everyone in Ireland can speak English is not enough to keep manufacturing jobs here, because companies can simply pay non-English speakers far less to do the required work.

The confusion and uncertainty around Brexit has also been seized upon by many people in Ireland as a gilt-edged chance to improve our economic position. "We will be the only English speaking nation left in the EU", they say "and all of the jobs that have to be moved from Britain will shift across the Irish Sea to us." Firstly, this ignores poor Malta, which also has English as an official language. But more importantly, it shows a failure to appreciate that, in the eyes of the business world, there isn't much difference between people who speak English as their first language, and people who speak it well.

When Britain voted to leave the European Union in 2016, experts pointed that some banking jobs in London, Europe's financial hub, would have to be moved to other countries in the EU. Dublin, Amsterdam, Frankfurt and Paris were highlighted as cities that could pry thousands of jobs in the financial sector out of the UK. Interestingly, almost every Irish writer or media outlet that discussed this story highlighted that Dublin was an English-speaking city. European commentators were less inclined to note this fact. The reason, once again, is that Irish people overestimate how important it is that English is our first language. There seems to have been an assumption, or at least a hope, that because London was an English-speaking city, Dublin was obviously the next best fit, and that the dominance of English would compensate for other factors that made Dublin less suitable.

And the outcome? Well, so far, disappointment for Ireland. As of September 2017, various banks had announced they were to move nearly 5,000 jobs out of London. Where were these jobs going? 3,050 to Frankfurt, 1,700 to Paris, and only 150 to Dublin. Why would this be so? Undoubtedly, the ability to speak English would be essential for all of these jobs. How come we couldn't lure them to Ireland? The reality is that we don't have the clear edge in terms of producing English speakers that we think we have. According to one report from 2006, 56% of Germans said they could hold a conversation in English, 90% of Dutch people said they could, and even 39% of the French population (not renowned lovers of English) self-identified as English speakers. If you want to find English speakers in the EU, you don't have to come to Ireland.

This isn't to say that there aren't businesses in Ireland that don't directly rely on the fact that we speak English to make a profit. Of course, there are. The most obvious one is the English language schools that have grown in considerable number over the last 20 years. Although a couple of these have turned out to be nothing more than scams, the TEFL industry definitely provides much needed jobs, and attracts students who contribute to the wider economy. One of the most important pillars of the Irish economy is one that benefits considerably from the fact that we are an English-speaking nation, but the value of English in this regard is often overlooked. I am talking about tourism. According to Fáilte Ireland, between 2012 and 2015, about 60% of overseas tourists who visited Ireland came from other English-speaking countries like the UK or the US. Bearing in mind what we have said about English speakers often being uncomfortable around people who speak other languages, that isn't surprising. Ireland is exotic, but not too exotic, for many of these visitors. 35% of our tourists come from continental Europe. Many, perhaps most, of these visitors will be able to speak some English, which gives them confidence that they can get around the country without any problem. As tourism is worth about €5 billion annually to the Irish economy, the contribution of English in this sector is vital.

The main point of this chapter, then, has been to argue that the fact that everyone in Ireland speaks English is not as beneficial to the country as a whole as most people imagine. But beyond this, there are actually some instances when our first language actually has negative economic consequences, at least for some of us. This is particularly obvious in the field of culture and entertainment. While people like Bono have enjoyed tremendous success as a result of being part of the English-speaking world, there is another side to that story, which is that many Irish writers, musicians and filmmakers struggle to make a living because they have to compete with counterparts from other English-speaking countries. Much of the money in Bono's bank account originally came from the US or Britain, but the tradeoff for U2's success is that British and American acts are also hugely popular in Ireland.

Whether this is a good or a bad thing depends on your perspective. Irish music fans presumably just want to purchase the best music, and don't care where the artist comes from. But an Irish musician, trying to make a career, is all too aware that they have to compete with international bands for airtime and sales. Of course, it will be noted that English language music is also very popular in non-English speaking countries, but most of these countries also have a demand for music in their native languages. This isn't true in Ireland, however, where a singer, be he or she from Woking or Wichita, is just as appealing as, and indistinguishable from, a singer from Wicklow. Indeed, just for this very reason, TD Willie Penrose proposed introducing a bill to ensure that 40% of the music played on Irish radio stations had to be made by Irish artists. Penrose claimed that this would create eight to ten thousand new jobs in the Irish music industry.

The same principle also applies for the television and film industry in Ireland. The Irish population in general benefits from being able to watch the best movies and TV shows made in the English-speaking world. But this also makes it harder for Irish people, be they actors, cinematographers, directors or producers, trying to break into these businesses and forge careers. Likewise, Irish writers have fewer opportunities than, say Finnish writers, because there isn't a domestic audience that they have sole access to. For every Colm Toibín or Edna O'Brien who gains worldwide fame through their penmanship, there are thousands of aspiring Irish writers who either can't get published or struggle to sell their books. Sean de Fréine, in *The Great Silence,* explained why this happens: "The circulation of so much printed material from abroad considerably reduces the home market for Irish-produced material. Reduced markets for Irish productions means reduced advertising revenue for them. This in turn means that payments for Irish contributors to native publications must be less than what they could earn by writing for foreign publications."[37]

It is actually quite difficult to get an estimate of how many books are published in Ireland each year. Searching online, the only number I could find was from someone who wrote a Masters thesis on the topic. They claimed that 1,099 books were published in Ireland in 2007 (120 of them in Irish). If this is accurate, then we are publishing slightly more books than Cyprus (estimated at 930 books in 1996) and less than Iceland (1,402 in 2014), despite having a much larger population than either. Finland, with a slightly larger population than ours, publishes between 13,000 and 14,000 books annually. Ireland might not be publishing many books, but we are certainly buying them. According to a survey of the European Federation of Publishers, which focused on 28 countries, Ireland spent the eighth highest amount of money per capita on books, and we were also in the top seven, proportionally speaking, for number of book stores in the country. Obviously if we are spending more on average on books than our European neighbours, but publishing less than them, this means we are largely buying books published overseas. Irish readers might be the winners, but Irish writers are certainly the losers in this exchange.

The most obvious drawback for Ireland in having an English-speaking population is that our first language facilitates "brain

---

37 Seán De Fréine, *The Great Silence,* op. cit.

drain". The history of emigration from Ireland is quite complex, with different factors in different eras pushing people towards going overseas. But language has undeniably played a considerable role in this. Since the mid 19th Century, Irish emigrants have travelled almost exclusively to English speaking states. One doesn't need to be a social scientist to figure out why. As Seán de Fréine observes "People are far more reluctant to cross cultural barriers than political ones."[38] When Irish people decide to leave their native land, they want to go to a place where they already speak the local language.

Of course, it would be wrong to see emigration as exclusively "good" or exclusively "bad". In times of hardship, opportunities for people to leave can be good for both the individual and the country as a whole. We could think of emigration as a kind of "safety valve" in this regard, helping Ireland navigate the worst of economic recession and decline. But the ability to move to other English-speaking countries can also act as an "eject button" for our citizens, and that is not always a good thing for the nation as a whole. Speaking broadly, many Irish people with ambition and determination feel that the quickest way for them to succeed in life is to simply leave Ireland. This means that other countries are often the ones to benefit from the talent, tenacity and innovative thinking of Irish citizens. In blunt terms, Ireland would be better off if these people stayed behind and tried to forge their way through whatever difficulties they encountered at home, instead of heading across the sea. Trying to quantify it would be almost impossible, but it seems likely that a disproportionate number of Ireland's best and brightest, compared to our European neighbours, take their talents to foreign shores. The English language facilitates this loss.

This returns us to the idea of our ability to speak English being great for us individually, but perhaps not so for us collectively. Undoubtedly there are thousands of Irish men and women all around

38   Ibid.

the world (but mostly in English speaking countries) who are very happy that speaking English gave them the opportunity to have the life they now have. Indeed, at the time of writing, it looks like I will spend most of my adult life in the United States, so it would be hypocritical not to point out that I have benefitted greatly from having English as my first language. Nevertheless, it is undeniable that our proficiency in English has a major downside for our nation in that our reservoir of human talent is too easily tapped by other countries. To point this out isn't to call for an effort to repress English in Ireland to stop this from happening. That ship has already sailed. Even if we revive Irish, English will still be widely spoken and highly educated and driven individuals will continue to leave. To highlight this fact is simply to note that the presence of English in Ireland has not been the unblemished treasure that some people view it as.

The emigration figures in the wake of the 2008 economic collapse give an interesting insight into how language shapes the decisions made by those who decide to leave Ireland. Between 2009 and 2015, 265,000 Irish citizens left the country, with 120,000 returning. This meant a net loss of 143,000 Irish citizens (excluding foreign nationals, who moved to Ireland and then subsequently left), equivalent to 3% of the country's population based on the 2016 census. A survey done by the UCC Émigré Project found that 62% had received a third level education, meaning the people leaving Ireland tended to be better educated than the general population, of which 47% have some kind of tertiary educational qualification. Throughout this period, more college-educated people were leaving than arriving in Ireland. According to the Central Statistics Office, Ireland had a net loss of 13,400 people with third level qualifications in 2011, for example. However, this was reversed in 2016, with 6,200 more college graduates entering the country than leaving. This is evidence that while English facilitates the "brain drain" of Irish citizens, it also allows us to attract well-educated migrants from other countries. It seems reasonable to assume that most college-educated immigrants to Ireland speak a reasonable level of English, and that the status of English here factored into their decision to come to our country.

So where did these migrants go and why did they leave? In 2013, 89,000 people left Ireland. About 22,000 went to the UK, with 26,000 going to continental Europe. 15,000 went to Australia, 5,000 to Canada, 6,000 to the USA, and 15,000 travelled to the other parts of the world. At first glance, these figures suggest that Irish people traveled to a wide range of countries with different languages. But there is a catch. Of that 89,000, only 51,000 were Irish citizens, with the remaining people being foreign nationals who had previously migrated to Ireland. When we consider that the number of people who left Ireland for English speaking countries in 2013 was about 48,000, it is evident what is happened. Irish citizens mostly departed for some other part of the Anglophone world, while foreign nationals largely went somewhere else.

A more complicated question is why did these migrants leave Ireland? According to the UCC Émigré survey, half of those who left Ireland had a full-time job at the time of leaving. This isn't to say that economic factors weren't behind the decision of these people to leave, as limited advancement prospects, poor pay or a partner's inability to find a job would all provide sound financial reasons for moving. But non-economic reasons also undoubtedly played a role. 40% of those who departed stated that the desire to travel or experience another culture was behind their decision. In other words, a significant amount of these emigrants left by choice, as opposed to being forced out due to a lack of employment. This was a major reason why, in 2013, Ireland became the European state with the highest level of net emigration (only six years after having the highest level of net immigration).

For every 1,000 people in Ireland, there was a net migration loss of 7.6 people. In comparison, the rate in Lithuania was 7.1, with Latvia

(5.8), Greece (4), Portugal (3.6) and Spain (3.5) the next countries with the highest rate of net emigration. Of course, Spain, Greece and Portugal all suffered financial collapse at around the same time as Ireland. Why was our migration level much higher? Again, this is a complex question, but the fact that Irish people could travel to more prosperous, English-speaking countries undeniably played a considerable role. Indeed, it is worth pointing out that of all the people who left Spain in 2012, 83% of them were foreign nationals. Spanish, Portuguese and Greek nationals did not depart their homelands in anything like the same numbers, proportionally speaking, as their Irish counterparts. As a result, Irish unemployment levels did not climb as high as those countries at the height of the "Great Recession". Unemployment rose as high as 15% in Ireland, but climbed to 18% in Portugal, 26% in Spain and 27% in Greece. In the short term, then, the fact that Ireland is part of the English-speaking world was undoubtedly of enormous help to the country. But whether the permanent loss of thousands of our well-educated and talented citizens is worth that trade-off certainly can be debated.

In conclusion, then, the English language undoubtedly has its benefits for Ireland, but it is a mixed blessing. It gives tremendous flexibility to every Irish person in global terms, allowing them to effortlessly become "citizens of the world". This does not translate into unending success for the Irish nation collectively, however, as speaking English does not give us the edge over our economic competitors as many Irish people think. Indeed, our first language enables other countries to siphon off the cream of the crop of our workforce. Admiration for the advantages English brings us is no bad thing, but Béarla worship blinds us to the fact that the language brings downsides as well.

CHAPTER 7

A MISCELLANY OF MYTHS

A lot of myths, misinformed opinions and, in some cases, outright lies about the Irish language are in wide circulation today. Many of them have already been addressed in earlier chapters, and a couple more will be discussed before the conclusion of the book. But this chapter will deconstruct an eclectic mix of nonsensical beliefs that, for one reason or another, didn't fit smoothly into other parts of the book. A couple of these myths have a powerful grip on the Irish imagination and really need to be challenged.

Myth One: We spend over €1 billion on the Irish language

The idea that €1.2 billion is spent on Irish every year has gained widespread acceptance in Ireland, particularly within the media. Kevin Myers, a well-known advocate for the removal of state support for Irish, has described the money spent on Irish as "...€1.2 billion down the drain every year. Mad, and immoral". In an article in *Belfast Newsletter* in 2017, Robin Bury wrote "Today it is estimated the cost of force-feeding Irish is €1.2 billion a year, which includes teaching, printing government publications, road signage, maintenance of Gaeltacht areas and recruitment of Irish translators." In a 2016 YouTube video entitled "An Bhfuil Cead Agam", journalist Eoin Butler said "The government currently spends about €1.2 billion per annum supporting the language through education, the media, various government quangos and government bureaucracy." And this figure is regularly repeated whenever any debate on the Irish language takes place. But the figure is false. It is what I like to call "the phantom billion euro". But where did this number come from?

The man responsible for the €1.2 billion figure is Dr. Ed Walsh, the former president of the University of Limerick. Walsh first made this claim in 2010, and it has been repeated with regularity since then. The first thing that should be noted is that, contrary to what Robin Bury and Eoin Butler thought, Ed Walsh was not claiming that this figure represented all the money spent by the state on Irish. Instead, Walsh stated that this figure represented, as he noted in an article in the *Irish Times* in 2011, the money "committed each year to teaching Irish." In other words, the true cost of Irish to the state would be more than €1.2 billion, because it didn't include the money spent on translating government documents into Irish, or on, say, funding TG4. But this figure always struck me as being suspiciously high. To give it some context, the Irish state spent €55 billion in 2016, and the annual Garda budget amounts to about €1.4 billion. If Ed Walsh's figure is correct, then Ireland spends 2% of its entire national budget, or about the same amount it spends on its entire police force, teaching one subject within its school system.

I reached out to Ed Walsh via email and asked him how this figure had been worked out. He replied that it had been calculated by "pro-rating the proportion of the school week dedicated to teaching Irish in the school against the total budget for the school system." To some people, this might seem like a very reasonable way of figuring out the state's financial commitment to the Irish language. However, some problems with Walsh's number become obvious once one looks a little closer.

The first issue is actually Walsh's verb choice. He described this as money that was "committed" to the Irish language, while people like Eoin Butler have said that this money is "spent" on Irish. Walsh's number is not actually a calculation for how much is "committed" or "spent" on Irish, but rather a valuation of the time dedicated to teaching Irish, nothing more. This might sound like semantic quibbling, but the difference is actually very important. When people hear that a billion euro is spent on Irish every year, they insist that this money should be spent on something else, such as improving our roads, or upgrading our hospitals, or something like that. After all, the verb "spend" implies that we can stop spending money on one thing, and instead spend it on something else.

But there is no billion euro pot of gold just waiting to be productively redistributed. If we stopped teaching Irish in primary schools tomorrow, we wouldn't pay our primary teachers any less. We could fire our Irish teachers in secondary schools, but then we would have to hire teachers of some other subject to fill that gap in the timetable. Removing Irish entirely from our curriculum would not free up vast amounts of money. Debating the position of Irish in schools can only be a question of whether we replace it with another school subject, not what we could do with all that "money" going to "waste". This isn't to say that the Irish state hasn't made a significant investment in the Irish language by including it in our school system. Clearly it has, but its investment is one of time (on the part of students and teachers) rather than money. Trying to put a value on this time and then claiming it is money being "spent" on Irish misleads people and creates further resentment toward the language.

The proof of this can be seen if we take Walsh's method and apply it in trying to find a value for some of the other ways time at school is spent. Let's say about a quarter of the time dedicated to English, and a quarter of the time dedicated to Irish, focuses on the teaching of poetry. Using the same logic that Walsh applied to Irish, we could claim that the Irish state "spends" €600 million every year on poetry. Can you imagine the outrage if Irish people thought that was true? Or what about break time when students are in school? After all, that takes place on school grounds and is supervised by teachers, so we should be able to place a monetary value on what the cost of this is

GAEILGE: A RADICAL REVOLUTION

to the state. When I was in school, our morning break and lunchtime took up 14.5% of the day. Prorated against the education budget, this would plausibly allow us to say that Ireland "spends" €1.3 billion every year on students playing hopscotch and soccer, smoking and sexting, eating cheese sandwiches and drinking milk. No one would take any of these numbers seriously, but when they are applied to the Irish language, it is very much a different story.

The other issue with Walsh's number is how the figure itself was calculated. In 2010, the entire budget for the Department of Education was estimated at about €8.7 billion. Walsh's estimate of €1.2 billion would represent a seventh of this total. It looks, to all intents and purposes, that the €1.2 billion estimate was calculated by dividing the entire budget for the Department of Education by seven. Why seven? Well, generally, most Leaving Cert students take seven subjects, so this may have been felt to be an adequate representative of class time dedicated to Irish. However, it should firstly be remembered that not all class time is dedicated to exam subjects, even in sixth year. When I was a Leaving Cert student, one eighth of classroom time was spent on Irish, so it is obvious that on this basis, allotting one seventh of the education budget to the teaching of Irish is too much.

But the true issue with this number becomes evident when we look at what the Department of Education's budget is actually spent on. Here is a breakdown of the major expenses in the 2015 education budget.

Teacher salaries: €3.1 billion
Skills development: €347 million
Third level grants: €1.4 billion
Infrastructure: €593 million
Department administration: €68 million
Special needs assistants: €407 million
Non-teaching staff: €100 million
Pension payments: €1 billion

Transportation costs: €175 million
Child abuse payments: €14 million
Grants to school and education boards: €393 million
Miscellaneous grants: €38 million
Teacher training: €25 million

Clearly many of these things have nothing at all to do with the Irish language, but all of them were factored into Ed Walsh's estimate for how much is spent on teaching Irish annually. Or to put it another way, this €1.2 billion includes, among other things, €200 million that is actually spent on third level education, €85 million that is actually spent on building and maintaining school buildings, €25 million that is actually spent on transporting children to and from school, €58 million that is actually spent on providing training assistants for students with learning disabilities, €14 million that is actually spent on paying cleaning staffs and secretaries, and €2 million that is actually spent paying compensation to people who suffered abuse while under the care of the Department of Education. This €1.2 billion is nothing but phantom money.

Another estimate for the amount of money spent on Irish that gained considerable attention came from Seán Ó Cuirreáin, Ireland's first Comisinéir Teanga. In his inaugural report in 2004, Ó Cuirreáin wrote "Hundreds of millions of euro are being invested – perhaps as much as €500m annually – in the teaching of Irish in the educational system." Describing this as an "opportunity cost" as opposed to an actual expenditure, Ó Cuirreáin said that it was calculated by prorating the amount of time dedicated to Irish against teacher salaries (as opposed to the entire budget for the Department of Education). In an email about this figure of €500 million, Ó Cuirreáin acknowledged that it was "a rough estimate". Indeed, if we take what the state paid teachers in 2015 (€3.1 billion) and divide it by eight (to represent the 1/8th of classroom time dedicated to Irish), we arrive at a figure of

€388 million, suggesting that Ó Cuirreáin's estimate was on the high side. Regardless of the number, however, Ó Cuirreáin points out that "as it is an 'opportunity cost' it is not money that could be saved if Irish were removed from the curriculum... It just demonstrates that the State appears to be saying that the language is important by allocating a significant amount of teaching time to it."

Nevertheless, the idea that hundreds of millions or even billions of euro are being wasted on Irish every year will be difficult to dispel. I had an argument online with journalist Eoin Butler after he published his video on the Irish language. One of my main criticisms was that he had taken Ed Walsh's figure at face value, without checking to see how it had been arrived at. After I had pointed out the obvious flaws in how this number was reached, Butler acknowledged that the calculation was "crude" and "imperfect", but nevertheless he said "I'm quite sure if the true figure would be calculated it would be north of €1bn." This kind of thinking has been satirised by Stephen Colbert, when he coined the word "truthiness". Truthiness means that evidence to support the accuracy of something is irrelevant, so long as a person believes in their gut that it is right. For a lot of people in Ireland, the idea that we spend more than €1 billion euro a year on Irish feels right. Thus, arguments to the contrary can be dismissed. Even if Ed Walsh's figure is wrong, it is still, somehow, correct for some people.

Myth Two: We spend tens of millions of euros each year on Irish translations

As with the €1.2 billion euro claim, this idea is widely circulated and widely believed. In his video "An Bhfuil Cead Agam", Eoin Butler stated "Every year in this country, over 150 public bodies spend tens of millions of euros hiring private companies to translate everything from fishing regulations to flood planning contingency documents into Irish." TD John Deasy, who has been a vocal critic of the government's policy to produce bilingual documents, claimed in the Dáil in November 2007 that "tens of millions" of euros were being wasted on Irish translations. The fact that the figure being claimed is particularly vague (tens of millions could mean anything from 20 to 99 million) suggests that these numbers are assumptions or guesses, rather than an accurate representation of how much is spent on Irish. By referring to "tens of millions" in the plural, we are at least talking about €20 million euro. So, do we spend at least €20 million a year translating documents into Irish?

The short answer is no, although with the caveat that trying to get an accurate grasp on how much is spent on Irish is difficult. Let's start with the government itself. Here are the figures provided by the Department of Justice and the Department of Foreign Affairs for their Irish language translation costs from 2011 to 2013.

	2011	2012	2013
DEPT. OF JUSTICE	€34,471	€23,391	€18,312
DEPT. OF FOREIGN AFFAIRS	€12,525	€19,316	€123,318

There is obviously a lot of disparity there from year to year. It should be noted that Eamon Gilmore, the Minister for Foreign Affairs who reported the figures for his department to the Dáil, noted that their costs for 2013 were exceptionally high to due to a series of one-off translations. If we use the figures for the Department of Justice to try to come up with an average number per department, we get a number of about €25,000.

There are 16 government departments, so we multiply €25,000 by 16 to get an estimate that the government spends €400,000 euros a year on Irish language translations. Then there is Rannóg an Aistriúchán. This is the government service that, among other things, provides translations in the Dáil when TDs speak in Irish and translates all acts of the Dáil into Irish. I contacted Rannóg an Aistriúchan about their budget, and was told that it was €1.5 million euro for 2017. If we combine that number with our estimate for how much government departments spend on Irish, we can say the government spends approximately €1.9 million euro every year on translating documents into Irish.

However, the government is not the only entity that has to translate documents. Public bodies like county councils and various regulatory boards also provide Irish language translations. However, getting to grips with how much each of these spend is a daunting task. For a start, some of these bodies don't keep track of how much they spend on Irish translations. Let me give you an example. Based on a freedom of information request asking how much the Gardaí Síochána spent on Irish language translations each year, the following figures were produced.

o 2013: €1,807,006

o 2014: €1,676,306

o 2015: €1,477,292

There was a catch to these numbers, however, the Gardaí said they did not track translation costs for individual languages. These figures represented the total sum of money spent on translation services in all languages. How much of this money was spent on Irish is hard to say, although when we consider that the London Metropolitan Police spend £7.1 million sterling each year (and clearly they aren't translating things as Gaeilge), it seems fair to assume most of the Gardaí translation costs are not related to Irish. The point of giving these figures is to show that getting an accurate figure for how much public bodies spend on Irish might be impossible.

The other issue is that, unlike government departments, which we might assume have similar translation costs, there seems to be very different practices towards Irish in some of these public bodies. Just searching through some of their websites, it is noticeable that while some have bilingual websites and publish reports in Irish as well as English, others don't have a word of Irish on their website and only publish documents in English.

Two of the public bodies I emailed that had bilingual websites, the Irish Film Board and the Chester Beatty library, reported that they spent €1,400 and €2,000 respectively on Irish translations (the Irish Film Board also noted that, despite the fact that their staff are presumably native English speakers, they send all of their English language publications to professional proof readers as well). I also contacted several public bodies that, judging from their website, did not have any Irish language publications. None of these replied to my enquiry about how much money they spent on translating documents into Irish, which suggested to me that they probably don't have anything translated, but didn't want to draw attention to this fact.

The Sun reported in 2013 that it found that 63 public bodies had spent €1.6 million on translating documents into Irish the previous year. However, over half of this was spent by one body, the State Examinations Office, which spent €900,000 on translating things like marking schemes and exams into Irish. Interestingly, *The Sun* claimed in the same article that Kerry County Council had 21 Irish language officers! However, while Kerry does have one full time Irish Development Officer, the other 20 people are simply officials employed by the Kerry County Council who speak fluent Irish and could deal with the public as Gaeilge if requested.

Anyway, if we exclude the State Examinations Office as an outlier, we are left with 62 public bodies who spent about €700,000 between them in translating documents into Irish. This would give us an average translation cost per public body of €11,290. Whether this is an accurate average might be debated. Many of the 63 public bodies referred to in *The Sun* article appear to be county councils, whose translation costs might be expected to be higher than, say, the National Milk Agency. As noted above, two of the public bodies I spoke with directly had translation costs far lower than €11,290, while others showed no evidence of translating anything into Irish and ignored my requests for information on their translation costs.

In other words, if accurate numbers could be obtained for all public bodies, it is quite likely the average would be lower, possibly significantly so. But using €11,290 for convenience's sake, we can calculate that the translation costs for all 296 public bodies combined amount to €3.3 million. When we add what the State Examinations Office spends, alongside our estimate for the government's translation costs, we get a grand total of €6.1 million spent on Irish translations every year. Whether that is money well spent or not might be debated, but clearly the number is a long, long way short of €20 million plus.

Hang on a minute, I hear you say, what about Irish language translations in the EU? Well so far, only a limited amount of translating has been going on. In 2016, the EU announced it was going to hire 62 Irish language translators, who were going to be paid €52,600 a year. Eventually this will increase to 180 translators. The cost of hiring these translators then will come to €9.5 million euro.

So here is the question. How can the EU plan to translate all of its laws into Irish for under €10 million a year if the Irish state is spending "tens of millions" a year translating what should be a much smaller number of documents? Obviously, the complexity of EU bureaucracy and regulations means that there are far more documents to be translated in Brussels than in Dublin. Some people might seize this as proof that "tens of millions" are indeed spent translating documents into Irish. Firstly, this is an estimate for a future cost. Right now, most of that money is not being spent. Secondly, even if we add that figure to our estimate for how much the

A MISCELLANY OF MYTHS

Irish state spends on translating documents, we are still shy of €20 million. And finally, with the departure of the UK from the EU, there is a strong chance that Ireland will have to drop Irish as its official EU language and revert to English.

This does give rise to the question, however, of how much money is actually spent on Irish in total by the Irish state. By "spend", I specifically mean money that is currently going towards some aspect of the Irish language, but which we could re-divert towards anything else if we chose to do so. In doing so, I do not attempt to factor in any estimated financial value for the teaching of Irish in our school system. This isn't to ignore the teaching of Irish. As I have already said, it is far and away the state's biggest commitment to the language. But, as noted earlier, trying to estimate a cash value for the time dedicated to Irish in class misleads people into thinking there is a financial bonanza awaiting the Irish state if we just kick Irish out of schools. There isn't. That all being said, here are the Irish state's main financial commitments to the Irish language.

o The Department of the Gaeltacht (2014 budget): €45 million
o TG4 (2012 budget): €32 million
o Raidió na Gaeltachta (2012 budget): €11 million
o Foras na Gaeilge (2015 budget): €11 million
o Translations (as estimated here): €6.1 million
Total: €105.1 million

Some might quibble with the use of the entire TG4 and Department of the Gaeltacht budget. After all, TG4 shows a lot of English language programming, so should its entire budget be counted as money spent on Irish? Seán Ó Cuirreáin, in an email he sent to me, pointed out that a considerable portion of the money allocated to the Department of the Gaeltacht is spent on improving infrastructure and subsidising travel costs for Ireland's island communities

181

and can't really be seen as an expense on the Irish language. But it is easier to include these numbers in their entirety. This figure of €105.1 million is almost identical to the one given by Manchán Magan in the second series of his show "No Béarla". The amount, according to Magan, was €105.9 million in 2006, and producer Rossa Ó Síordáin said the number was provided by the Department of Community, Rural and Gaeltacht Affair.

Now €105 million euros, to the average person, seems like an enormous fortune, but it should be understood in the context of government spending generally. Magan, on "No Béarla", pointed out that in 2006, the Irish government spent more than twice as much, €216.5 million, on stationary. Or to put it another way, let's say we decided to redistribute this money in some other way. Many of our public servants, like Gardaí and nurses, are underpaid. What if we used that €105 million spent on Irish to give a pay rise to everyone employed by the Irish state instead? The result would be a pay increase for all state employees of €6.70 a week. And that would be it. The money would all be gone. No doubt many of our public servants deserve a pay raise, but, to me at least, it wouldn't seem to be worth it to jettison the Irish language so some people could afford an extra pint once a week.

Myth Three: The language is not called Irish/is not called Gaelic

It can be argued that there is no undisputed name in English for An Ghaeilge, because I have seen people dispute the idea that either 'Irish' or 'Gaelic' is an accurate title for the language. However, the people who reject one of these names are usually coming at it from a different point of view from people who have a problem with the alternative name.

The main issue that people take with 'Gaelic' is that Americans use it. And we love nothing more than telling Americans that they are wrong about something. We insist that they are annoyingly misinformed when they call it 'Gaelic', and we point out that the actual name of the language is 'Irish' and that "nobody" in Ireland calls it Gaelic.

Actually, the latter isn't true, but a quick history lesson might help explain how these Americans became so misinformed. Up until the end of the 19th Century, the tongues we know today as Irish and Scots Gaelic were generally regarded as the one and the same language. The name used in English was 'Gaelic', although it was (and still is) pronounced differently in Ireland and Scotland. It was sometimes referred to as Irish or Erse in Scotland, while in Ireland, 'Irish' and 'Gaelic' were used interchangeably in the 19th Century. This is evident when we remember that the organisation that was set up in 1893 to try and preserve the language called itself the Gaelic League. The 19th Century was also a time of high immigration to the United States, and when Irish emigrants moved there, they kept calling the language what they had always called it: 'Gaelic'.

Back in Ireland, however, the growing differences (especially due to spelling reform) between the Gaelic languages of Ireland and Scotland meant that 'Irish' became a more accurate label. Furthermore, the newly independent state, in trying to assert its identity, tended to only refer to the language as Irish. Thus, a rift emerged between what Irish people called the language, and what Irish Americans did, as 'Gaelic' has not gone out of fashion on the other side of the Atlantic (and, of course, it is more commonly used in Scotland to describe 'Scots Gaelic'). However, it is not accurate to say that the word 'Gaelic' is not used in Ireland today when referring to 'Irish'. If one pays attention, one will find it is employed quite regularly by Irish writers. There also seems to be a tendency among people from the northern half of the country, and among older Irish people, to still use 'Gaelic' instead of 'Irish' from time to time.

It is less common to come across people who take an issue with calling the language 'Irish', but if you follow the comments section on anything online related to the language, you will occasionally encounter such thinking. The logic is basically this: French people speak French and Spanish people speak Spanish, but as most Irish people cannot/do not speak Irish, the language does not belong to the Irish people and therefore cannot be called 'Irish'. I once came across the following comment "I am Irish and I don't speak that language, so how can it be called Irish?". It appears this person hadn't followed his logic to its obvious conclusion to discover what his true identity therefore must be, based on the language he did speak!

What motivates people to reject calling the language 'Irish'? This question can be answered by studying the Language Freedom Movement. This organisation was formed in the 1960s and was committed to overturning certain aspects of the state's policy towards Irish, in particular the requirement to pass a language exam to get a job in the civil service. Frank Crummey was a member of this group. In an interview in 2015, he commented that "For the Language Freedom Movement, 'Irish' and 'Gaelic' were the same language, but we preferred the term Gaelic because we viewed it as the language of the past, not a modern language." Even if we accept Crummey's argument that Irish isn't a modern language, why would that mean the name of the language had to be changed?

Maolsheachlainn Ó Caollaí, the former president of Conradh na Gaeilge, points out that if the Language Freedom Movement was solely interested in rolling back state support for Irish, it wouldn't have engaged in semantic games. Instead, there was an obvious ideological ploy afoot. Ó Caollaí notes that the Language Freedom Movement exclusively called it 'Gaelic' and not 'Irish' because they were trying to separate the connection between the language and 'Irish' identity. If the language is not called 'Irish', then it is easier to argue that it is not an important part of 'Irishness'.

This goes back to the collective identity crisis caused by the very existence of a 'national' language that we cannot speak. So long as the language is called 'Irish', then it is hard to argue that it is not the 'native' language of the 'Irish' people. But calling it 'Gaelic' creates a linguistic separation between the people (the 'Irish') and the language. This then has the potential to drive a wedge between the historic, Gaelic cultural identity of our island, and the new, 'different', 'modern' Irish one. If the country's ancient past and culture can be prised apart from its modern identity (as has happened in places like Australia and the US), then the identity crisis is resolved and people can forget about Irish because they no longer will see it as 'their' language. It is for this reason that, although outright rejection of the name 'Irish' is not regularly voiced, certain people who are known to have little positive feelings towards the language are far more likely to call it 'Gaelic' than 'Irish'. The debate between calling it 'Irish' or 'Gaelic' might seem like a semantic squabble, but it is actually a battle to define the very meaning of Irishness.

Myth Four: Our National Language is "Hiberno-English"

This one isn't so much a myth, but there are some interesting paradoxes in the thinking of people who put forward this idea. I am a fan of "Hiberno-English". Living in the United States for several years now, I oftentimes find myself reminiscing about the wonderful words and turns of phrase that I heard every day growing up in a council housing estate just outside Cork City. Indeed, I see no contradiction between cherishing the Irish language and admiring the various dialects of English spoken in Ireland, as both are part of Ireland's linguistic heritage. But it has seemed to me that most of the people who insist on calling the English language in Ireland "Hiberno-English" also have nothing but disdain for Irish. The logic of the champions of "Hiberno-English" has always been perplexing to me, however, for several reasons:

They usually dismiss supporters of the Irish language as mindless "nationalists", and yet then turn around and try to put a nationalist sheen on the name they give the English dialects of Ireland. These people who want Ireland to have its own unique mode of expression, but who can't actually speak Irish, seek to shunt the Gaelic language to the margins while trying to insist that the English spoken in Ireland merits quasi-language status. Indeed, to call English spoken in Ireland "Hiberno-English" is to ultimately concede the point that Ireland should have its own unique national language, and to suggest that there is something uncomfortable about Irish people speaking "just" English.

Almost everything that makes "Hiberno-English" unique and distinctive is due to the influence of the Irish language. Indeed, learning Irish as an adult, it has been fascinating to realise that many of the words I spoke growing up were lifted directly from Irish and mixed into our English speech. But fawning over the unique aspects of "Hiberno-English" while despising the actual source of its distinctiveness has always struck me as an odd contradiction.

On the one hand, the "Hiberno-English" crew point out that English is invaluable because it is a global language that is understood by millions. True. Yet on the other hand, they admire the idioms and pronunciation that often make us unintelligible to the rest of the English-speaking world. There isn't much point arguing for the utilitarian value of English while also encouraging speech that not only makes it hard for others to understand us, but frankly is often interpreted by people outside Ireland as a sign that we are stupid.

There also seems to be some misguided ideas about the vitality and strength of "Hiberno-English". I once came across an online comment claiming that while the government struggled to save Irish "Hiberno-English is thriving without any support from the state". He must have meant other than the fact that it is "shoved down our throats" every day in school or in any interaction we ever have with the Irish state? But the idea that "Hiberno-English" is "thriving" is open to debate. Like the Scots language over the last couple of centuries, many of the distinctive features of "Hiberno-English" are being bleached out as we increasingly adopt more general forms of British, and especially American, English.

Since I left Ireland in 2006, it has been fascinating to see (mostly through what people write online) the growing influence of Americanisms in how Irish people speak. In 2005, Pat the Baker ran a TV advertisement which showed an Irish youth (Jon Kenny) wearing typically American clothes and saying American things like "Awesome, Dude!" His aunt comments "Fancy lingo you...and you only in America for the weekend." I wonder today though would young Irish people even get the joke, as it seems they say "Awesome, Dude" as much as any American teenager. In other words, the form of English we speak in Ireland will only come to sound more and more like that of the rest of the English-speaking world, and will not stand out as an expression of our "national distinctiveness".

Myth Five: Irish Was Never Spoken in Dublin

This claim is similar to that made by individuals who say that their ancestors never spoke Irish. It is another attempt to resolve the identity crisis caused by the existence of Irish. By denying that Irish was ever a part of "their" past, these people resolve any tension they might feel about not speaking Irish by insisting that they actually are a continuous part of an English-speaking community stretching way back into the past. They are giving historical legitimacy to the fact that they speak English while denying that Irish ever played a role in their identity. This is a very similar tactic to what we see in Scotland, where there is a blanket denial that Gaelic was ever spoken in large parts of that country, ignoring all historical and place-name evidence to the contrary.

The mindset behind the deployment of this argument is interesting, however. From a practical point of view (and "practicality" is usually the centre piece of any argument made by English speakers against Irish), it shouldn't matter if we were all monoglot Irish speakers up until half an hour ago, so long as most of us can only speak English now. The fact that people choose to try and fight the "language battle" on historic grounds shows that, subconsciously at least, they see the idea that Irish should be spoken today because it was spoken in the past by our ancestors has some validity. Thus, they feel the need to write Irish out of their personal or regional past, as a way of denying the language's claim on them.

The idea that Irish was never spoken in Dublin is so stupid that it doesn't merit being refuted on its own. The inaccuracy of the claim can be shown in challenging more nuanced versions of a similar argument. In his *A History of the Irish Language,* Aidan Doyle claims "Irish was never spoken by the power elites in Dublin and other urban centres."[39] Certainly, Dublin was founded by Vikings, and we imagine in the beginning that Norse was the primary language there. But as the city was surrounded entirely by an Irish speaking hinterland, it seems farfetched to think the language would have remained unknown to the ordinary people of the city.

The idea that the "power elites" never spoke Irish is inaccurate. Firstly, the Norse were driven out of the city for a period in the early 10th Century. The Vikings returned, but through intermarriage and adoption of Irish customs, they became known as the *Gall-Ghael* or Norse-Irish. These "power elites" certainly would have spoken Irish, in some cases possibly as their first language. Furthermore, in the 11th and 12th Centuries, Dublin was often ruled by Gaelic rulers. Why would we think men named Murchad Mac Diarmata, Diarmait Mac Maél na mBó, Muirchertach Ua Briain, or Énna Mac Murchada didn't speak Irish? Unless the Kings of Dublin didn't count among the "power elites"?

Journalist Victoria White, who read Doyle's book, has made a similar argument, writing "In Dublin, Cork and Belfast, Irish has

39 Aidan Doyle, *A History of the Irish Language,* op. cit.

not been the dominant language since at least the 12th Century, if not before." White appears to be alluding to the Norman Conquest here, suggesting that once they arrived, their language dominated these urban centres. But the Normans only arrived in 1169. The last year of the 12th Century was 1200. White seems to assume that an enormous language shift took place in Irish towns over half the life-time of one generation. Certainly, the importance of Irish in Dublin decreased as time went on, but its position there would hardly have collapsed in a mere 30 years. Furthermore, Belfast didn't exist in the 12th Century, so there wasn't a city there for Irish not to be the dominant language of.

Meanwhile, Irish retained a strong influence in Cork well into the 19th Century. The English writer Edward Wakefield, who wrote a book about Ireland, commented of Cork City in 1812 "The Irish language is so much spoken among the common people...that an Englishman is apt to forget where he is and to consider himself in a foreign country." In *An Irish-Speaking Island,* historian Nicholas Wolf notes that Irish language translators were required to work at voting stations in Cork City into the 1820s, and Father Mathew had people swear temperance oaths in Irish there in the 1840s.[40] In other words, the historical absence of Irish from the country's major urban centres has been greatly exaggerated.

Myth Six: Irish is a Difficult Language

This is an important myth to challenge, because it acts as a mental stumbling block for many people learning Irish. Yet it is an idea that is widely accepted. Even Aidan Doyle, who is a linguist, wrote in the *Irish Times* that "it is a difficult language". The "difficulty" of the language is often one reason cited for why Irish school children fail to learn it in school. I have even seen people suggest online that Irish was abandoned *because* it was a difficult language, as if native speak-

---

40 Nicholas Wolf, *An Irish-Speaking Island,* op. cit.

ers could no longer bear the struggle of their impossible tongue and went off searching for an easier alternative.

But what makes a language difficult? When it comes to learning a second language, there isn't really a neutral, objective point from which we can judge the level of difficulty. The reason for this is that we all already speak one language. Therefore, the degree of difficulty in learning a language is almost entirely dependent on how similar it is to your first language, or other languages you have already learned.

The vast majority of people who try to learn Irish speak English natively. It is worth reflecting for a moment on the history of English, to understand why people might see Irish as a "difficult" language to learn. The original English language was essentially a dialect of German. The path of the language changed course dramatically with the arrival of French speaking Norman invaders in 1066. Eventually a new version of English emerged, with a large number of French and Latin words adopted into the language. Some people have argued that this new English was actually a pidgin language, a combination of English and French with a dramatically simplified grammar structure.

Fast forward to today. It seems safe to assume that the most common languages for English speakers to learn in the 21st Century are French, Spanish or German. But, in linguistic terms, the difference between English and these three languages is not so wide. The Norman influence means that English shares a great deal of its vocabulary with French and Spanish. Not only does English have many similar words to German, but the two languages also resemble one another in terms of sentence structure and word order. Irish, on the other hand, has a greater degree of difference from English than these other languages. In other words, since the experience of most English speakers is learning a language (French, German or Spanish) that has considerable overlap with their own, then the lack of similarity between Irish and English will naturally make it seem more difficult.

There certainly are aspects of Irish that are unusual in terms of global languages, In particular, the fact that the front of a word is pronounced differently in certain situations is something that Irish has in common with other Celtic languages, but it is not something found in most languages in the world. Therefore, an English speaker will find features like this to be unusual, and therefore see Irish as "difficult". A Welsh speaker, on the other hand, will find Irish reasonably straightforward, because the grammar and syntax of the two languages are very similar. But the "difficulty" of Irish needs to be put in perspective. It might seem more challenging than French or German, but for an English speaker it is almost certainly an "easier" language to learn than say Hindi or Korean, because it is at least distantly related to English. Remember, the girl in Loreto Bray who had learned both Irish and Chinese assured her classmates that Irish was by far the easier language to learn.

But related to the idea that Irish is a "difficult" language is a perception that it is an "irrational" or "crazy" language. This is mostly based on the relationship between how Irish words are pronounced, and how they are spelled, with similarly negative attitudes also being shown towards Welsh for the same reason. The root of this lies in the arrogance of English speakers in assuming that the English pronunciation of the Roman alphabet is the "natural" way letters are supposed to be pronounced, and any other pronunciations are "illogical". Over 130 languages use the Roman alphabet, and all of them have different variations on how certain letters are pronounced. Spanish speakers pronounce the letter 'j' like an English 'h', and German speakers pronounce the letter 'w' like an English 'v'. There is no one right way for the Roman alphabet to be pronounced. This is also true for the sounds made by combinations of letters. There is nothing more or less logical about pronouncing "bh" in Irish as a 'w' or 'v' sound than pronouncing 'gh' or 'ph' in English as an 'f' sound.

As the Irish (and Welsh) language associates very different sounds with combinations of certain letters to what the English language does, it is not surprising that English speakers find the appearance of written Irish words to be bewildering. Unfortunately, this easily leads people to think that the language (and by extension, the culture that produced it) is backwards.

Sadly, we Irish people are at times happy to indulge such demeaning attitudes. When Saoirse Ronan appeared on the Late Show with Stephen Colbert in 2016, Colbert produced a card to show the audience how her name was pronounced. Ronan responded by saying "Doesn't make any sense...it's a ridiculous name." Colbert then produced a series of cards with other Irish names for Ronan to pronounce. One of them was Siobhan, which Colbert already knew how to pronounce, but which he found to be "ridiculous by the way". I'm sure Colbert and Ronan would argue that this was just a bit of lighthearted fun, but sadly both were reinforcing an old prejudice regarding the backwards nature of the Irish language and Gaelic culture, which is still perfectly acceptable to demean. I look forward to seeing Shaquille O'Neal on the Late Show someday and I can't wait for Colbert to produce cards with "crazy" African American names on them so O'Neal can pronounce them for the general amusement of the audience.

Indeed, we ourselves seem so ashamed by our Gaelic culture that we often distort our own past rather than dealing with the parts of it that seem too alien to us. Like most Irish school children, I learned about a man called Dermot MacMurrough, who "betrayed" the Irish people by inviting Norman barons to come to Ireland and help him recover his lost kingdom. MacMurrough is viewed as the villain of Irish history, because he is deemed to be the one responsible for making Ireland an English colony. It was only years later that I realised that MacMurrough never existed. Along similar lines, the *Irish Times* published an article in 2018, recounting 25 remarkable women in Irish history. Among them were Margaret O'Carroll and Grace O'Malley, two notable Gaelic women who lived in medieval Ireland. But why do we refer to these women by these names, when they would have spent their entire lives thinking of themselves as Mairgréag Ní Chearbhaill and Gráinne Ní Mháille? Possibly Mairgréag and Gráinne heard an anglicised version of their names, but we can be certain that Diarmait Mac Murchada never caught wind of any person called "Dermot MacMurrough". Embarrassed by all of those "unnecessary" letters and fadas, we find it easier to impose anglicised names upon our ancestors rather than showing them the respect of referring to them by the names they themselves used.

The ironic thing about mocking how Irish words are pronounced is that while Irish pronunciation certainly has its irregularities, once someone has learned the rules of pronunciation of Irish, it is generally more consistent than English. Or as Aidan Doyle puts it "English orthography is just as cumbersome and misleading as Irish, or perhaps even more so."[41] A pet hate of mine is when people ask for the pronunciation of an Irish word to be written "phonetically". What they mean, of course, is if it can be spelled as it would be pronounced in English.

But English is not a phonetic language. Want proof? Take ten Irish words or phrases, and then ask ten people separately to spell out their pronunciations "phonetically" in English. The results will not be identical. Learners of English find it incredibly frustrating that English words that should sound the same, based on the rules of pronunciation, don't, and that similar sounds are often spelled differently. English has two words, "you" and "ewe", that are pronounced identically but don't even share a single letter in common. It also calls for different pronunciations of the word "live" depending on whether you are talking about somewhere you reside, or whether the event you are watching on TV is actually happening

---

41 Aidan Doyle, *A History of the Irish Language*, op. cit.

at the moment you view it. Try explaining to a non-native English speaker why words like "once", "knight" or "choir" are pronounced the way they are. Indeed, even adult native speakers of English often find that words they have often seen written are pronounced very differently to what they had thought. The point of this isn't to say that English is stupid for its inconsistencies, but that the idea that it is somehow phonetic and Irish isn't is laughable.

Myth Seven: The One About Mick Wallace

In March 2015, an exchange between Enda Kenny and Mick Wallce in the Dáil gained national, and even international attention. The *Daily Express* reported the story under the headline "Irish PM REFUSES to speak English after minister loses translation headset". Eoin Butler, in his video "An Bhfuil Cead Agam", described the incident as follows: "In the Dáil, when TD Mick Wallace raised awkward questions about American drone strikes with Enda Kenny, the Taoiseach chose to respond in Irish, knowing Deputy Wallace didn't speak the language." United People, a group dedicated to greater participatory democracy in Ireland, uploaded a video of the exchange to YouTube under the title "Enda Kenny refusing to speak English". They labelled Kenny's behavior "disgusting" because he was "deliberately being unwilling to accommodate others" and of his "refusal to try better communicating with elected representatives." Several Irish media outlets reported the exchange as being one where Kenny "refused" to speak English.

The sum of these reports gave the general impression that Kenny stubbornly chose to speak Irish in order to avoid having to answer Mick Wallace's questions and ignorantly ignored Wallace's pleas to speak in English, thereby effectively not answering the question since Wallace didn't understand the answer.

But this is a dishonest misrepresentation of what happened. Firstly, the exchange took place on a day on which it had been designated that all questions and answers to the Taoiseach would be in Irish (as part of Seachtain na Gaeilge), something that Eoin Butler and United People failed to mention in their depiction of events. It was actually Wallace who had broken with the protocol of the day by asking the question in English. Outraged articles about Wallace's refusal to speak Irish didn't materialise for some reason, however. As for the idea that Kenny was trying to avoid answering the question, well let's take a look at a transcript of the conversation between the two.

KENNY (*in Irish*): "...and American foreign policy."

Wallace signals that he cannot understand what Kenny is saying.

KENNY (*in Irish*): "Put on your translation system. You have one there."

CLAIRE BYRNE: "He hasn't got any."

MICK WALLACE: "I haven't got one here...I apologise that I can't speak Irish."

KENNY (*in Irish*): "Well there is one available in the next seat."

WALLACE: "I would appreciate it if you would answer me in English."

KENNY (*in Irish*): "You have one there. When Jim White, God rest his soul, was there years ago, he was over there and I was beside him, and a minister was speaking in Irish and Jim said it was an insult to his "faith", and a translation system was put in place after that. (*Switches to English*) So put on your translation system. This is our national language and this is Lá na Gaeilge (*in Irish*) so they tell me. (*In English*) Put it on there...put it on there. Now (*switches to Irish*) turn the...turn the...turn the knob. Michael my friend can you hear me...can you hear me...can you hear me? The translation is taking place."

(*Still in Irish and answering the original question*) "Three things were mentioned then. Human rights, military affairs and American foreign policy."

Wallace, wearing a headset, indicates that no translation is coming through.

KENNY (*in English*): "Can you hear me? (*In Irish*) Someone is translating everything that is said in Irish. (*In English*) Is it switched on?....Wallace strikes again! In any event, you raise three issues: Human rights...em...em the American military machine, and American politics internationally..."

Someone indicates that the translation system is now working

KENNY (*In Irish*): "Is it working now? (Turns to someone sitting behind him) Is it working for you? (*The person answers "Yes"*). (*Addressing Wallace in Irish*) Put it on again...put it on again and turn the button then."

WALLACE: "You are wasting our time as well."

KENNY (*In Irish*): "I'm not wasting your time at all...isn't it working?...Put it on you...Put it on you...Now is it working now Michael? OK, thank you."

Kenny then proceeds to answer the question in Irish while Wallace hears the translation through the headset provided for him.

To sum up what happened then. Kenny began answering the question in Irish, and then tried to get Wallace to listen to the translation in English. When Kenny thinks the translation system isn't working, he switches to English. He reverts to Irish when he hears the system is working after all. He then answers Wallace's question while Wallace listens to the translation. There was no attempt to avoid answering the question, nor any refusal to speak English despite "knowing" the translation system wasn't working. Some people have viewed the incident as one where Kenny belittles Wallace for not speaking Irish. Certainly there is no love lost between the two men, but if Kenny was "belittling" Wallace, it was for his inability to operate the translation system, not for his inability to speak Irish.

However, discussing the Mick Wallace myth isn't important from the point of view of accurately finding out what happened. Rather it should be seen as a template for how any story involving the Irish language is prone to being distorted in such a manner to suit the agenda of the anti-Irish lobby. It also gained attention because it fed into the persecution complex English speakers seem to have when it comes to other languages.

Note the use of all capital letters for the word "refuses" in the *Daily Express's* headline, an expression of outraged indignation that anyone who could speak English would ever choose not to. As soon as any Irish speaker makes any kind of stand for a language, the description of what happened will certainly be twisted by some in such a way as to maximise the "offense" in the eyes of the monoglot English speakers. The mindset that warped what happened between Mick Wallace and Enda Kenny is the same one that convinced people there was a barman in the Flying Enterprise in Cork who was refusing to speak English to customers. It is the same one that somehow came to believe that the Kerry County Council employs 21 full time Irish language officers. It is the one that will continue to fabricate anti-Irish myths for the foreseeable future.

CHAPTER EIGHT:

LANGUAGE REVIVALS ELSEWHERE

Of course, Irish is not the first language that people have sought to promote or revive in the face of some stiff challenges. The purpose of this chapter is to examine some other case studies to see what lessons can be learned and applied to Irish in order to ensure a bright future for the language.

CASE STUDY ONE: WELSH

Whenever the question of how Irish can be revived is raised, the example of the Welsh language is often put forward. In the weeks before the 2016 general election in Ireland, the short-lived political party Renua issued its party manifesto. In reference to the party's Irish language policy, they stated, "We believe that the modern revival of the Welsh language provides a roadmap for a revitalisation of the Irish language. Ireland can and will rediscover the pride it has for its native tongue and the great cultural and artistic history that goes with it." That same year, former TD Dan Boyle commented that "I was really impressed with how the Welsh have made their language a living language. From what I could see this has been because of the emphasis on spoken language, as opposed to the defeatist emphasis on grammar in how Irish is taught... Most of the interactions the Welsh have with their language are seen to be positive."

But all of this discussion about the relevance of a Welsh revival for Irish leaves one important question unasked. Was there a Welsh revival? The short answer is no. Indeed, this idea of a magical reversal of fortunes for the Welsh language has a long history in Ireland. My own research on the Gaelic League at the turn of the 20th Century has shown that members of that organisation promoted the belief that Wales offered an important linguistic lesson for Ireland. Gaelic Leaguers claimed that Welsh had suffered a dramatic decline in the 18th Century, to the point that it was almost no longer spoken. However, through hard work and dedication, Welsh had been restored as the national language by the 20th Century.

It was a great story, one full of inspiration for those trying to promote the Irish language. But it was also a complete fabrication. There had been no dramatic Welsh collapse. Now there had been a dramatic change in the Welsh language in the 18th Century, namely, that through the work of Welsh religious groups, literacy in the Welsh language had increased in leaps and bounds. It seems that this tale of a Welsh literary renaissance morphed, whether by accident or design, into an account of the spoken language being rescued from imminent death.

The legacy of this Welsh tale told by Irish language activists still lingers in Ireland, but there are other contributing factors to its persistence. One is the continuing strength of Welsh in certain areas of Wales. Irish people today who travel through Gwynedd, for example, are probably astounded at how much Welsh they hear. What they might fail to understand is that this is not so much an example of Welsh being revived, but rather the legacy of Welsh having not declined as quickly as Irish.

Furthermore, as in Ireland, there has been a renewed interest in the indigenous tongue of Wales in recent decades, which includes the growth of Welsh medium schools in areas that were largely English speaking (like the Gaelscoileanna in Ireland). But while this has produced more people who can (although not who necessarily do) speak Welsh, this isn't exactly a revival in the true sense of the term. No part of Wales that had become largely English speaking has reverted to Welsh, for example. It seems that some Irish people, seeing how strong Welsh is in some parts of Wales and hearing about a growth of interest in Welsh generally, believe the latter caused the former. But these things are not directly linked, and sadly, Welsh appears to be in decline as a daily spoken language in its traditional heartlands. The Welsh revival is largely a figment of Irish imaginations.

That isn't to say that Wales is not worth studying, from an Irish perspective. While the long-term survival of Welsh is not guaranteed, the language is in a much stronger position than Irish today by any measure. Understanding why the Cymric language has attained this superior position relative to Irish might offer insights into how the language of Ireland could be revived.

The history of Irish and Welsh can be said to have followed a broadly similar path up until the time of the Reformation. The fact that Ireland largely stuck with Catholicism while Wales embraced Protestantism was to have significant consequences for the respective indigenous languages of both nations. The Catholic faith of Ireland's Gaelic lords, and in particular the efforts of these aristocrats to build alliances with European Catholics, meant they were deeply distrusted by the newly Protestant English state. The solution to this problem, from the crown's point of view, was plantation. Over the course of the 1600s, an Irish-speaking, landowning elite was replaced by an English-speaking one, either directly through planation, or out of necessity, as landowners with Gaelic ancestry switched to speaking English to enhance their prospects. This caused a major decline in the status of Irish. No equivalent social, cultural and economic upheaval took place in Wales. Although the largest and wealthiest landowners in Wales had largely turned towards English in the 18th Century, Welsh remained the language of most social classes, and as such could still be viewed as a language of prosperity in a way Irish no longer could.

A second important consequence of the Reformation was the growth of literacy. A central tenet of Protestantism generally is that people should be able to read and understand the Bible for themselves. A Welsh Bible appeared over a century before an Irish one did. This push for literacy intensified in the 18th Century. Welsh Nonconformists, seeking to convert the masses to a less-centralised, but more stringent, form of Protestantism, established travelling schools to teach Welsh peasants how to read. By the end of the century, Wales had one of the highest rates of literacy in the world, and a growing market for Welsh language books. Furthermore, Welsh was entrenched as the medium of worship for most of Wales, and its strong association with faith only added to the prestige associated with the language.

In contrast, the Catholic Church in Ireland did not play a similar role for Irish. Firstly, Catholicism did not place the same emphasis on literacy amongst ordinary people, so there was no zeal for teaching Irish peasants how to read Irish. Secondly, the Catholic Church was and is a hierarchical body, and whatever language its higher officials did business in would become the language of the clergy in general. The penal laws meant that aspiring priests had to be educated on the continent, which led to the wealthier Irish classes being disproportionally represented in the Irish clergy. This meant that they were largely from English speaking homes, and not surprisingly the hierarchy of the Irish Catholic Church did its business in English. The Catholic Church in Ireland gave added status to English, because if you wanted to advance in that institution, you had to speak English. In Welsh Nonconformism, however, there wasn't really a ladder to climb. Certainly, many Irish priests also spoke Irish well into the 19th Century, but to a man they spoke English. In Wales, on the other hand, there were Nonconformist ministers who were Welsh monoglots.

By 1800 then, some noticeable differences between Irish and Welsh were emerging. Welsh was still the language of respectable people, and was essential for participation in many religious congregations in the country. In addition, it was a language with a modern literature in print. Irish was increasingly viewed as the language of the poor and destitute. English had replaced Irish in all positions of status and power in Ireland, and the fact that hardly anyone could read or write in it added to the sense that it was more patois than a "proper" language. More people spoke Irish than Welsh at the beginning of the 19th Century, but the languages were clearly heading in different directions. Wales had a population of just over half a million in 1800. Accurate figures are impossible, but it seems likely that between 80% and 90% of the population spoke Welsh. The Irish population was about 5 million people at that time, but as noted earlier, it seems that only between 45% and 55% of the population spoke Irish then.

We know what happened to Irish in the 19th Century, but what about Welsh? Given the description above, one would think the language was in an almost unassailable position. While the disastrous Great Famine accelerated the decline of Irish, ironically it was the prosperity of Wales, in particular its mineral resources, that undermined the dominance of Welsh. The coalfields of South Wales attracted large numbers of emigrants from England, which over the course of the 19th Century tipped the linguistic balance from Welsh to English in many parts of the country. The number of people who spoke Welsh actually doubled over the course of the 19th Century, at a time that Irish was in complete freefall.

The problem was that the number of English speakers increased 70-fold over that same time period, with the Welsh population in general quadrupling in that time. So, while the 1911 census showed that just shy of one million people in Wales spoke Welsh, it also revealed that only 43% of Welsh people spoke Welsh. In other words, while the number of Welsh speakers had been growing, the percentage of the population who spoke Welsh had fallen. Like Irish in 1845, Welsh in 1911 was simultaneously at its strongest and weakest point as a community language.

However, the influx of English speakers into Wales is only part of the reason that Welsh went into decline in the 19th Century. After all, millions of Spanish speakers have emigrated to the US in recent decades, but it seems extremely unlikely this will cause the kind of language switch that we have seen take place in Ireland and Wales. The explanation for this lies in the fact that Wales was within the United Kingdom. Had Wales been an independent country in the 19th Century, it is conceivable that the English migrants would eventually have been absorbed into the Welsh speaking population. But these emigrants not only spoke the same language as the powerful business magnates who industrialised South Wales, but they also spoke the language of the state, namely English.

With all western states becoming more involved in the day to day lives of their people, locals found themselves under pressure to speak the language of the emigrants, rather than vice versa. When the British government introduced compulsory primary school education into Wales in 1870, teaching was done exclusively through English. Some of the Nonconformist chapels, seeking to win new converts, switched from Welsh to English services. As English became essential in Wales, parents stopped raising their children through Welsh and began speaking English at home instead. These trends continued into the 20th Century. The percentage of Welsh speakers fell to about 20% in 1971, where it has more or less stayed since. Yet in the strongest Welsh speaking areas today, there are signs that the language is in trouble as the number of people who speak it on a daily basis continues to fall. In 2017, the Welsh government announced a plan to create one million Welsh speakers by 2050. It is certainly an ambitious plan, although whether it will succeed in reversing the decline in the fortunes of Welsh remains to be seen.

In short then, while there has not yet been a dramatic Welsh revival that we in Ireland can learn from, understanding what happened to Welsh in the first place can offer some clues regarding what can be done for Irish.

CASE STUDY TWO: URDU

Doing a quick internet search about Urdu, I came across the following comments. I bet they will sound very familiar to anyone with an interest in the Irish language.

> "There is no developed country in the world that uses a foreign language as medium of education, administration or judiciary, only us."

> "If a European kid can learn 3 languages in school, why are we too lazy to learn Urdu AND English. Scandinavia can serve as a good example. They are keeping their languages, however small and they all learn very good English."

> "I wish I had put more effort in learning my own language. Living in a foreign country has also made me appreciate Urdu. I have heard people suggest that we should do away with Urdu altogether and should make English the national language. Their argument is that Urdu serves no purpose and is not widely spoken around the world."

> "I didn't really learn how to speak Urdu as a child, and never did well in that subject at school either. What's embarrassing is, I was born and brought up in Pakistan and Urdu should come naturally to me, but 'hey English has always been the cooler language' – right? When I was in school I never thought twice about Urdu. I mean why would I? I would never really need Urdu, right?"

If we substituted the words "Irish" and "Ireland" for "Urdu" and "Pakistan", these sentences would be remarkable only for their unremarkableness, given how often we read or hear these sentiments in Ireland. Indeed, perhaps there is no better parallel to the national debate about Irish than the complex issues regarding Urdu's position as Pakistan's official language.

Although the origins of Urdu can be traced back for centuries to the Indian subcontinent, its classification as a separate language is actually quite recent. As a result of several Islamic invasions of India, the Hindustani language of north-central India was influenced by the Turkish, Arabic and Persian languages. It was the language of elites, both Muslim and Hindi, in large parts of India when the British arrived. Muslims wrote in Hindustani using the Persian script, but over time Hindus began writing the same language using the traditional Sanskrit, or Devanagari alphabet. Tensions over this difference began to escalate when the British East India Company made Hindustani, written in the Persian alphabet, the official language in parts of northern India in 1837.

Those who used the Sanskrit script felt they were at a disadvantage in applying for government jobs, and demanded that their version of Hindustani also be made an official language. Meanwhile, Muslim scholars sought to remove words with an obvious Sanskrit origin from their version of Hindustani, while Hindi writers similarly tried to purify their one by banishing words that had been borrowed from Persian or Arabic. In place of these outcast words, writers sought more "authentic" Perso-Arabic or Sanskrit replacements (depending on their religious orientation), widening the gap between the two dialects. In 1900, the British agreed to make Hindustani written with the Sanskrit alphabet an official language in the North West alongside its Persian counterpart. Thus Hindustani had been officially split into two languages, with Urdu used mostly by Muslims, and Hindi by Hindus. Nevertheless, speakers of the two languages can mostly understand one another today (although they cannot read each other's writing), while both sides claim that their dialect is the authentic heir of Hindustani.

As a result of this conflict, the Urdu language became an important symbol of Islamic distinctiveness on the Indian subcontinent. However, it was only spoken by Muslims in certain parts of India. Several other areas that had large Muslim majorities spoke their own language. As the demand for Indian independence from Britain grew in the 20th Century, questions were raised about whether Muslims should remain in independent India, or create their own state. In 1947, the British government agreed to split the subcontinent into the independent states of Pakistan and India. Enormous violence erupted as Hindus and Muslims were driven out of their homes because they were now seen as living in the "wrong" country. Up to 12 million people were displaced and possibly as many as two million people were killed in the chaos.

Those in favour of creating an independent Pakistan believed that Urdu was the best choice as the nation's official language. In their eyes, Urdu was the most "Islamic" language of all the tongues spoken in Pakistan, and therefore was the best choice to unite an Islamic country that was linguistically divided. But there was a complication to this idea. The areas where Urdu was spoken as a first language ended up in India. Urdu wasn't spoken exclusively in any region of Pakistan, and most of the Urdu speakers in the new state were refugees fleeing religious persecution in India. Only 7% of Pakistanis spoke Urdu in the first few years after independence.

Upon achieving independence, Urdu was declared the national language of Pakistan, but English would serve as the official language until Urdu could be spoken more extensively by the population. Of course, this sounds pretty similar to what happened in Ireland upon independence. But there are a couple of differences. While only a small percentage of the population spoke Urdu, this amounted to over two million people in a nation as large as Pakistan. Further-more, English was chosen not because it was the language everyone spoke (as in Ireland) but because to have chosen one of Pakistan's larger regional languages would have stirred resentment among supporters of the languages that missed out. English was a useful "neutral" language in that sense. But certainly, newly independent Ireland and Pakistan were very similar in that they hoped to see a language spoken by a small minority of people become the dominant linguistic force in the new nation.

So did Pakistan fare any better than ourselves in this mission? Yes, but perhaps not as significantly as it might first appear. Today it is estimated that there are about 14.5 million speakers of Urdu in Pakistan, which would represent about a seven-fold increase since 1951. Compared to Ireland, that seems like a staggering achievement. The problem is that most of these gains can be explained by Paki-stan's population explosion. Proportionally speaking, the percentage of people who speak Urdu has risen from about 7% in 1951 to 7.5% today. One factor that explains this modest growth is the loss of East Pakistan. Over half of Pakistan's native Urdu speakers in 1947 lived in East Pakistan, which became the independent state of Bangladesh in 1972. So in reality, the percentage of Pakistanis who speak Urdu as their first language has risen from 3.3% at the moment of independ-ence to 7.5% today. One might be tempted to see that as an amazing achievement compared to the efforts of the Irish state, where the number of daily speakers in the Gaeltacht has certainly declined in the century since independence. But Urdu and Irish were not in sim-ilar positions when Ireland and Pakistan became independent.

Irish was a language at the tail-end of a dramatic decline, spoken by a decreasing number of poor people in rural areas. Despite the efforts of the Gaelic League to change attitudes towards it, there were still plenty of people who could be described as indifferent, if not outrightly hostile, towards Irish. Urdu, on the other hand, was a highly prestigious language in British India. While the people who brought Urdu to Pakistan were refugees (known today as "Muhajir"), they tended to be very well educated and quickly became successful in their new surroundings. The fact that many of these Muhajir settled in and around the cities of Karachi and Hyderabad, instead of spreading across Pakistan, helped maintain a large, Urdu speaking community.

Furthermore, Urdu was still spoken by millions of speakers in India, so the speakers in Pakistan never felt a sense of despair that their language was in decline. Indeed, between India and Pakistan, about 66 million people speak Urdu, leaving it just outside the top 20 most spoken languages in the world today. Additionally, Urdu speakers can largely understand Hindi, the globe's fourth largest language, so Urdu could never be dismissed as a "useless" language. Given all that, it can hardly be judged a major success that the proportion of people who spoke Urdu didn't fall, as there was no reason that it should have.

The next obvious question then is how did Pakistan try to promote Urdu and why was this policy not successful? As noted earlier, Pakistan declared that Urdu was the nation's national language in 1947, but announced that English would serve as the official language temporarily. That sounds a lot like what happened in Ireland, but Pakistan was very different in that about 70 languages were spoken across the country. Bengali (55%) and Punjabi (28%) dwarfed the number of people who could speak Urdu, while Sindhi (5.3%) and Pushtu (6.6%) also had more native speakers. While 14.7% of people claimed they could speak Urdu, only 3.3% spoke it (excluding Urdu speakers in East Pakistan) as their first language.

Not surprisingly, a lot of people were unhappy at the prominence given to Urdu at the expense of their language. While Urdu was central to the vision of Pakistan before it became independent, the reality of partition meant that areas where Urdu was a community language were not included within the borders of the new nation. Unlike Ireland, where even those who resent the language don't dispute that it was spoken across the island for centuries, some Pakistanis saw Urdu as an outside language. In East Pakistan especially, Bengal speakers were outraged that their language did not receive official recognition, and four Bengali students were shot dead by government forces during language riots in 1952. While Bengali was made an official language in 1956, its speakers never felt it was placed on an equal footing with Urdu, and this contributed to the bloody civil war that led to East Pakistan ceding and becoming Bangladesh. Urdu, then, has an even more complicated place in the identity of Pakistan than Irish has in Ireland.

So what did Pakistan do to promote Urdu? As in Ireland, it was largely left to the education system. While the government of Pakistan largely functioned through English, state schools began to teach through the medium of Urdu. Dismayed by the lack of progress for Urdu, the new Pakistani constitution of 1973 declared that Urdu would replace English as the official language within 15 years. But nothing happened. Dr. Fateh Muhammad Malik was the chair of the National Language Authority, which was set up to facilitate the government switching from English to Urdu. He said that the 15-year declaration was made because "senior bureaucrats at the time thought they would have already retired before that period expired. That is why they did not object to the clause, thinking that dealing with it would be the headache of their successors and not their own". This certainly sounds like what happened in Ireland, with politicians undoubtedly sincere in their desire to see the language flourish, but believing the work would be done by others down the road, not themselves.

As in Ireland, the main obstacle to the growth of Urdu is the role played by English. Unlike in Ireland, this isn't because the majority of people speak English, but because English is the language of the elite in Pakistan. The government largely functions through English. If you want a government job, you need to speak English. All Pakistani universities teach through the medium of English, so if you want a higher-level education, English is required. Although government schools teach through Urdu, private schools generally use English as the language of instruction. And all of this is before we factor in the importance of English in a global economy. Where parents have a choice, they prefer their children are educated through English rather than Urdu. Urdu simply doesn't offer the same opportunities. Akhtar Raza Saleemi, an Urdu novelist, notes that "Those who know Urdu cannot do much except write or teach." The same problem largely exists with Irish, except that writing isn't even an option.

So how widespread is the knowledge of Urdu in Pakistan, outside of native speakers? Because it is used as the language of instruction in state schools, it is probably fair to assume that your average Pakistani can speak more Urdu than your average Irish citizen can speak Irish. But given that large numbers of children don't even finish primary school in Pakistan, and that low literacy rates and a poor quality of education generally is characteristic of Pakistani schools, it would be a mistake to think that everyone who attends a state school becomes fluent in Urdu. Aside from school, the government does encourage the use of Urdu in state television and newspapers, so Pakistanis hear and see Urdu in their daily lives in a way that we don't see with Irish.

There is anecdotal evidence that some parents in certain cities in Pakistan are making Urdu their home language, but without updated census returns, it is hard to tell how widespread that phenomenon is. Yet, as we saw in the comments at the beginning of this section, there are also many Pakistanis who do not speak Urdu as well as they would like. Some of these people undoubtedly came through the English language schools, where they were taught Urdu as a school subject, but as we know in Ireland, that doesn't really mean much in the long run.

Indeed, despite the fact that Urdu clearly has a more vibrant presence in Pakistan than Irish does in Ireland, many people, especially from the wealthier classes, feel they can get on fine without it.

What lessons can we take from the efforts to promote Urdu then? The main one is that even improving people's knowledge of a language (in this case, by using the language as the main teaching language in schools) will not significantly change how people use that language if a more important (in the socio-economic and political sense) language exists in that society. Secondly, declaring that a language will in the future be the national language isn't really going to change anything if no plan is put in place to facilitate that change. But in Ireland, we already knew that.

CASE STUDY THREE: FRENCH IN QUÉBEC

The association of the French language with North America is a long one, with French-speaking settlers having arrived in what today is Canada as far back as the 16th Century. However, the British victory over France in the Seven Years War meant that French Canadians have lived under the rule of English speakers since 1763. As a result, French speakers have long felt that their language and identity are in danger of being swept aside by the growth of English in Canada.

While French-speaking minorities exist in various parts of Canada, Québec has remained predominantly Francophone. As such, French occupies a bit of a weird position in Canada, in that its speakers are a minority nationally, but form a substantial majority in the largest Canadian province.

Canada has always struggled to accommodate its French-speaking citizens, in trying to find a way of expressing Canadian identity that includes everyone, without detracting from the cultural distinctiveness of its Francophones. To this end, the Canadian government introduced the Official Languages Act in 1969. This gave equal status to French and English in Canada, which guaranteed that Canadian citizens could receive all services from the federal government in either language.

But for many people in Québec, this was not enough. They were less interested in a bilingual Canada, and more concerned in preserving the dominance of French in Québec. For much of the 20th Century, the percentage of Québécois who spoke French as their first language hovered around 80%. But there were signs that a decline could be imminent. The 1961 census showed that 81.2% of people in Québec spoke French as their first language, while 13.4% spoke English. But the 1971 census revealed that the numbers speaking French had fallen to 80.7% and 13% for English speakers. The fact that the percentage of both French and English speakers fell reflected that Québec was attracting immigrants who did not speak either language natively (these people are known in Canada as allophones). French speakers were concerned, however, that these immigrants made far greater efforts to learn English than French. They feared that this trend, coupled with the fact that Canada was a predominantly English-speaking nation anyway, could be enough to eventually cause Québec to switch from being a Francophone to Anglophone province.

To preserve and strengthen the position of French in Québec, the provincial government brought in the Charter for the French Language in 1977. According to the Charter, its purpose was "to make French the language of Government and the Law, as well as the normal and everyday language of work, instruction, communication, commerce and business." It made French the sole official language of Québec, and introduced a series of provisions to encourage the use of French in the workplace. These included:

o All public utilities had to provide service in the French language.

o Making the knowledge of a language other than French mandatory for a job became illegal, unless the nature of the position
specifically demanded an employee spoke another language.

o An employee could not be dismissed or demoted for only
speaking French, or for demanding his or her right to work
through the French language.

o All printed material produced by businesses must be in
French, or, if bilingual, must keep the prominence of French
equivalent.

o Primary and secondary education was to be conducted through
the French language, with English a mandatory subject at all
grade levels.

o Only students whose parents had received an education
through the English language in Canada were entitled to be
educated through English.

The last provision was viewed as particularly important, as it
sought to ensure that the children of any immigrants who came to
Québec would become French, not English, speakers. The Charter,
also known as Law 101, was hugely controversial. Indeed, it is remarkable that no one had read enough Orwell to realise that calling it Law
101 would strike a particularly ominous note. Some estimates have
suggested that up to a quarter of a million English speakers have left
Québec since the 1970s, while some prominent businesses also relo-
cated to other parts of Canada to avoid the language requirements
placed on them. Many immigrants were also unhappy that if they
wanted their children to receive a public education, they could only
get it through French.

So, thirty years after the Charter of the French Language was
introduced, what has been the outcome? The short answer is that
while the position of French in Québec has not gotten weaker, it has
not grown much either. According to the 2016 census, 78.4% of the

inhabitants of the province speak French as their first language. But the number of people who speak English as their first language is rising again after a post-1977 drop. That figure in 2016 stood at 9.6%, while almost 20% of the people in Québec said they speak English at least sometimes at home.

For defenders of the French language, this is evidence that the Charter for the French Language is not working. Eric Bouchard of the Mouvment Québec Francais said that the 2016 census was a disaster for French in Canada's largest province. He called for the end of "institutional bilingualism" in order to preserve the French language. Bouchard pointed out that because all state services were supplied in English as well as French, there wasn't any incentive to learn French. His solution was for the Québec provincial government to operate through French only. "If nothing is done, French will be over", he said. "The francophone elites need to take their head out of the sand."

Of course, there are considerable differences between the position of Irish in Ireland and that of French in Québec. Indeed, what people look upon as a crisis for French would be seen as a dream scenario for the Irish language. Yet the Charter of the French Language has been studied by many other nationalities who are seeking to protect or promote their language, and considered reflection of what has and has not worked in Québec might offer useful lessons for what can be done with Irish.

CASE STUDY FOUR: CATALAN

As in the case of Welsh, the Catalan language revival is often mentioned as a possible role model that Irish could follow. Unlike the case of Wales, however, labelling what has happened in Catalonia in recent decades a "revival" seems appropriate, and as such, those interested in promoting Irish could learn from it.

The Catalan language is spoken in various parts of Spain, France, Italy and Andorra, but in this instance we will be examining its recent history in Catalonia. With the rise of the Bourbon monarchy in the early 18th Century, the Spanish state took increasing measures to limit the official use of Catalan. However, Catalonia remained a relatively prosperous region of Spain, and the wealthier Catalonians (as well as the rest of the population) continued to speak Catalan as their daily language. Already one can see a significant difference in the history of Catalan and Irish, in that Catalans did not feel the heavy economic pressure that Irish speakers did to switch languages in order to get ahead. Indeed, a literary revival in the 19th Century further strengthened the position of the language, and at the turn of the 20th Century, Catalan was in a very healthy position in Catalonia.

However, two significant changes weakened the position of the language. The first was the development of authoritarian, centralist governments in Madrid. First Miguel Primo de Rivera in the 1920s, and then General Franco from the mid-1930s onward, insisted on Spanish being the sole administrative language in Catalonia. Where possible, the Spanish state actively discouraged the use of Catalan, and all education was through the medium of Spanish.

Social and economic factors also played a role in undermining Catalan. Just as the mineral wealth of Wales had attracted large numbers of English-speaking migrants into Wales, so the economic prosperity of Catalonia drew people from all across Spain into the region. The population of Catalonia increased 110% between 1940 and 1980, with much of this growth attributable to migration from the rest of Spain. With state policy heavily favouring Spanish and a growing number of Spanish speakers living in Catalonia, the Catalan language began to flag. In 1939, 90% of the population of Catalonia could speak Catalan, but by the time of Franco's death in 1975, this had fallen to 60%.

As Spain transitioned to democracy in the 1970s, many in Catalonia were determined to reverse what they felt had been the unfair treatment of their language. Compulsory Catalan classes were introduced for all school children in 1978, but some felt this was not enough (perhaps the example of Ireland was even used as proof that this was the case?). Therefore, in 1983, the Language Normalisation Act was passed. This was a three-pronged approach to reviving Catalan. Firstly, the Catalonian government would carry out its daily operations in the Catalan language. To get a job with the Catalan state, one had to be able to speak Catalan. Secondly, the Act committed the Catalonian government to using the Catalan language in communicating with the public, and within a few months, a state-run TV and radio station, using the medium of Catalan, had been established. Thirdly, primary and secondary education in Catalonia would be delivered through the Catalan language. Catalan was no longer to be a school subject, but rather the language of instruction in Catalan schools.

So, 35 years after the passage of this act, have these efforts been successful? The short answer is yes. Where 60% of the population spoke Catalan in 1975, 75% of the population say they can speak Catalan today, which rises to 90% among people under thirty. It should be understood, however, that the figures for both 1975 and today refer to people who speak Catalan as both their first and second language, as opposed to just their "native" tongue. One survey in 2001 revealed that 95% of Catalans can understand Spanish, reflecting the bilingual nature of the region in that this includes Spanish speakers who can understand the language, but not actually speak it.

Other figures reveal interesting numbers. According to one 2013 survey, 7% of people in Catalonia say they speak both languages natively, with 36.4% speaking Catalan as their first language, and 47.5% speaking Spanish. In total, it is estimated there are about four million people in Europe who speak Catalan as their first language, and five million who speak it as a second language. Clearly, the use of the language is trending in a positive direction. Indeed, complaints are starting to grow from Spanish-speaking parents that their children are not mastering Spanish in school. At the same time, the fact that Catalan is a minority first language even within Catalonia means that its defenders feel efforts must be ongoing before they feel the future of their language is completely safe. The Catalan political crisis of 2017 may also have a significant influence in future years, with those supporting Catalan becoming more attached to the language while the Spanish state will feel that too much emphasis on Catalan has created a subversive element and may need to be challenged.

CASE STUDY FIVE: BAHASA INDONESIA

Bahasa Indonesia, or Indonesian, is a fascinating example of a language that has seen an enormous growth in the number of speakers over the last 70 years. As was the case with Urdu, it can't really be termed a "revival", as the language was never spoken as a national language all across Indonesia. But the Indonesian government has had far more success than its Pakistani counterpart in increasing the percentage of people who speak the "national" language at home.

Indonesian is closely related to Malay, and for most of its history, it was simply recognised as a dialect of Malay, rather than being seen as a separate language. Malay had been an important trading language in Southeast Asia for centuries, and while most Indonesians did not speak it as their first language, many were able to speak at least a little in order to facilitate trade.

Beginning in the 17th Century, the Dutch began exerting a colonial influence in Indonesia. They found that Malay was a useful lingua franca in trying to communicate with the incredibly linguistically diverse people in Indonesia, and they encouraged its use among Indonesians, rather than trying to replace it with Dutch. Indeed, in order to use the language as part of educating the people of Indonesia, the Dutch helped produce dictionaries and standardised the language in the 19th Century. This, combined with the influence of Dutch on Malay over time, helped create a distinct Indonesian dialect of the language.

In the 20th Century, Indonesian nationalists began dreaming of a homeland free of Dutch rule. Indeed, it could be argued that the idea of "Indonesia" was a European invention. Made up of over 17,000 islands, 300 ethnic groups and with a mind-boggling number of languages (estimates vary, but it is assumed that between 300 and 700 languages are spoken natively across the archipelago), about the only thing that tied everything together was the fact that it was ruled as a single colony by the Dutch. Indeed, the very name Indonesia was coined by European academics.

One might say that the Dutch imagined Indonesia into existence, but if so, Indonesian nationalists nevertheless wanted to remove Dutch influence and create an independent Indonesian state. They were the first ones to insist that the dialect of Malay spoken in the region was a separate language: Bahasa Indonesia, or the language of Indonesia. When Indonesia acquired its independence in 1945, Indonesian was chosen as the national language.

This was not as logical a choice as it might first seem. Indonesian was only spoken as a first language by about 5% of the population. In contrast, possibly up to half of the 84 million new Indonesian citizens spoke Javanese, while other languages also had more native speakers than Indonesian.

But there was actually a good deal of wisdom in choosing Indonesian. Firstly, while only a small number of people spoke it as their native tongue, a lot of people across Indonesia had some familiarity with it because it had always been a useful language to learn. And because the language was not considered to be the language of any one ethnic group (unlike, say, Javanese), then it was easier for Indonesians to accept it as "their" national language, as opposed to "someone" else's language being imposed on them. This is in marked contrast to how many people in Pakistan viewed the decision to make Urdu the official state language. It has often been said that the reason Hebrew was revived was because there was a need for a common language in Israel among speakers of different languages. As we will shortly see, that isn't actually true of Hebrew, but it certainly fits what happened in Indonesia.

How was the language to be spread? Quite simply, it was used from day one as the language of government and education in Indonesia. In areas where one language dominated, the government permitted the local language to be used for teaching up until children were about eight, and then they switched to Indonesian. In areas where there was more than one language, Indonesian was the language of instruction from the moment children began school. The effects of this policy took greater effect from the 1970s onwards, when the Indonesian government stepped up its efforts to provide at least primary-level education for all children.

However, there was a problem with adopting Indonesian as the national language. The fact that it was only spoken by a small percentage of the population, or had been used as a trading language, meant that it did not have the vocabulary to deal with all walks of modern life. So the Indonesian government set about creating this vocabulary. Since Indonesia became independent, government linguists have coined 150,000 scientific and technical terms, another 70,000 words to describe economic activities. 35,000 administrative or bureaucratic words have been created, as well as thousands more in fields that Indonesian once had no words for at all. As a result, not only does Indonesian have the breadth of range of any major language, but (unlike Irish) it is also the language most Indonesians have to master in order to participate in the modern world.

Given all that, then, how successful has the Indonesian government been in promoting its language? Well in 1945, it is estimated there were

4.2 million native speakers of Indonesian. Today there are 43 million. As with the increase of Urdu in Pakistan, some of this can be explained by booming population growth. But the percentage of Indonesians who speak Indonesian as their first language has risen from 4.9% in 1945 to about 10% in 1990 to 20% today. On top of that another 156 million say they can speak Indonesian as a second language, while the 2010 census indicates that 92% of Indonesians can speak the language in one form or another. Most Indonesians speak their own regional language as well as Indonesian, although the number of people who speak it as their first language seems set to grow further. Of all the language promotion efforts we have looked at so far, this would be the most successful in terms of the spectacular growth in the number and percentage of speakers of the language.

Case Study Six: Hebrew

Hebrew is the only example in human history of a "dead" language being revived. Logically, one would think that if one were interested in reviving Irish, drawing lessons from what happened to Hebrew would be a natural starting point. But we can't.

The situation that led to the revival of Hebrew was and is totally different to that of Irish. As a result, they can't be compared.

At least, that is what we are told. Opponents of an Irish revival naturally make this point over and over, eager to depict any effort to increase the use of Irish appear as hopeless. But they are not the only ones. Reg Hindley, author of *The Death of the Irish Language,* was largely sympathetic to the plight of Irish in his book. Nevertheless, he wrote "The need for a lingua franca for the multilingual Jews who refounded Israel has no parallel in Ireland, and for all Ireland's suffering there is no Irish equivalent of the Jewish reason for abandoning the main Jewish language, which was Yiddish (Jüdisch), the German Jewish dialect which received the full force of Nazi extermination policies and was also latterly repressed under Stalin."[42]

Tomás Mac Síomóin is an ardent defender of the Irish language who is eager to promote the language. Yet he is adamant that "the cases of Hebrew and Irish revival are about as comparable as chalk and cheese... Jewish colonists in Palestine, the later Israel, needed a common tongue since the Jewish colonists living there were of different linguistic backgrounds."[43]

The message is simple. Hebrew was only revived for practical reasons. The new Israeli state had to find a common language because the Jews who emigrated there all spoke different languages. The desire to revive Irish is entirely ideologically motivated, and therefore incomparable with Hebrew.

This argument is repeated whenever the example of the Hebrew revival is mentioned in Ireland. It is largely accepted as conventional wisdom. And it is based on a complete misunderstanding of when and why Hebrew was revived.

Firstly, as we will see, the revival of Hebrew began decades before Israel was established. The Israeli state was created by Hebrew speakers, not the other way around.

Secondly, there was nothing practical about reviving Hebrew. Indeed, a little reflection on the subject would show exactly how illogical this belief is. After all, if practicality was the only grounds on which Jewish immigrants chose a new language, then surely the language of the largest group of speakers, even if this only amounted to 10% of the population, would have made more sense? Secondly, how can reviving a dead language ever be considered practical? We saw in the case of Bahasa Indonesia that despite the fact that some people spoke it as their first language, thousands upon thousands of new words had to be created to make the lan-

---

42 Reg Hindley, *The Death of the Irish Language*, op. cit.

43 Tomás Mac Síomóin, *The Broken Harp*, op. cit.

guage practical for all aspects of life. How much more necessary would this have been for a language that was lacking native daily speakers for centuries?

No, Hebrew was not chosen for practical reasons. There was one language that most of the Jewish migrants to Palestine already spoke. The choice to switch to Hebrew was ideological, not practical. There certainly are differences between the case of Irish and of Hebrew, but the notion of practicality is not one of them.

Hebrew was the language spoken by the ancient Israelis. It seems to have been gradually been replaced by Aramaic, and scholars estimate that Hebrew ceased to be anyone's first, native language around 200 AD. However, it is not really accurate to say it was a "dead language". Hebrew retained a ceremonial use within the Judaic faith and many Jews would have had some familiarity with the language through learning Jewish prayers and reading the Torah. Furthermore, Jewish scholars continued to write in the language and new literature in Hebrew constantly appeared. Jack Fellman estimates that by 1879 over 50% of male Jews around the world could understand the Bible and daily prayers, while 25% of male Jews could read a Hebrew book of average difficulty. Occasionally, if Jews who had no other common language met, they could use Hebrew to communicate to some extent. Hebrew was only dead in the sense that no community of daily Hebrew speakers existed.

By the 19th Century, most of the world's Jews lived in Europe, especially Eastern Europe. However, a series of anti-Jewish pogroms in the Russian Empire caused many Jews to flee. While America was the most popular destination, some Jews felt it might be time to create a Jewish homeland, where Jews could live free of persecution. Palestine, then a province of the Ottoman Empire, seemed the logical choice for such a homeland, as it was where the ancient Israeli state had once existed. Beginning in the 1880s, thousands of Jews began migrating to Palestine.

One of them was a man named Eliezer Ben Yehuda. Like other Jewish migrants, Ben Yehuda believed that moving to Palestine was the first step toward creating a Jewish homeland. But Ben Yehuda didn't just want to revive Israel, he also wanted to restore the ancient Hebrew language. In desiring this, he was almost alone. Theodor Herzl, who founded the World Zionist Organisation to promote Jewish migration to Palestine, scoffed at Ben Yehuda's idea. Herzl asked "surely we cannot speak Hebrew with one another? Who among us knows enough Hebrew to ask for a train ticket in this language?"

Undaunted, Ben Yehuda and his wife moved to Palestine in 1881. When they had a son the following year, Ben Yehuda vowed to only speak Hebrew to him. As a result, Itamar Ben-Avi became the first native speaker of Hebrew in over a thousand years. The burdens brought on by this decision are actually staggering to think about. Ben Yehuda had studied Hebrew for years, so he was reasonably well-prepared for the task, but his wife, Dvora, did not know any Hebrew. Since Eliezer forbade her from speaking any other language to her son, she could only speak to her son in a language she was learning herself. In a biography he wrote about his father, Itamar remembered a lonely childhood, during which his parents would not allow him to speak to other children because they feared he would pick up other languages besides Hebrew. When Dvora died of tuberculous in 1891 (with the same disease also claiming three of her five children that same year), Eliezer married her sister, Hemda. But Hemda did not speak Hebrew either, and had to throw herself into picking it up in order to integrate with the only family in the world that spoke the language.

These challenges were daunting themselves, but there were two other factors that made the situation even more difficult. Firstly, many of the Jews who lived in Jerusalem (where the Ben Yehudas lived), were strictly Orthodox in practicing their faith. They believed that Hebrew was a divine language and should not be tarnished by being used for daily life. As such, they were disgusted by what Ben Yehuda and his family were attempting to do, and refused to interact with them.

Secondly, because Hebrew had mostly only been used for religious purposes, it lacked the vocabulary for day to day use. Ben Yehuda realised this, of course. He wondered what the Hebrew word was for a spinning top, one of the first toys his son Itamar had. In order to solve this problem, Eliezer threw himself into the task of creating a modern Hebrew dictionary. He basically had to coin (or invent) thousands of new words in Hebrew. In order to do this, he scoured ancient and medieval Hebrew dictionaries, creating either compound words or repurposing old Hebrew words for modern concepts. He was also willing to borrow from Aramic or Arabic, as these languages were related to Hebrew. Ben Yehuda dedicated his life to writing this dictionary, but had not completed it by the time he died in 1922.

Initially, Ben Yehuda's efforts bore little fruit. While he was successful in making Hebrew the language of his own family, he only managed to convince a few other families in Jerusalem to copy his example. But word of his project had spread among the other Jewish communities in Palestine, as well as back to Eastern Europe. Many were astonished at his family's dedication to the cause, and some decided to follow in their footsteps.

But how could a revival of Hebrew be achieved? For Ben Yehuda, the answer was obvious: education. He had experienced the policy of *Russification* in the Russian Empire, when the Tsarist state sought to impose the Russian language on a linguistically diverse population. Ben Yehuda noted "We know that the schools play a large role in turning a nation entirely over to one... language, as the Russian language has quickly become the language of an entire new generation in Russia." If Jewish settlers in Palestine wanted to revive Hebrew, they would have to create an education system operating entirely through Hebrew.

But was that even possible? Palestine was part of the Ottoman Empire, and as such there was not an extensive state education system within the province. The education of Jews in Palestine fell on rabbinical schools or those established by international Jewish philanthropic organisations like the Alliance Israélite Universelle. Such schools taught in French or English however, and Ben Yehuda criticised them for this, insisting that the language of instruction had to be Hebrew. Many were skeptical that this could be done, but Ben Yehuda took a teaching position in an Alliance school in 1883 and taught his classes by speaking only Hebrew. Although ill-health forced Ben Yehuda to give up after a few months, he had proved his point that children could be educated through Hebrew. This belief in the importance of teaching through Hebrew spread to the immigrant colonies that were springing up around Palestine. By 1903 Hebrew was the language of instruction in almost every colony school, while Hebrew kindergartens similar to one established in Rishon Le Zion in 1898 began appearing across Palestine.

Of course, for reasons we have already outlined, teaching through Hebrew demanded extraordinary sacrifices on the part of teachers and students. These difficulties were outlined by David Yudeleviz, one of the first teachers of these Hebrew-language schools. He wrote "without books, expressions, words, verbs and hundreds of nouns we had to begin...teaching. It is impossible to describe or imagine under what pressure the first seeds were planted...The Hebrew teaching materials for elementary education were limited...We were half mute, stuttering, we spoke without hands and eyes."

Slowly then, Hebrew began to take hold among the children of the agricultural colonies. But the revival effort received a boost from a new wave of Jewish immigrants that began to arrive at the turn of the 20th Century. Many of them had been inspired by Ben Yehuda's example and were determined to move to Palestine and make Hebrew their first language. Indeed, some began learning conversational Hebrew before they departed. David Ben Gurion, who would become the first Prime Minister of Israel, established a youth group to help Jewish teenagers in Poland learn Hebrew before moving to Palestine. As the number of Jews in Palestine grew, so did the number of Ben Yehuda's followers.

The arrival of the *Hilfsverein der deutschen Juden* (Aid Association for German Jews) in Palestine was to have a dramatic influence on the language movement. Formed in 1901, the Hilfsverein was an organisation that worked for the relief of underprivileged and repressed Jews. The hardships experienced by many immigrants in Palestine and the lack of educational opportunities for their children moved the organisation to intervene. A well organised and well-funded group working on behalf of philanthropic German Jews, the Hilfsverein began building up an extensive network of educational institutes in Palestine. Although German was initially the language of instruction in these schools, the Hilfsverein proved responsive to popular sentiment in Palestine, and Hebrew was increasingly accommodated within their schools. In 1908 Dr. Paul Nathan, vice president of the Hilfsverein, stated that a European language should only be taught in major urban centres to facilitate future trade, and that Hebrew and Arabic alone should be taught in the colonies.

The Hilfsverein also established kindergartens and permitted girls to attend. This was a crucial sign of support for the Hebrew revival, as Ben Yehuda had been lambasted by Orthodox Jews for calling on female as well as male children to be educated in Hebrew. By 1912 the Hilfsverein had an impressive portfolio of schools under its umbrella, maintaining over 50 educational institutes responsible for 6,500 students. This included 13 kindergartens, six boys' schools, two girls' schools, a secondary school, a high school, a teachers' seminary and a kindergarten training school. Thus, by this date, it was possible for a child to be educated entirely through Hebrew. All that was missing as a capstone was an institution of higher learning, and work had already begun in bringing this to fruition.

In 1909, the Hilfsverein announced that it planned to build a technical institute, with a focus on third-level science and engineering, in Palestine to serve the growing Jewish population. The question of what language the college would use for teaching was left unanswered, but many assumed that Hebrew would be chosen. Indeed, comments were already being made about the remarkable progress of the language revival. One teacher living in Jerusalem, David Yellin, reported in 1910 that Hebrew was now a common language around Jerusalem, particularly among children, while it was also the principal language being used by Jews in the colonies. Another Jewish teacher who had left Jerusalem in 1905 and returned in 1912 was astonished at the transformation, commenting that when he had left, he doubted whether any students could converse in Hebrew, but that he returned to find the language to be widely spoken by children. As building progressed and the project neared completion, supporters of the Hebrew revival believed that the emergence of a third-level educational institute operating through Hebrew would serve as proof that the language had been revived.

However, in 1913, it was announced that the core subjects of the new college, science and mathematics, were going to be taught through German. Paul Nathan, director of the Hilfsverein, argued that the preference of German over Hebrew was a practical one. According to him, there was not a single textbook in Hebrew through which science and engineering could be taught. Furthermore, most of the textbooks which had been donated to the Technion were written in German. In his mind, there was no other choice but German. As the compiler of the modern Hebrew dictionary, Ben Yehuda believed he was the best equipped to answer Nathan's assertion. While he admitted that Hebrew was somewhat lacking in scientific terminology, he was adamant that this situation would be resolved in months, owing primarily to his own endeavours. He warned Nathan that the decision against Hebrew "would be accompanied by bloodshed."

Blood was not shed, but there was a great deal of anger at the decision to use German in the new college (which was named the Technion). Protests and strikes were held at Hilfsverein schools across Palestine. In response, it was announced in February 1914 that the Technion would become a completely Hebrew institute within seven years, while mathematics would immediately be taught through Hebrew. Although it would be nearly ten years until the institute actually opened, owing to the outbreak of the First World War and complex wrangling about ownership of the building after the war, a decisive victory had been won for the Hebrew language. As well as serving as a unifying banner that all elements of the fledging Jewish community in Palestine could rally around, it had been confirmed as the future language of economic, political and intellectual power. The 1916 census showed that 40% of the Jewish community in Palestine claimed Hebrew as their daily language, with this percentage rising in the ensuing decades. The British government, which took over the management of Palestine from the Ottomans after World War One, made Hebrew, alongside Arabic and English, the official language of the territory in 1922. The revival, to all intents and purposes, was complete.

As we can see, the revival of Hebrew took place before the Israeli state existed. The other myth that needs to be dispelled is that Hebrew was revived out of a practical need to create a way to communicate between a diverse collection of Jewish immigrants who did not have a common language. The problem with this idea is that, for the most part, a common language did exist between these people, and it was Yiddish. Firstly, a Jewish community existed in Jerusalem before the mass migrations that began in the late 19th Century. It is estimated that 10,000 Jews lived in the city in 1875. The majority of these people were either migrants, or descendants of migrants, who emigrated to Jerusalem in the 18th or early 19th Century. These people came from Eastern Europe, where Yiddish was the native language of Jews. Exact figures are impossible, but an educated guess would suggest that perhaps 70% of the Jewish population in 1870s Jerusalem used Yiddish as their daily language.

Then came a surge of Jewish migration to Palestine. Between 1880 and 1940, just under half a million Jews settled in Palestine. Not all of them stayed, but enough did to help grow the Jewish population in Palestine to about 475,000 by 1940. Once again, precise figures are hard to come by, but all of the evidence suggests that a large majority of these migrants came from Eastern Europe or Russia, where Yiddish was the Jewish community language. Adopting a conservative approach, estimating that 60% of the migrants who came to Palestine were Yiddish speakers seems more than plausible. Jewish Palestine before the formation of Israel was no Tower of Babel. A dominant language clearly existed within the Jewish community there.

Given that, people might reasonably ask why Yiddish, and not Hebrew, did not become the national language of Israel. The problem was that Yiddish, despite centuries of rich tradition and association with Jewish faith and culture, was seen by some as problematic. It emerged as a distinctly Jewish language in Europe in the Middle Ages, as a blend of Hebraic, Aramic, Germanic and Slavic elements. But from the point of view of Zionists, it was tainted. Yiddish had only emerged because the Jews had been forced to leave the Holy Land. Those who wished to create a new Israel did not want to make Yiddish the national language of this area because its existence was a reminder of their expulsion in the first place. It was, in the words of David Ben Gurion, a "language of humiliation". One could draw comparisons with the attitudes of some Irish people towards English. Despite the fact that everyone speaks English in Ireland, its dominance is still associated, in some minds at least, with the conquest, colonisation and humiliation of Ireland.

In other words, the decision to try and revive Hebrew as the language of Jews living in Palestine was based entirely on ideology, not practicality. Indeed, the earliest efforts to revive Hebrew were disproportionally made by people who already had a common language. Ghil'ad Zuckermann, an Israeli linguist, writes that "Yiddish...was the mother tongue of the vast majority of revivalists and first pioneers in *Ersetz Ysrael*".[44] Zuckermann notes that in 1916 62% of Ashkenazi children and 28.5% of Ashkenazi adults were speaking Hebrew (Yiddish was the language of Ashkenazi Jews), but for Sephardic Jews, (who spoke Ladino, a Jewish language with a heavy Spanish influence), the figures were only 18.3% and 8.4% respectively. Hebrew was not really being used to facilitate communication between groups who did not speak a common language, but instead was being learned mostly by people who wanted to switch from one language to another one. Zuckermann concludes that those who switched languages "were extremely ideological and made a huge effort to revive Hebrew."[45]

Thus, when Israel was formed in 1948, it was dedicated to maintaining the Hebrew revival, not kick-starting it. In fact, far from needing to find a language to unite the polyglot wave of Jewish refugees moving in to Israel, the government was afraid that too many of the newcomers already spoke a language that threatened to wash away the gains Hebrew had made. Once again, that language was Yiddish. Between 1948 and 1953, just under 700,000 Jewish refugees migrated to Israel. The backgrounds of these Jews were more diverse than those of the immigrants who came before 1940, but nevertheless, the single biggest group (about 45% of the total) came from Yiddish-speaking Eastern Europe. To give some idea of how

44 Ghil'ad Zuckermann, 'Hybridity versus Reliability: Multiple Causation, Forms and Patterns,'*Journal of Language Contact: Varia 2,* (2009), pp. 40 – 67.

45 Ibid.

strong Yiddish was in that part of the world, it should be noted that it is estimated that 85% of the Jews who were murdered in the Holocaust spoke Yiddish. The Israeli government was so concerned that Yiddish might undermine Hebrew that it closed down Yiddish theatres and prevented Yiddish from being broadcast on radio stations until the 1970s.

Obviously, there are differences between the efforts to revive Hebrew and revive Irish. The biggest one is several languages were spoken in Palestine when the revival began. Turkish was the language of the government, Arabic the language of the market place, while English, French and German were the languages used in education. The point here isn't that Hebrew was "necessary" in this environment, but rather that no single powerful language dominated to repress its use. In contrast, the effort to revive Irish has always been hindered by the powerful position of English in all walks of life.

A second difference was the imperial context. Palestine was in the Ottoman Empire, which, unlike its western counterparts, was not as interested in using education to create loyalty to the empire. Ben Yehuda himself acknowledged his relief that Palestine was part of the Ottoman Empire rather than one of the 'enlightened' western ones, where greater cultural and linguistic assimilation was expected of subjects of the empire. As no state education system existed in Palestine, Jews were free to create their own and mould it as they saw fit. This differed with the situation in Ireland, where the British government controlled the education system. As such, Irish revivalists were dedicated to simply introducing Irish as a school subject. Indeed, even a century after Ireland obtained independence, not much has changed, as efforts to revive Irish are still largely focused on how to improve the way it is taught.

So there certainly are differences between the case of Hebrew and Irish. But the "practicality" argument holds no water. The revival of Hebrew is, at its core, a story of how a group of people switched from a language they already spoke to a new one. And that, of course, is very relevant if one wants to ask how Irish can be revived.

But there is one last aspect of the Hebrew revival that we have not discussed yet that deserves more attention. After all, Irish medium primary and secondary schools have existed since the foundation of the state, and their number has been increasing in recent decades. Yet while they have undoubtedly helped increase the number of people who can speak Irish, it seems fair to say that there has not been a noticeable increase in the number of people using Irish on a daily basis. This is quite different from the Hebrew revival, where, as we have seen, people commented on a noticeable difference in how much Hebrew was spoken in Jerusalem over five years. So, what is the difference?

It is a small one, but a significant one. Basically, many of the parents who sent their children to Hebrew-speaking schools insisted that the children taught them what they had learned when they returned from school. Some of these parents, to the best of their ability, tried to make Hebrew the language of their homes. In doing so, they resembled Irish-speaking parents in the 19th Century, who tried to raise their children though whatever English they had. As noted in an earlier chapter, in order for language shift to take place, there needs to be a generation that is willing to live their lives through a language that is not their mother tongue. While the Hebrew medium schools helped the children learn Hebrew fluently, it was the sacrifices many of their parents made in trying to speak Hebrew themselves that allowed the language to be a natural part of their children's lives outside of school as well. When these children grew up, it was completely natural for them to raise their families through Hebrew. Of course, the grandchildren of those revivalists usually did not learn Yiddish at all, in the same way that Irish-speaking grandparents ended up with grandchildren who couldn't speak Irish.

In contrast, the recent surge of Irish-language schools has not had the same effect. And the reason for this is obvious. Parents send their children to Gaelscoileanna so they can learn Irish in addition to English. There is no expectation, or desire, for Irish to replace English as their primary language. Certainly, some parents have taken advantage of their children's attendance in Irish-language schools to brush up on their own Irish, but it seems likely that only a tiny number might try to switch their home language from English to Irish.

As such, Irish remains trapped in the classroom, with students switching to English as they leave the school grounds. Once these students leave school, their Irish wanes unless they make an active effort to use it. When they have children, they almost certainly raise them through English. They might send their children to a Gaelscoil as well, but then these children are just back at the same spot that their parents started in. In terms of progress, the language remains stuck in a rut, having to be learned from scratch by each generation. The third generation do not emerge as natural, native speakers of the language in the same way that Hebrew speakers (or even English speakers in Ireland) did. As such, widespread use of Irish remains impossible because almost everyone, across generations, is much more comfortable using English than Irish. But could something be done to change this dynamic?

CHAPTER 9

WHAT IS TO BE DONE?

The previous chapter showed a variety of strategies that have been adopted to try and promote different languages in various parts of the world. What is notable, however, is that none of these approaches were based on a foundation of simply teaching the language as a regular school subject. If we want to revive Irish, we need to change tactics. But to what?

Obviously, some suggestions have already been made over the years. Before I lay out what I think needs to be done to revive Irish, I will highlight a couple of other ideas that have been put forward. The first one is the Irish government's own "Twenty Year Strategy, 2010-2030". This document has been largely panned for setting unrealistic expectations and some feel it is a disingenuous effort to show a false concern for the future of the language. My own assessment is that document (available online) has value in that it correctly identifies some of the reasons that the "revival" has failed so far, but only contains vague ideas in how to address these issues.

The plan begins by stating that "the Government's aim is to ensure that as many citizens as possible are bilingual in both Irish and English", and that "'Normalisation' of the language is required in order to expand the use of Irish". Ultimately, the goal of the government is to "increase the number of families throughout the country who use Irish as the daily language of communication.... The transmission of Irish as a living language within the family and between the generations is critically important."

Although these are broad principles, there is at least evidence of some understanding of what will be necessary for reviving Irish. The goal of ensuring "as many citizens as possible are bilingual" is vague, and frankly "as possible" seems to be code for "whoever wants to be", but at least it expresses a desire to increase the use of Irish. The expressed goal of "normalising" Irish and increasing its presence as a family language is encouraging from the point of view of recognising that any revival of Irish will depend on more than just teaching Irish as a school subject. By identifying the importance of making Irish a living language within individual families, and one that is transmitted through the generations, the authors are certainly on the right track. As we have already seen, the switch from Irish to English in the 19th Century, as well as the switch from Yiddish to Hebrew in Palestine, were dependent upon family languages changing. Put simply, the key to any successful Irish revival will be the ability of Irish to emerge as a home language for at least a substantial percentage of the population.

The problem, however, is that the strategies suggested by the document are either small modifications on existing plans, or are just vague and general without specific details. We are told that the government will continue to seek improvements in how Irish is taught (not a bad thing, but surely the last century has taught us that tweaking teaching methods cannot lead to the "normalisation" of Irish use), provision of Irish medium education for those who want it (a modest enough ambition in the context of reviving Irish, yet one that the government appears to be struggling to achieve), and ensuring that whoever wants to use Irish through the state can do so (a situation which, by Irish law, is already supposed to exist).

There is also a call for developing Irish in the universities and the defense forces, although what this means and how it will ultimately lead to 250,000 people speaking Irish by 2030 (the stated goal of the strategy) is not explained. It notes that 25% of primary school teachers have only weak Irish themselves, and wants to address this (which is a positive goal, but once more is largely focused on teaching Irish as a school subject). Then we see some more original ideas, but ones in which no details are offered for when or how they will be implemented. These include all students being taught at least some subjects through Irish during their education, promoting a youth culture with Irish having a central role in it as a way of making the use of Irish more natural among the young, advertising the value of bilingualism to parents & encouraging at least one parent to use Irish at home, providing adults with opportunities to learn Irish, and encouraging communities outside the Gaeltacht (but with a Gaelcholáiste) to use more Irish in public.

All of these are commendable ideas, but the issue is that they really are not given any more explanation beyond what I outline here. Furthermore, the exact manner in which these individual goals will provide synergy for a more general revival of Irish is lacking. These solutions are very much in the tradition of throwing mud at a wall and seeing what will stick. There is no "joined-up" thinking on how these separate aims will build upon and reinforce one another, rising the tide of the Irish language in general. Furthermore, they share the flaw at the heart of all revivalist thinking in Ireland since the formation of the Gaelic League: the belief that Irish is held back because people either have not had a chance to learn it or are just a little shy about using what they have learned. If only we could just teach a little more Irish and tweak people's attitudes towards speaking it, then the language would suddenly come gushing forth out of the ground and spread across the country, like an oil strike. No attention seems to have been given to the fact that all political, economic, social and cultural forces in Ireland are geared towards maintaining the dominance of English. Until those issues are addressed and some balance in favour of Irish is restored, then the number of people who will try to raise their children through Irish will remain tiny, because there is no practical benefit to doing so.

A different path for revitalising the Irish language has been put forward by Tomás Mac Síomóin in his book *The Broken Harp*. One of Mac Síomóin's biggest gripes is "the repackaging of the entire language revival project as 'Irish is Fun' – i.e. Irish as almost an exclusively pastime language, is seriously held by many Irish 'enthusiasts' as being the only way to secure the survival of the language."[46] In this sentence, Mac Síomóin has hit upon two examples of flawed thinking on the part of the Irish public generally when it comes to the Irish language. The desire to "Make Irish Fun" is born from the belief that all of the problems of the language stem from "the way it is taught". The idea is that in the "old days", the learning of Irish was like swallowing cod liver oil: it tasted horrible, so everyone hated it. If we could just make Irish fun (i.e. if we could make it taste like ice cream instead), then everyone would completely immerse themselves (i.e. start guzzling the stuff) and the language would flourish once more.

Mac Síomóin believes that Irish "enthusiasts" are the ones who view Irish as essentially a pastime or hobby, but I think this is actually how most of the population sees the language, not so much in how they term the use of Irish by fluent speakers (although certainly some do hold that view), but in what they ideally want for themselves. By pastime, I mean they want to be able to pull out their Irish whenever it is convenient for them, but not to speak it on a regular basis. In other words, they want the Irish language "app" in their brain. This then can be used for things like being able to understand the snatch of Irish they hear when they accidentally tune into RnaG, or impressing a few foreigners while on holidays. And the "Irish is Fun" bit is important in this. By making the language fun, students will pick it up easily, and then never lose it (or so the theory goes). Irish is to be conveniently effortless, both in acquiring it and in retaining it. Indeed, in order for Irish revival to succeed, this must

46 Tomás Mac Síomóin, *The Broken Harp*, op. cit.

be the long-term goal. But that will require a lot more than tweaking our teaching strategies.

Mac Síomóin, however, attacks one of the central tenets of Irish revivialism, namely what he calls "the Irish for Everybody" approach. He says that the idea that most, or all, Irish people could become Irish speakers in the future is deluded. Instead, he calls for all efforts to be focused on creating a smaller community of committed Irish speakers, which could eventually involve up to 20% of the population. Mac Síomóin's proposals are radical if for no other reason that he has set a clear benchmark for what a "revival" would constitute.

So, what does Mac Síomóin propose? Basically, he calls for Irish speakers who are committed to growing the language to be identified and brought together in local circles or networks. They will then create community centres in their area to serve as rallying points, both to provide a meeting point for Irish activists and a place to recruit and educate new supporters. A national organisation will be required to coordinate efforts between these networks, although they will be primarily focused on local initiatives. He also calls for a national advertising campaign to alert the people of Ireland to the danger facing the language, in the hope that some people who don't speak Irish will be prompted to learn it and take up the cause.

The most important aspect of Mac Síomóin's proposals is that he is advocating self-reliance for Irish activists, as opposed to looking to the government for assistance. Indeed, in Mac Síomóin's view, the Irish government is indifferent at best to any Irish revival, and will never be a force of positive change for the language. One could certainly make the argument that those who wish to see Irish prosper have focused too much of their attention in lobbying the government since the formation of the state. As we saw in the previous chapter, the revival of Hebrew was largely achieved through a grassroots effort without any state support.

Similarly, in his book *Coming Home*, Michael McCaughan points out that the vibrancy and success of the Irish language movement in Northern Ireland seems to spring directly from the fact that people had to do things for themselves as they knew no state support for Irish would ever materialise. Although I believe that the government will have to be centrally involved in an Irish revival, I think Mac Síomóin is not wrong in trying to push activists to think how they could bring about change themselves, instead of looking to Leinster House for solutions.

That being said, there are some problems evident in Mac Síomóin's proposals. The first is that his ideas will require a large number of English speakers to switch over to using Irish daily. That need not be an issue, except that Mac Síomóin himself is a believer in preserving the purity of the Irish language as well. Throughout his book, he decries the *Gaeilge easnamhach* (deficient Irish) that is being produced by the Gaelscoileanna. However, it remains unclear how thousands of English speakers can become Irish speakers and adhere completely to the style of Irish spoken in the Gaeltacht that he champions. The explosion of daily speakers required to meet Mac Síomóin's aim of 20% of the population speaking primarily through Irish would inevitably bring dramatic changes to how the language is spoken. It is difficult to see how this can be squared with the particular type of Irish Mac Síomóin wishes to see promoted.

The second problem is that when it comes to surmounting the biggest challenge facing his own suggestions, Mac Síomóin really has nothing to say. Although he feels that his proposals are more realistic than those traditionally associated with the revival, that is not to say they are easily achieved. If 1% of the Irish population are daily speakers of Irish today, is calling for a 19-fold increase of this really any more realistic than a 99-fold increase, when we have yet to see evidence that we can even double that number? How can such a dramatic rise in the number of Irish speakers be brought about? In brief, Mac Síomóin says that "Irish language organisations" will need to try new approaches and tactics to help the surge of new students that will hopefully come to master the language. In other words, he leaves it to others to figure out how 19% of the population can attain the fluency they are going to require to speak Irish on a daily basis. For all the insights he provides us, Mac Síomóin does not offer a clear pathway to how even a truncated revival can be achieved.

Journalist Ger Colleran has offered another suggestion for how Irish could be revived. In a radio interview on Newstalk in 2017, Colleran suggested that the best course of action would be to make every primary school in Ireland a Gaelscoil, thereby ensuring that every child in Ireland would be immersed in Irish for the first eight years of education. Colleran is not alone in putting forward this idea, and it is probably fair to say that anyone who has given serious thought on how to revive Irish has considered some plan along these lines. The attractiveness of the idea is that it would be relatively straightforward to implement, since all primary school teachers are competent in the language, and it would undoubtedly mean that almost all students who went through the Irish education system would end up with a higher degree of fluency in Irish than those who currently receive their education through English.

Well then, problem solved? Not exactly. I would certainly welcome any move in this direction by the government, but it must be acknowledged that there are some issues with the plan. Firstly, Irish primary school teachers have a widely different range of abilities in the Irish language. Based on studies on the competency of primary teachers in Irish, we would probably need to improve the language skills of at least 25% of the workforce before the idea could be implemented. Besides this, resistance on the part of teachers would be likely, as for many it would involve a dramatic change in their working lives. Nor would teachers be the only ones complaining. There is a very vocal anti-Irish language lobby, especially in certain sections of the Irish media, and virulent criticism from those quarters would be inevitable.

Then there is the question of whether such a move would be the right one for all of our students. There is no doubt that Gaelscoile-anna have been tremendously successful in terms of student achieve-ment, but all of the parents have chosen to send their children to these schools, and can be said to be supportive of Irish-medium education. This support would not exist in all cases if every school became a Gaelscoil. This would be a problem in particular for disad-vantaged students. As things currently stand, there are already chil-dren who are doomed to fail in our education system. It is possible that this number could grow substantially were the language of edu-cation changed. For some Irish children, it is already an uphill strug-gle to receive an education, and being taught through a language that they are unfamiliar with certainly will not ease that burden.

But the bigger question is what would this change achieve? It would probably mean that almost every Irish person would become fluent in Irish for at least a period of time in their lives. From this foundation, we would probably see a larger number of secondary students take an interest in Irish than we currently do, and a modest increase in the number of daily speakers of Irish would be plausi-ble eventually. But would we see a revolution in how much Irish is spoken on a day-to-day basis across Ireland? Almost certainly not. Once students enter secondary school, they would speak better Irish than our secondary students today do, but they wouldn't speak it any more regularly, because they would have no real reason to. The vast majority of these students would receive their secondary and tertiary education through English, then work through English, and raise their children through English.

That wouldn't be so bad though, would it? At least everyone would have Irish in their back pocket and can use it whenever they chose? And after all, isn't the point of an Irish revival ultimately about giving people the choice to use as much Irish as they want, whenever they want? The answer to these questions, in reverse order, is yes and no. Students who speak Irish fluently at twelve might hold on to much of their Irish ability through secondary school, but it would fade relatively quickly after that unless they spoke Irish regularly. Remember, there are lots of people, like Conor McGregor, who received both their primary and secondary education through Irish, but within a decade of leaving school they have lost the ability to speak Irish fluidly. Having everyone receive their primary education through Irish will not remedy this. Reviving Irish does not simply mean ensuring everyone can reach a level of fluency. It also means creating a society where many people use it naturally and its use remains effortless throughout the life of the average Irish citizen.

Before we explore what needs to be done to revolutionise the position of Irish, let's start small. What changes could be enacted to make the current strategy (i.e. hoping that people take it upon themselves to learn and use Irish) more successful than it has been up to this date? I would like to make two modest proposals. The first one is that the Irish government should recruit Irish citizens whom young people look up to front an ongoing promotional campaign to encourage people to use Irish. In short, the celebrity appeal of certain citizens will be harnessed to try and make Irish "cool" in the eyes of our youth. Of course, this would not happen for free. These celebrities would first require intensive tutoring to become fluent Irish speakers themselves, and of course they would have to be paid. Obviously, this isn't exactly a new idea. Certain GAA players like Ciarán Kilkenny have been vocal about their passion for Irish. Former boxing world champion Bernard Dunne has used his national profile to promote the language and encourage others to use it. But these efforts have always involved (1) people who are reasonably well-known in Ireland, but could hardly be called international celebrities, and (2) people who already spoke fluent Irish.

What I am talking about is targeting the upper echelons of the Irish celebrity world, people who have considerable credibility in the eyes of the young people of Ireland. Of course, it may be that some of these people have a negative attitude towards Irish and would not be interested, but on the other hand, there are some who would probably be excited at the prospect of becoming fluent Irish speakers. So who do I have in mind? Well when I was younger, I know I would have been incredibly impressed by someone like Roy Keane speaking Irish and encouraging others to do so. Brian O'Driscoll or Niall Horan would have had immense appeal as Irish language ambassadors to people slightly younger than myself. Saoirse Ronan, Conor McGregor, or Katie Taylor would also be fantastic people to have involved in something like this. I will not embarrass myself by trying to suggest other names, but my point is clear enough. Involving celebrities with superstar status would be enormously beneficial. I don't want to claim that this approach would, by itself, create hundreds of thousands of new Irish speakers. But I do believe that it would help counteract some of the negative images that many of our young people have of Irish, and hopefully push some towards using Irish more regularly.

So much for the salesmanship of trying to get people to want to speak more Irish. What could we do to help people who want to learn Irish? They say that youth is wasted on the young. Certainly, when it comes to teaching Irish, we seem to waste our time providing lessons for the demographic that is least interested in learning it. Both from an anecdotal point of view and based on findings in the 2015 ERSI survey on attitudes towards Irish, there is a lot of evidence that people develop a more positive view of Irish after they leave school and regret not having learned it. Yet what does the state do to help these adults who want to learn Irish? Absolutely nothing. Which is odd since every major political party claims it is dedicated to the promotion and development of Irish. Yet any adult who wishes to play their small part in "developing" Irish by learning it themselves finds they have to reach into their own pocket to pay for private lessons. Surely, we can do better than that?

Providing free Irish lessons is the obvious answer, but can that be done without placing an undue burden on the Irish exchequer? Yes, by creating an online platform that has lessons aimed at all levels of Irish speakers, and through which a learner can progress from being a complete beginner to someone with a reasonable level of proficiency. Obviously, a number of free online options exist for Irish language learning, but most of them are limited to a few lessons. Probably the most successful option in this field is Duolingo, but even that has its limitations.

What I am suggesting is that the government create a comprehensive and extensive online learning centre, aimed exclusively at teaching Irish. The idea would be that anyone who completed all the lessons available on the website would have a much greater knowledge of the language than they can currently receive from available online courses. Full time tutors should be hired to help answer questions that people might have as they progress through lessons. Of course, learning a language ultimately requires communication with other human beings, so lessons online can only take someone so far. But the idea is that whatever the upper limit is on people learning a language in this way, it should be reached through this medium.

It must be kept in mind that creating such a comprehensive learning tool would involve some cost, perhaps (as an estimate) €20 million euro to develop and then €2 - €3 million euro a year to maintain. To some that might sound like a lot of money, but if it helps Irish citizens who want to improve their Irish to do so, then it would be justified. An alternative option to building a new Irish language website is to support a program that Dublin City University has been working on for the last few years. Called "Fáilte ar Líne", the team at DCU is developing a programme (or MOOC – Massive Online Open

Course) that would allow people to progress from being complete beginners to earning a degree in Irish entirely online and free of charge. At the time of writing, only the introductory level course was available. But with a substantial increased investment on the part of the government (the Department of Culture, Heritage and the Gaeltacht already provides some funding), the broader vision of those who are trying to create this platform could be realised, to the enormous benefit of Irish citizens and members of the Irish diaspora who want to learn Irish as a way of exploring their heritage.

But these suggestions are only aimed at some moderate improvement in the current position of Irish. Ultimately, I am more interested in discussing something much more radical: the revival of the Irish language. As set out in the introduction, my main goal in writing this book was to answer the question of whether Irish could be revived. I hope that the previous chapter, in particular the case studies involving Bahasa Indonesia and Hebrew have shown that the answer is certainly yes (although in the case of Bahasa Indonesia, it was more a case of dramatic growth, rather than a revival as such).

The first thing we need to do is to define what we mean by a revival. If someone ever joins a gym and starts working with a personal trainer, the first thing the trainer will ask is "what are your goals?". The reason for this is pretty simple. By having a clear idea of what you want to achieve, the trainer can then put together a plan to help you get where you want to go. It often strikes me that whenever the idea of an "Irish revival" is discussed, it is rarely accompanied by a concrete vision of what this will involve. Does it mean that everyone in Ireland will speak only Irish, and English will largely disappear? Does it mean that everyone in Irish will predominantly use English in their day-to-day life, but can revert to Irish when desired? Or something in between?

Firstly, when one talks about reviving Irish, that should not be read as some attack on the English language. My ideal vision is an

Irish society that is completely bilingual, and this means that every Irish citizen should speak English fluently. This of course can mean different things in different contexts, but at its core it means that even people in the future who mostly speak Irish both at home and at work will also retain a strong command of the English language. In other words, the proposals that follow are not intended to push English out of Ireland. However, in order to revive Irish, certain functions that the English language is currently used for in Ireland need to be turned over to Irish in the long term. This is explained in more detail below.

It is worth bearing in mind that some people are very skeptical that such a bilingual society can ever be created. Linguists often argue that a bilingual society is simply one in the middle of language shift from an old language to a new one. Perhaps. But I believe that bilingualism can be created by necessity. In other words, if it is advantageous to speak two languages fluently, people will do so. The advantages for English are already obvious and need not trouble us further. The question is how to make the acquisition of Irish necessary and desirable. We will address that shortly.

Back to the revival question. What exactly is our goal when we say we want to revive Irish? On a basic level, I think reviving Irish means that everyone who wants to speak it fluently can do so. The online surveys mentioned in a previous chapter (and acknowledging their flaws) indicated that 70% of the Irish population wants to speak Irish, with another 5% or so already speaking it fluently. So, to put a number to our revival goal, this means an "Irish revival" involves 75% of the population having the ability to speak Irish fluently. Of course, if these levels could be attained, it seems natural to assume that much of the remaining 25% would also see view the ability to speak Irish as more desirable than they currently do.

Or perhaps Malta can be our model? Malta is a highly bilingual society, with two official languages: Maltese and English. It is estimated that 88% of the population speaks English, and 98% speak Maltese. Having most of the population comfortable in speaking two languages is exactly what I would like to see replicated in Ireland. The fact that Malta (with a population of less than half a million people) can achieve this without losing its native language suggests this goal is achievable.

OK, we have some broad numbers in relation to the percentage of the population we would like to see being able to speak Irish. But, as we saw in earlier chapters, what it means to "speak" a language can be ambiguous. What would the breakdown of "speakers" look like in such a scenario? If we take the figure of 75% of the population being able to speak Irish, perhaps we would see 20% to 25% of the population being native Irish speakers, in the sense that they are born and raised through Irish, and speak Irish at home. Then we might have another 50% of the population who, although predominantly using English at home and at work, can converse on any topic in Irish and make use of this ability on a semi-regular basis. We would then be left with 25% of the population who speak limited or no Irish, who live their lives entirely through English, as most of the population today does.

Of course, these numbers are entirely guesswork. I believe we can greatly increase the amount of Irish spoken in Ireland and have a high rate of fluency among the general population, but once the conditions are in place to facilitate this, it is impossible to say what patterns might emerge. It may be that only a tiny percentage (under 5%) make Irish their home language, but that the vast majority of the population (90%) would become proficient in Irish. Or it may be that a high percentage (say 40%) use Irish as their first language, but that another 50% use English exclusively, with only a small number (10%) speaking English primarily but becoming fluent in Irish. What is important, however, is creating a society in which acquiring Irish is easy and useful, with people thereafter making the decision on how often they use it.

But what can be done to bring about such a drastic change in the fortunes of the Irish language? As has already been noted, improving how Irish is taught in school really won't change much of anything. Seán De Fréine notes that "For tangible results in language teaching a definite motive is needed." We see this with the teaching of maths as well. For most of us, the only maths we learned in school that we can still use are things like addition, subtraction, multiplication and percentages. We forget things like calculus and trigonometry. Why is that? Is it because our teachers found a magic formula for teaching percentages that we can't forget, but not geometry? Of course not. It is that we use percentages regularly in the normal course of our lives, but most of us don't have any reason to use geometry.

The thing we most "effectively" teach in schools is literacy. Why do we succeed with this? In part because schools are basically literacy "immersion environments", in that students practice reading and writing in almost every class every day. But what is far more important is that students use the skills of reading and writing all the time in their daily lives. Even students who hate reading books in school will still communicate with friends through texting or social media messaging. Obviously, some people do end up with weak literacy skills, but compared to the teaching of Irish, or even maths, our schools are almost 100% successful at producing people who are functionally literate. This is not due to better teaching tactics, but because in our society, these skills are indispensable.

In other words, we need to do more than just making Irish a more attractive school subject. The role of Irish within the education system will be very important for reviving the language, but the focus first needs to be on what we do outside the education system to make Irish something worth learning. Furthermore, as should be evident from the previous chapter, the key to any revival will depend on encouraging parents to use Irish as the main language they speak at home with their children. We want to reverse the language shift that took place in Ireland over the course of the 18th and 19th Century, with one key difference, namely that the old language (English) be retained alongside the new one.

This of course would require considerable sacrifice on the part of parents whose first language is English. The belief that has underpinned the effort to revive Irish is that if Irish is taught well enough, then students who learn it in school will use it outside of school and the transition to a more Irish-speaking society will occur naturally and easily. But as the example of the shift from Irish to English, or Yiddish to Hebrew, shows, a major change in language use requires a generation to use a language that is not their first language. There needs to be a generation that "takes one for the team" as it were. Anyone who wants to see the Irish language grow and prosper needs to realise this and ask what they can do to help.

Would parents be willing to make such a change? I think there are many who would, if they felt they had the linguistic competence to do it, because they feel a sense of pride in their Irish identity. There are others who could be persuaded if there were clear advantages to ensuring their children spoke Irish fluently. But as things stand in Ireland today, there is very little incentive to do so. Even among parents who potentially could choose to use Irish at home, English is almost always viewed as a better choice. Mastery of English is essential in Ireland. We need to find a way to level the playing field in order to make mastery of Irish as important.

The obvious answer is that Irish needs to be economically useful. But how can that be done? Some people might feel that we should encourage businesses to make more use of Irish. One friend of mine suggested offering tax concessions to businesses that allow customers to do business through Irish. That would certainly be welcomed by people who already speak Irish, although I don't know if it would do much to increase the number of speakers, as most people will continue to do business in English. Others might think that copying

Quebec's Law 101 might be helpful, in making all businesses display all information in Irish as well as English. Again, while increased visibility might help create a more positive attitude towards Irish, it certainly wouldn't make it essential to learn. Personally, I believe that we shouldn't bring in any regulations that try to force private businesses to use Irish. If we can encourage more widespread use of Irish elsewhere, businesses will respond in time.

How do we make the acquisition of Irish economically beneficial then? In an earlier chapter, I asked why France or Norway have not seen language shift in the 20th Century, whereby people stopped speaking French or Norwegian at home, and switched to English instead? After all, a majority of people in both countries reported that they could speak English, which in global terms is more useful than their native languages. So why do Norwegian and French parents insist on speaking their languages at home? The answer is that both languages are still essential to advance in French and Norwegian society. Why are they essential? Not just because everyone can speak them. After all, especially in the case of Norway, we know that most people also speak English as well. It is because the French and Norwegian states operate through their respective national languages. In order to get a state education or to be employed by the state, you need to speak French or Norwegian.

And there is the answer to the question we have asked throughout this book. In order to revive Irish, in order to encourage parents to speak Irish at home with their children, we need to Gaelicise the Irish state. We need to make Irish the sole language through which the Irish government functions.

As radical as this sounds, it actually ties in with how the revival of Irish has always been envisioned by those who supported such an effort. The assumption was that the transition of the Irish government from being a body that primarily used English to one that used Irish would occur naturally over time. Once people, having learned Irish in school, began using Irish socially, then the Irish government would become Irish-speaking as well. As we know, that is not what happened.

Because most Irish people are not fluent in Irish, suggesting that we try to make Irish the only language of the state is seemingly to suggest the impossible. It is to put the cart before that horse. But that is exactly the point. In order to increase the use of Irish, you have to put the cart before the horse. English was imposed as the state language in Ireland at a time when most people in the country did not speak it at all. Hebrew was made the language of instruction in Palestine's first third level institution even though the language lacked the vocabulary to be immediately effective in that regard. The same was true of the decision to make Bahasa Indonesia the state language of Indonesia. But by granting these languages privileged positions, any shortcomings they may have had were quickly overcome. The same is true for Irish. There is no point waiting for enough people to be able to speak Irish to make such a change, because that moment will never come. But commit to making this change (implemented in stages, of course), and the supply of qualified Irish speakers will rise to meet the demand.

To some people, it might sound like this idea has been tried before, and failed. It is true that in order to be employed in the Irish civil service, up until the 1970s, you had to pass an Irish language exam. But what I am talking about goes far beyond that. I am saying that in the Irish civil service of the future, EVERYTHING will be done THROUGH the Irish language. That is something very different from everything being done through English by people who passed an Irish exam.

In his book *Coming Home*, Michael McCaughan writes "The first session of the Irish parliament, sitting in rebellion in 1919, was conducted entirely in Irish. There was, perhaps, an opportunity for consensus and a major switch, not overnight but within a generation."[47] The suggestion seems to be that the Irish government in the early years of independence missed an opportunity. McCaughan implies that if the members of the first Dáil had insisted on making Irish the language of government at that time, then Ireland would likely be a genuine bilingual country today, with most people able of speaking both languages. He also seems to suggest that this unique chance to revive Irish, has now passed.

I disagree. Making Irish the sole state language today is no less difficult than it would have been in the 1920s. Indeed, in terms of the percentage of the population who have some competency in Irish, as well the number of people educated through Irish, conditions today are probably more favourable. And if we did make this change in our lifetimes, future generations would be forever grateful to us.

So how would switching the state language to Irish make a difference? It would do so in two ways. Firstly, the Irish state is the country's largest employer, employing about 300,000 people out of a total workforce of two million people. This would make the ability to speak Irish economically attractive, and encourage parents to take steps to ensure their children were competent in Irish and English. Of course, if someone had no interest in getting a job in the public sector, then Irish would not be economically necessary for them and they would be unlikely to master it.

Which brings us to the second way that making Irish the sole language of government will help increase its use, namely that eventually citizens will have to deal with the Irish government through the medium of Irish. For example, in this scenario, if someone wanted to apply for a passport, they could only do so through an Irish form. This naturally would be a controversial idea, and of course would entail removing rights that people who speak English in Ireland currently have. The debate that would have to be had would focus on what rights English speakers should have to deal with their govern-

---

47 Michael McCaughan, *Coming Home*, op. cit.

ment if it switched to operating through Irish. In simple terms, the more necessary it is to have Irish to interact with the government, the more widespread the knowledge and use of Irish would become. Conversely, the greater the opportunity people have to deal with the government solely through English, the fewer people who will become fluent Irish speakers.

Let me give an example of what kind of scenarios could play out. Take the Irish legal system. In proposing that Irish become the sole state language, I am saying that this eventually means that Irish courts will operate only through Irish. But what about if someone who only speaks English comes before the court charged with something? That is where the question of how far the rights of the monoglot English speaker are to be extended. Let's lay out a couple of suggestions for how this would work, moving from the greatest recognition of English to the least. In scenario A, if an English speaker comes before the court, all court business would be conducted solely through English. Naturally, it is envisioned that everyone who becomes a fluent Irish speaker in the future will also be fully fluent in English, so switching language to suit our hypothetical monoglot would not be a problem. In scenario B, the language used when dealing directly with the defendant would be English, but otherwise would be Irish. So, the judge might make the defendant aware of his or her rights in English, but cross-examination of a witness to the matter at hand might be done in Irish (assuming of course the witness speaks Irish). Scenario C would see Irish having the greatest presence in the court. The defendant would be allowed speak in English, but with everything else, including the questions directed to him or her, being in Irish. The defendant would require either his or her solicitor, or a translator, to translate for them.

Most people would probably feel that scenario A is the best solution here. Perhaps. But in the context of discussing how to promote a more widespread use of Irish, the point I am trying to make is that the extent of the long-term growth of the language will be directly proportional to whether scenario A, B or C becomes the reality in a future Ireland in which Irish has been revived. The more essential Irish is, the more it will be spoken, and spoken to a high standard. The more unnecessary it is, the less it will be spoken. Thus, anyone who says they want to see Irish revived has to decide where they feel the ideal balance is between taking steps to encourage the use of Irish and respecting the rights of people who don't want to speak Irish.

Let's stick with the legal system a moment to further demonstrate how the increased use of Irish as the language of government will stimulate the growth of the language beyond the bounds of government. If, after the introduction of Irish as the sole language of government, scenario A was how Irish courts operated, then it is fair to assume that only a small number of Irish solicitors would make any effort to learn Irish, because most Irish people would probably exercise their right to have legal proceedings conducted in English. But if scenario C became the reality, things would be different. Now all Irish solicitors (estimated to number 10,000 in 2017) would by necessity speak Irish fluently. The legal profession is of course one of high status. We might well imagine that most of these solicitors would either raise their children through Irish, or at least have them attend Irish-speaking schools. Law courses in Irish universities would eventually have to transition to offering their courses through Irish rather than English, because there wouldn't be much point in training people through a language that they will not have to use in practice. Thus, granting a practical use to Irish has the knock-on effect of creating other practical uses for it (in this case, the teaching of law in universities), as well as making the language more desirable for socio-economic reasons (because in this case it increasingly becomes the language of legal "elites").

It should be stressed (if it isn't already apparent) that I am talking about such dramatic changes being implemented gradually in stages, for a couple of reasons. Firstly, we obviously don't have enough people who speak Irish to the degree required that we could change the government language from Irish to English in the short term. Secondly, even if we did have enough speakers that this change could be made quickly, there is a question of fairness of disadvantaging citizens who never had any need to speak Irish up until now. The balance we would have to strike would be between making Irish the language of government as soon as possible while providing ample opportunity for those who might need to learn Irish to do so. The key would be to set ambitious future goals (with dates clearly outlined) for how the switch to Irish as the language of government would be done in stages. If we were to start the process tomorrow, the idea would be that only those children who are about to start their education would be the ones who would be expected to work through Irish if employed by the state as adults. If we started tomorrow, this means that scenario C discussed above (if that was the end goal agreed upon by those who start the revival process) would not happen for decades. Perhaps as many as 50 years.

Of course, therein lies the challenge. How can we gradually change languages while steadily increasing the importance of Irish and decreasing that of English in a way that the change we wish to see actually comes about? Simply setting a date for the change to happen will not work. We have already seen this in the case of the Pakistani government which promised to make Urdu the only language of government within 15 years, and then basically did nothing (because they thought that the next generation of politicians would figure it out). To avoid this mistake, a great deal of planning would be required, but what kind of road-map would be needed?

The key to creating a workforce of hundreds of thousands of people who can operate through Irish lies in education, in particular Irish-medium education. But therein lies something of a problem for the revival of Irish. In order to operate solely through the Irish language, the government would require the number of people enrolled in Irish language education to increase dramatically. But in order to increase these numbers dramatically, the government needs to make Irish its every day language so that parents will seek an education through Irish for their children. How do we square that particular circle?

The first step is to make an Irish-language education appear to be economically valuable. This would begin by making an announcement that in 15 years' time, one quarter of new government jobs must be given to people who have received their primary and secondary education through Irish. This number can then be increased, so that in, say, 30 years' time, anyone who wishes to be employed by the Irish state must have received their first and second level education through Irish. This change would serve two functions. Firstly, it will lead to a large increase in the number of people being educated entirely through Irish. Secondly, it would eventually make the functioning of the Irish government through Irish possible.

It should be emphasised at this point that making Irish the language through which all government officials work is essential to this plan. One might be tempted to think that by simply employing people who are educated through Irish, the Irish government can revive Irish without actually having to change its own day-to-day language. Making an Irish-language education a requirement for state employment would certainly help create more 18 year olds who speak Irish fluently, but it probably wouldn't lead to an enormous change in how Irish is used in wider society. In order to encourage more people to raise their children through Irish, and thereby create a culture where many (though not necessarily all) Irish people socialise through Irish, we need to ensure that there are hundreds of thousands of people who spend much of their living day thinking, talking, reading and writing in Irish.

We will come back to the mechanics of how the Irish government will actually oversee such a language shift a little later on. For now, we need to figure out how to cope with an increased demand for Irish-medium education. There is already a shortage of places in Irish-language schools, so wouldn't this demand require a massive investment to build many new schools to accommodate the future demand of parents? Not necessarily. A simpler solution, at least in the short term, would be the creation of Irish-language units or streams within English-language primary schools. These Aonaid Lán-Ghaeilge already exist in several schools around the country. If every primary school had such a unit, then access to Irish-medium education would be available to far more students than it currently is. Furthermore, while we have already discussed how some primary school teachers do not have a high standard of Irish themselves, there are obviously others who do, so opening up Irish units in English-language schools should not present a problem in terms of finding competent teachers.

It should be noted that some people feel that an Irish language stream in an English language school will not provide students with the same grounding in the language that they would get in a Gaelscoil. This is probably true, but such a move would hopefully only represent a transitional stage. Once the level of demand in response to the changing of the government's language is clear, then more suitable permanent arrangements can be made. If the demand for Irish-medium education becomes enormous, then it may be that most primary schools simply become Gaelscoileanna over time. If the demand for English and Irish medium schools is more or less equivalent, then rather than having Irish streams in each English-language school, it would make more sense, if a locality had two primary schools for example, to designate one for English-language instruction and one for Irish-language instruction.

Similarly, there would not be a great need to build new secondary schools at first, as Irish-language units could also be created in existing schools (which again is something that already exists in certain schools). However, unlike our primary schools, making such streams in secondary schools would present a major challenge because most secondary teachers do not speak Irish. Indeed, existing Gaelcholáistí already find it very difficult to find teachers who speak Irish and are qualified to teach subjects like science. This problem would eventually be solved when a large segment of the Irish population receives its education through Irish, but it certainly would present a significant challenge in the short term.

Right now, there is a shortage of secondary school teachers in general for subjects like Irish, maths, science and foreign languages, so these issues need to be addressed first. Once this has been resolved, we need to look at how to create more teachers qualified to teach through Irish. To fix this, the government would need to create institutions (similar to the ulpan used in Israel to help new immigrants learn Hebrew quickly) where these teachers could intensively learn Irish, to prepare them for jobs teaching through Irish. I think many of these teachers would be willing to go on such courses (which may last a year or two) if they were guaranteed employment at the end of them. In this way, the initial shortage of secondary teachers capable of teaching through Irish would be overcome and anyone who wished to receive their secondary education through Irish could do so. However, creating institutions where would-be teachers could immerse themselves in Irish, and possibly offering incentives to encourage people to learn enough Irish to teach through the language, would obviously require a significant investment by the government.

But once our education system is capable of producing thousands of competent Irish speakers, how will the government make the transition from functioning through English to functioning through Irish? After all, this can't be done overnight, and we want to do it in a way that people without Irish don't lose their jobs. I will focus on how such a change might be implemented in one state institution, which would offer ideas on how a wider program could be implemented along similar lines throughout the government. How would we plan to make An Garda Síochána, with 13,000 members, a body that operates through Irish rather than English?

The first step will be ensuring that all new gardaí can speak Irish. This means first introducing more Irish into the curriculum at Templemore, as a part of the formal studies trainee gardaí complete there. This would only be a short-term measure, however, to prepare future gardaí for a time when they would be expected to use more Irish in their work. Eventually (let's use the same 15 year time period mentioned above), all training at Templemore would be undertaken through Irish, thereby ensuring that new gardaí at least could work entirely through Irish.

At the same time as these changes are being made at Templemore, efforts would be undertaken to implement Irish as the day to day language of gardaí where possible. In the beginning, the ability to do this would be limited, but some steps nevertheless could be undertaken. Let's say that currently there are about 200 gardaí who speak Irish daily (roughly equivalent to the percentage of the population who say they speak Irish every day on the census) and who are interested in working through Irish. These gardaí would be reassigned to work in stations whose language of operation would be Irish, not English. All of their day-to-day interactions with one another, written or oral, would be in Irish, although they would speak either English or Irish with the general public. All their paperwork would be completed in Irish, although obviously in communicating with gardaí from outside their station, they would speak in English. As more newly trained gardaí started coming through, they would be assigned to work together and more stations would convert to using Irish as their daily language, although some stations would have to operate bilingually for a time as more senior gardaí who are unable to speak Irish would oversee new gardaí who could. As time went on and the number of gardaí who could only speak English grew fewer, these English-speaking officers would be assigned to work together in certain stations or units within An Garda Síochána.

However, converting the rank and file gardaí to Irish would only be part of the process. An effort to appoint Irish-speaking gardaí to the most senior positions within the force as soon as feasibly possible would also be needed. These officers would use Irish among themselves, while using English with those who didn't speak it. An Garda Síochána is led by a commissioner and two deputy commissioners. It would be imperative to fill these positions with Irish-speakers as soon as possible, and ensure that all communications between them were conducted in Irish. This Irish-speaking bureaucratic circle at the top of An Garda Síochána would then be extended further and further down the chain of command over the following decade or two until all the Garda hierarchy would operate through Irish. The use of English for official functions would be phased out until all gardaí could speak Irish, and then Irish alone would be the working language of An Garda Síochána.

Obviously different institutions within the Irish state operate along different lines, but the same broad plan would be introduced to each branch of the Irish government until the state bureaucracy functioned entirely through Irish. In this way, the entire process could be completed in 30 to 50 years.

Undoubtedly some people will say that converting the Irish government to an entirely Irish-speaking body is impossible. It isn't, but clearly it will require considerable planning to bring it about. But if changing 300,000 positions from being primarily English-speaking to primarily Irish-speaking sounds daunting, worry not, because we will start with a smaller number. 158 to be exact. Converting 158 government jobs that currently are mostly carried out in English to ones that are preformed mostly through Irish will be an important starting point for the revival.

The 158 positions I am referring to, of course, are the seats in Dáil Éireann. For a host of reasons, converting the Dáil to an Irish-only chamber will be vital to the success of the revival. As such, this conversion should take place as quickly as possible, perhaps within eight to ten years of the decision to replace English with Irish within the government. This would allow politicians with ambitions of working in the Dáil some time to master the Irish language. Intensive Irish-language courses could be created and offered to those who wish to bring their Irish ability up to the required standard to take part in debates in the chambers of the Dáil. Joe McHugh is an example of what is possible in this sense. When he was appointed as Minister to the Gaeltacht in 2014, he did not speak Irish fluently, but by 2018, he was able to take part in Dáil debates through the medium of Irish. By Gaelicising the Dáil, we will further enhance the status of Irish, making it the language of not just the legal but political elite as well, which will increase the value of the language in the eyes of parents and over time see some families switch from using English to Irish as the language of their home.

Another important step in the revival of the Irish language will be the creation of an Irish language university. Indeed, as things currently stand, there already is a need for one, as students who receive their primary and secondary school educations entirely through Irish find they must switch to English once they enter third level education. This is a problem because it threatens to undermine the recent growth in Irish-medium schools once parents realise that, for all the advantages of being educated through Irish, having to adjust to learning through English once one moves into the third level sector is a disadvantage. Adrian Kelly, in his book *Compulsory Irish*, feels that it was this very fact that saw the number of Irish-language secondary schools decline in the middle of the 20th Century, as parents came to feel that a secondary school education through English was the best preparation for a university education through the same language.

But if we want to improve the status of the Irish language in a way that makes the language desirable for people, then it needs to become a language through which one can receive a university education as well. To be clear, I am not saying that universities that currently exist switch over to teaching through Irish, but rather that a new university be built, which will operate solely through Irish from the moment it opens. This of course will require government investment, but the cost of this could be lowered by choosing a more affordable location outside of Ireland's cities. The goal would be to offer the same range of courses as any of our top universities, although course offerings would probably be modest at the beginning, concentrating on things like teacher-training, Irish or law. By eventually offering all regular college courses through Irish, the Irish-language will be valuable (and therefore, will be picked up more eagerly by students) because it will offer a pathway to a career that otherwise might not have been available. Take the study of medicine. This has traditionally been the most competitive degree course to earn a spot in, meaning that only the very top students get a place to study medicine. But if places are available to study for a medical degree through Irish, then receiving a primary and post-primary education through that language becomes more attractive. Furthermore, as the government converts to Irish, the value of a degree through Irish in certain subjects like government and public policy would increase. Thus, an Irish-language university is essential for helping raise the overall prestige of Irish, which will lead to wider use of it in Irish society.

"But what about English?", I hear my worried fellow citizens ask. "If we take all of these measures to promote Irish, might we not end up with English going into decline, just as Irish did in the 18th and

19th Century?" The answer is no. English is simply too valuable, both in Ireland and overseas, for people to consider abandoning it in the way that their forefathers abandoned Irish. In Ireland today, English dominates every way of life. The proposals above are designed to carve out some spaces for Irish to thrive alongside English, not instead of it. In order to build a truly bilingual society, different languages have to have practical benefits. In order for Irish to be revived, it must become the language of government, of law, of politics. But English would remain the main language of business and tourism. It would also largely remain the language of entertainment in Ireland. Hopefully we would see considerable growth of music, TV shows and movies in Irish, but English would naturally continue to be the main language in this regard.

In the field of education, Irish and English will co-exist. Parents will have the choice to have their children educated through either Irish or English. While we would hope to see the day where the majority of Irish parents choose to send their children to Irish-medium schools, most of our universities will remain-English speaking (although they may offer courses through Irish where there is a practical benefit to doing so in light of Irish becoming the sole language of government). In this society, speaking both languages will be important, and therefore most people will end up with a strong command of both. But what about life outside of school and work? Will that be Irish or English? What I would expect to see is far more people socialising through Irish than we see today, but with English probably remaining the language in most pubs and casual settings in Ireland. But how exactly these changes would play out is difficult to say for sure. We might see people raised in Irish-speaking homes preferring to socialise with other people who were raised in similar circumstances, with the same holding true for people raised through English, but as most people will be comfortable in both languages hearing a mix of both in most conversations would also be a possibility.

One final question worth reflecting on: what will happen to the Irish language if this revival effort succeeds? It would certainly mean that the type of Irish that would emerge would be noticeably different from that spoken by Peig Sayers and her generation. We know this from the revival of Hebrew. The Hebrew spoken in Israel today is so different from traditional Hebrew that one linguist, Ghil'ad Zuckermann, argues that the language should be called "Israeli" instead of Hebrew. When a population shifts from one language to another, the new language is heavily influenced by the old one. Thus, the influence of Yiddish has heavily influenced how Hebrew is spoken today.

Similarly, the type of English colloquially spoken in Ireland has many obvious traces of Irish. If Irish were revived, the English language would inevitably shape and mold this new Irish. In fact, it is already happening. In an article published in the *Irish Times*, linguist Brian Ó Broin pointed out that there is considerable divide emerging between Gaeltacht and urban speakers of Irish, to the point that urban speakers avoid Irish programmes where they expect to hear Gaeltacht speakers and vice-versa. Is this a problem? We have already discussed the views of Tomás Mac Síomóin, who feels that deviations from how Irish was traditionally spoken is a negative development. My own views are probably best summed up by another Irish linguist, James McCloskey. In describing the style of Irish that is already emerging from our new Gaelscoileanna, McCloskey says "we cannot be too fussy about what kind of language might emerge at the end of this strange experiment."[48] Hear, hear.

---

48 James McCloskey, *Voices Silenced*, op. cit.

CONCLUSION

So, there you have it. That is how Irish can be revived. In fact, it is the only way in which the language ever could be revived in a meaningful way. Imagine the linguistic environment of Ireland as a forest. English is represented by sequoia trees, these massive beings that dwarf everything else. Irish is represented by sunflowers, which need to bask in the sun's light to grow strong. But the sequoia trees block out the sunlight for everything else. Sunflowers can be found here and there throughout the forest, but most wither and die, lacking sunlight. Even where sunflowers flourish in small patches, they struggle to reproduce. New sunflowers have to be constantly replanted, but only a small few grow to their full extent. In order for the sunflowers to flourish alongside the sequoia trees, we need to give them a designated area by chopping down some sequoias. In other words, unless proactive steps are taken to clear some space for Irish to breathe, to allow it to be a useful and necessary language alongside English, then it will continue to languish.

But here is another question. Is this what Irish people want? Do they want the language revived? Let's look at the figures put forward in the survey conducted by Merike Darmody and Tania Daly on attitudes towards Irish in Ireland. They found that 43% of people wanted Ireland to be bilingual, with English as the main language. Another 5% wanted to see a bilingual Ireland where Irish was the dominant language, with another 1% saying they wished that Ireland was solely an Irish-speaking nation. In other words, if this survey holds true for the Irish population in general, then just under 50% of the people want to see Irish being revived in some capacity. As for the other half of people surveyed, 25% wanted to see Irish preserved, but not spoken (whatever that means!), 17% wanted to see it preserved in the Gaeltacht only, 1% think Irish should be abandoned completely, and 8% didn't know or care.

A large majority seemingly want to see Irish either revived or at least preserved. There doesn't seem to be a great appetite for the language to simply vanish. My own theory is that some of those people who have a positive view of the language but don't want it revived hold this position because they think that it would be too expensive to do it, or because it would threaten the position of English in Ireland (thereby weakening our economic competitiveness). As discussed in the previous chapter, reviving Irish does not mean attacking English. Both languages would coexist, and all Irish people would continue to be fully fluent in English.

Reviving Irish would certainly require the state to spend money on the project, but this would not involve the countless billions that naysayers would claim. In the plan laid out in the previous chapter, the emphasis is placed on stimulating the demand for Irish and encouraging people to do as much as they can themselves to learn the language. Certainly, the education system would be the primary vehicle through which people would learn Irish, at least at first, but this is primarily about making adjustments to a resource we already use, as opposed to inventing something new from scratch. To try and have every current government employee operate through Irish today would cost a fortune in terms of having to provide everyone with Irish language lessons. But by encouraging parents to make the maximum use of the education system to ensure their children are fluent in Irish, then transitioning to an Irish-language government bureaucracy over time can be done in a cost-effective way. This is not to claim that the state will not have to invest resources in reviving Irish – clearly it will – but with proper planning it can be done in a financially responsible manner.

But is this what the Irish people want? Who knows, but obviously there would need to be some consent on the part of the Irish people to begin such a radical transformation within the Irish state. Irish politicians certainly won't take the lead in enacting this plan. Since most of them don't speak Irish, we would effectively be asking turkeys to vote for Christmas. But here is what I would like to see happen. The government could draw up a plan along the lines I have outlined in this book. It would provide a detailed explanation of what the government would need to do to transfer over to working through Irish, what deadlines and benchmarks would be put in place, and how much this would cost over time. Then the plan would be put to the public for a vote. A plebiscite could be held on whether this plan should be put into action. Would people support it? It is impossible to say. Certainly, there would be fierce resistance to it from some quarters. But if people could be shown that this would work in restoring Irish to a place of prominence in Ireland, and that it could be done in a way that didn't bankrupt the state or cause people who don't speak Irish today to be disadvantaged, then I believe there would be support for this plan.

So, to answer the original question put forward in the introduction: can Irish be revived?

Yes.

Should we revive Irish?

Yes.

Why?

Because we can.

WORKS CONSULTED

Alyssa Ayres, *Speaking Like A State: Language and Nationalism in Pakistan*, Cambridge: Cambridge University Press, 2009.

Michael Billig, *Banal Nationalism (Theory, Culture and Society)*, New York: SAGE Publications, 1995.

Michael Cronin, *Irish in the New Century/An Ghaeilge San Aois Nua*, Dublin: Cois Life Teoranta, 2005.

Tony Crowley, *War of Words: The Politics of Language in Ireland 1537 to 2004*, Oxford: Oxford University Press, 2008.

Seán De Fréine, *The Great Silence: The Study of a Relationship Between Language and Nationality*, Dublin: Mercier Press, 1978.

Aidan Doyle, *A History of the Irish Language: From the Norman Invasion to Independence*, Oxford: Oxford University Press, 2015.

Tom Garvin, *Preventing The Future: Why Was Ireland So Poor For So Long?* Dublin: Gill and MacMillan, 2004.

Reg Hindley, *The Death of the Irish Language: A Qualified Obituary*, Oxford: Routledge, 1990.

Adrian Kelly, *Compulsory Irish: Language and Education in Ireland, 1870s – 1970s*, Dublin: Irish Academic Press, 2002.

James MacKillop, ed., *An Irish Literature Reader: Poetry, Prose, Drama*, New York: Syracuse University Press, 2006.

Tomás Mac Síomóin, *The Broken Harp: Identity and Language in Modern Ireland*, Dublin: Nuascéalta, 2014.

Michael McCaughan, *Coming Home: One Man's Return to the Irish Language*, Dublin: Gill Books, 2017.

James McCloskey, *Voices Silenced- Guthanna in Éag: Has Irish A Future- An Mhairfidh Gaeilge Beo?* Dublin: Cois Life Teoranta, 2001.

Caoilfhionn Nic Pháidín, Seán Ó Cearnaigh (eds), *A New View of the Irish Language*, Dublin: Cois Life Teoranta, 2008.

Muiris Ó Laoire, *Athbheochan na hEabhraise: Ceacht don Ghaeilge?* Dublin: An Clóchomar, 1999.

Gearóid Ó Tuathaigh, *I mBéal an Bháis: The Great Famine and the Language Shift in Nineteenth Century Ireland*,Conneticut: Quinnipiac University Press/ Ireland's Great Hunger Museum, 2015.

Nicholas Wolf, *An Irish-Speaking Island: State, Religion, Community and the Linguistic Landscape, 1770 – 1870*, Wisconsin: University of Wisconsin Press, 2014.

Ghil'ad Zuckermann, 'Hybridity versus Reliability: Multiple Causation, Forms and Patterns,'*Journal of Language Contact: Varia 2*, (2009), pp. 40-67.